红星奖荣誉宣言
Red Star Honorary Manifesto

“公平、公正、公益、高水平、国际化”是中国设计红星奖所代表的原则。

评审标准、评审程序均面向参评者和社会公开。评委按照评审标准所规定的指导原则对其所提交的资料和实物进行评审。为确保评审公平、公正和不受外界干扰，评审现场不对外开放，评委对产品进行试用和评估，以评委的独立判断为评审的最终结果。

评委代表着奖项的高水平，来自多个国家，包括资深设计师、院校教授、媒体和经济界人士，他们均在本领域有出色的表现并同意遵守评审的荣誉准则。奖项还不断地邀请新的专家加入评审，以其专业知识丰富决策，对于设计超越文化、国界，实现基于文化多样性的设计创新极具意义。每年的评委主席由著名的专家轮流担任。

红星奖是国家级的政府公益奖项，不向任何参评企业和个人收取报名费、评审费和宣传费用。同时，奖项还通过颁奖典礼、电视转播、网络新媒体、全球巡展和年鉴出版等形式，为参评者和企业提供尽可能多的宣传推广机会。

为保证红星奖的声誉和社会公信力，红星奖自创立之日起，评审结果就没有来自政府官员、红星奖主席、执行主席等奖项组织者的影响，今后也将一如既往。

中国设计红星奖委员会

Fairness, justice, commonweal, top-level and internationalization - these are the principles that China Red Star Design Award stands for.

The evaluation criteria and procedure is open to the participants and public. The jury board will evaluate the material and object of each individual entry based on the principles of the criteria. To ensure the process of screening is fair, impartial and undisturbed, the screening on site does not open to the public. Furthermore, the jurors would test and assess the products independently, and give the final results based on their own judgment.

The invited jurors represent the top-level of the event, all of whom are qualified designers, college professors, media and business experts from international range. They all perform outstandingly in professional fields and promise to abide by the code of honor during the screening. The event will continually invite new experts to join the jury committee with their participation can enrich the decision making, which is of great meaning for design to go beyond culture and nations, and to realize the design innovation based on culture diversity. Every year, the chairman of the juror committee is held in turn by experts on reputation.

China Red Star Design Award is a national award that is public welfare and supported by government. Therefore, the fee for entry, screening and promotion from individuals and businesses is not requested. And at the same time, the event will provide extra chance for publicity and promotion via the award ceremony, television relay, online media, world tour exhibition and the yearbook publication.

To ensure the reputation and credibility of Red Star Award, since Red Star's establishment, the fact that the competition result absolutely keep the impregnability from government side, the chairman of the award, executive chairman and the organizers. And we insist that we will always keep this belief.

China Red Star Design Award Committee

红星奖 Red Star Design Award

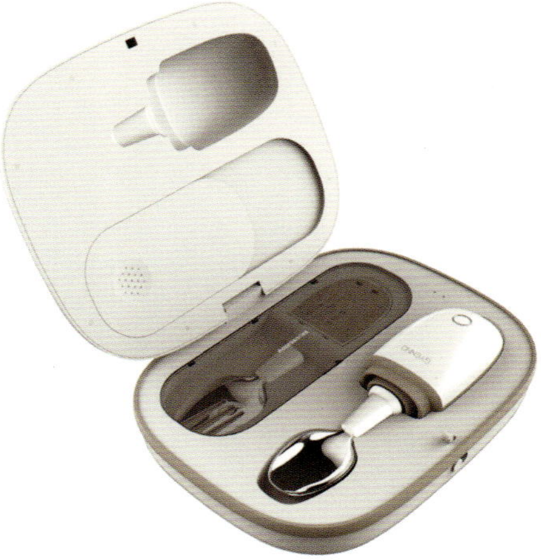

红星奖
Red Star Design Award

10th

2015
CHINA RED STAR DESIGN AWARD YEARBOOK
中国设计红星奖年鉴

主编 / 中国设计红星奖委员会
Edit / China Red Star Design Award Committee

中国书店
Cathay Bookshop

图书在版编目（CIP）数据

2015 中国设计红星奖年鉴 / 中国设计红星奖委员会主编. — 北京 : 中国书店, 2015.11
ISBN 978-7-5149-1400-9

Ⅰ. ①2… Ⅱ. ①中… Ⅲ. ①工业产品－造型设计－中国－ 2015 －年鉴 Ⅳ. ①B472-54

中国版本图书馆 CIP 数据核字（2015）第 247365 号

2015 中国设计红星奖年鉴

中国设计红星奖委员会 主编
责任编辑：木洛

出　版：中国书店
社　址：北京市西城区琉璃厂东街115号
邮　编：100050
印　刷：北京朝阳印刷有限公司
开　本：850mm×1168mm 1/12
版　次：2015 年 11 月第 1 版第 1 次印刷
印　张：22
书　号：ISBN 978-7-5149-1400-9
定　价：188.00 元

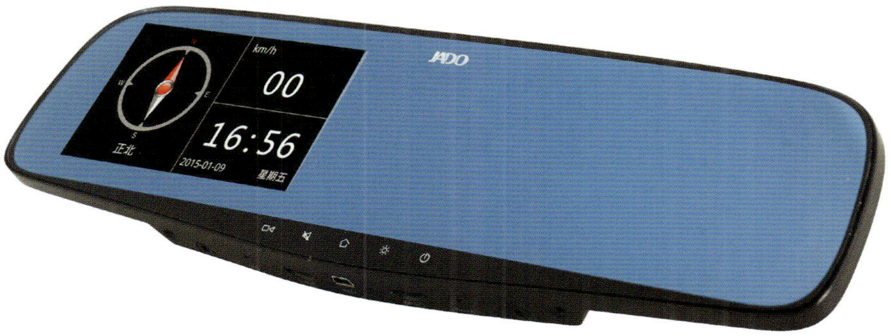

km/h
00
16:56
2015-01-09

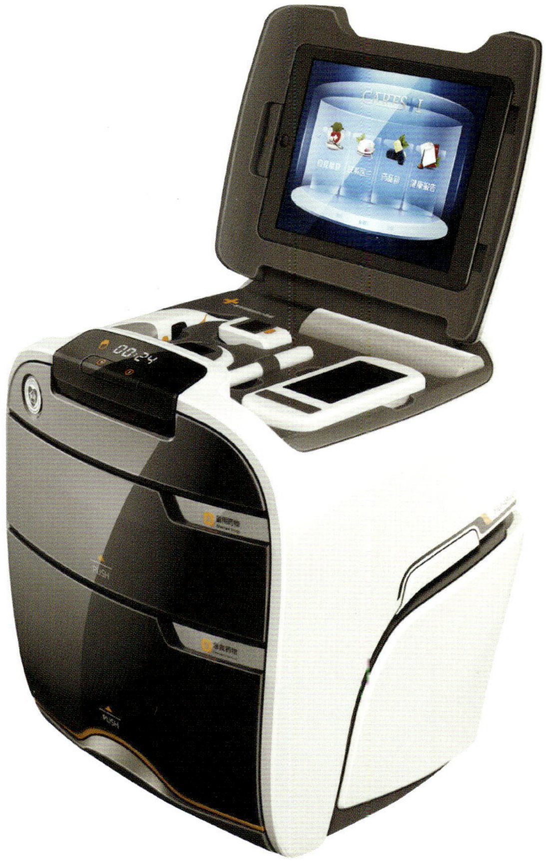

CHINA RED STAR DESIGN AWARD

Best of the Gold Prize

至尊金奖

lenovo
lenovo
skype

Yoga3 Pro

设计 / 联想设计与用户体验中心
生产 / 联想
Design / Lenovo
Manufacture / Lenovo

联想 Yoga3 Pro 是一款可变形笔记本电脑，轻薄且具有出色的功能。联想 Yoga 系列是近些年中国工业设计的代表作之一，建立了新的可变形笔记本产品的市场，而 Yoga3 Pro 可变形笔记本电脑更是让人眼前一亮。Yoga3 Pro 采用革命性的新铰链设计和直观的软件设计，使产品拥有良好的用户体验。产品具有笔记本电脑模式、站立模式、帐篷模式及平板电脑模式 4 种基本模式，满足工作和娱乐等多种使用要求，还可改变为其他模式以符合更多的场景和使用习惯。创新的设计与突破的工艺集中在 Yoga3 Pro 的表链式的轴设计，实现 360 度自由翻转，达到全角度使用模式，使用户在各种使用场景中轻松自如地切换使用模式，进一步提升产品的美学价值与感知精度。键盘使用软人造革材料，更具亲和力，同时起到保护作用。

As a representative product of Chinc industrial design, Yoga series is a highlight series of products of the market, building up the new convertible market. The Lenovo YOGA3 Pro is a new Laptop in this family. It is exceptionally thin & light, yet brilliantly intelligent, with a revolutionary new hinge design and intuitive software that responds to how you use it. Whether for work or play, YOGA3 Pro is adaptive to you with 4 basic ways to do almost anything: Laptop, Stand, Tent or Tablet. But not only 4 ways, but also you can find more usage ways base on different scenarios. This new hinge design likes watch band that can let the screen open from 0 degree to 360 degrees smoothly. This innovative design further enhance the aesthetic value and the perceived accuracy. Keyboard adopts soft leather, is more user-friendly, while the protective effects.

扫一扫查看产品 Pin3D 技术三维效果图
Scanning for the 3D image by Pin3D

CHINA RED STAR DESIGN AWARD

Gold Prize

金奖

海尔智能机器人
Haier Intelligent Robot

设计 / 青岛海尔智能家电科技有限公司
生产 / 青岛海尔智能家电科技有限公司
Design / Qingdao Haier Intelligent Home Appliance Technology Co.,Ltd
Manufacture / Qingdao Haier Intelligent Home Appliance Technology Co.,Ltd

海尔智能机器人是一款创新的优秀设计产品，可以满足老龄化社会照顾及陪伴的需求。该产品已成为海尔全系列产品完整生态体系的桥梁，未来海尔的产品都将能通过机器人进行有机关联。该机器人集成各种体贴功能，如控制屋内家电、安全警报、陪护儿童、为老人拿取药片等。产品内置多种传感器，可以对室内环境质量进行实时的全方面监控，包括温湿度、PM2.5 及 CO2 等。材质表面采用柔触感表面处理，头部组件运用特殊塑料，在保证良好外观的情况下，使红外信号很好地透过组件。产品设计为洁白圆润的主体，干净整洁，部分使用蓝灰色体现沉稳，赋有科技感。炯炯有神的眼睛，微笑的嘴角，好像一个可爱的小男孩。

As a good design product, Haier Intelligent Robot is a result of innovation, meet with the rapidly growing market demand to take care of an aging society and companionship needed. The product has become a bridge connecting the whole Haier ecosystem, all the future product will be able to link one another through this robot. The robot integrates a variety of thoughtful features, such as house appliances control, security alarm, accompany children, picking up pills for the elderly, etc. The built in sensors could accomplish real-time monitcring of all aspects of indoor environmental quality, including temperature and humidity, PM2.5, CO2, etc. Special plastics is adopted for the head part in order to convey the infrared signal. The outlook is like a cute little boy which brings affinity to the users.

CRH2G 时速 250 公里高寒动车组
The EMU Resistant to Freezing, Windy and Sandy Conditions

设计 / 南车青岛四方机车车辆股份有限公司
生产 / 南车青岛四方机车车辆股份有限公司
Design / Csr Qingdao Sifang Co.,Ltd
Manufacture / Csr Qqingdao Sifang Co.,Ltd

CRH2G 时速 250 公里高寒动车组是应用在恶劣环境下的集技术与速度于一体的列车，同时也是一款达到顶级设计水平的交通工具。该高寒动车组针对高寒等恶劣气候和线路，能够适应零下 40℃至零上 45℃的环境，可在各种环境条件下持续高速运行。该车设计轻量化、阻力低，最大限度利用再生制动，降低基础制动闸片磨耗。轮轨冲击小，外部噪声低。采用真空集便系统，实现废水污物零排放。动车内部空间宽敞，满足旅客中长途乘坐的需求。该动车组不仅拥有优雅的外观造型，同时兼具高贵的内饰，为乘客提供了良好的乘车体验。

The EMU CRH2G Train is a integration product for both a technical solution for high-speed mobility in unfriendly environment and a very well top level desired transportation product. The train is designed for the severe weather conditions under -40 to+45℃ , and the high speed operation can be maintained under different environment conditions. The lightweight train body is of low resistance, could be the advantaged of running in the severe condition. The train maximizes the usage of regenerative brake to reduce the abrasion of the brake. It has a mild impact between wheel and the pathway and the external noise is decreased to a low extend. The vacuum excretion collection system realizes a zero discharge. The bright and spacious catering area can offer a favorable servicing environment for passengers. It doesn not only has elegant exterior outline, but also a distinguished and functional interior design which offers great comfort for the passengers.

OLED 电视
OLED TV

设计 / 冠捷显示科技（厦门）有限公司创新中心 ID 设计团队
生产 / 冠捷显示科技（厦门）有限公司
Design / TPV XMIC ID Design Team
Manufacture / Top Display Technology (Xiamen) Co.,Ltd

OLED 电视的设计方案为通过未来感展示电视优点。产品采用薄型化喇叭设计、镂空底座设计和简洁美背设计，体现整机的超薄理念。产品极富美感的金属底座、超纤薄相框感的金属机身以及曲面大屏幕，让人不由心动。产品底座设计为细枝镂空，简洁稳固，适合在家中的多个环境摆放。简洁的背板使用磁吸盖板，使整机简洁，同时起到收纳线缆的作用。底座使用可回收金属进行磨砂与高亮的双质感处理，高端金属质感使产品充满科技感和奢华感。电视侧面与背面的完美处理，使产品设计进阶高端水准。

The OLED TV adopts design to demonstrates its futuristic. The product uses thin speaker design, hollow base design and simple beauty back design embodies the whole concept of ultra-thin. The highly aesthetic metal base, super slim metal body frame and curved sense the big screen brings is impressive. The base is designed hollow twigs, which is simple and stable for home display. Magnetic back cover is utilized to collect cables at the same time. The use of recyclable metal base is processed double scrub and highlight texture processing, the strong high-end metallic finish makes the product full of technology and luxury. Perfect finishing and the back side of the TV takes the product design to a high end.

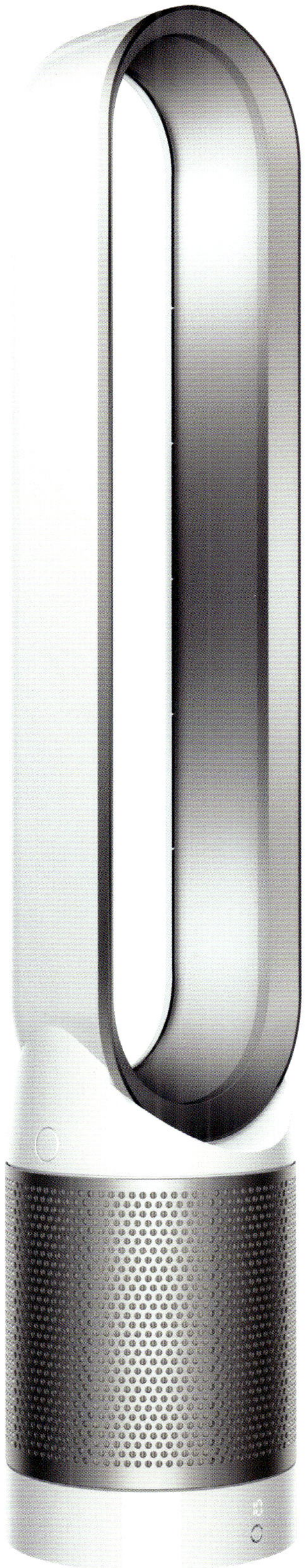

戴森 Pure Cool™ 空气净化风扇
Dyson Pure Cool

设计 / 戴森
生产 / 戴森
Design / Dyson
Manufacture / Dyson

该产品不同于以往的风扇，同时也是一台空气净化器。产品采用独特的戴森 360 度极细玻璃纤维 HEPA 滤网，有效捕捉 99.95% 的细微颗粒与有害物质，并能将其牢牢地锁在滤网中。产品将净化器与风扇功能完美融合，可将净化后的空气均匀、安静地吹送至屋内各个角落。此产品采用强大的气流倍增器技术，并使用风扇底部的混流叶轮吸入空气。产品采用修长的流线型设计，简洁轻盈的线条延续了戴森一贯的品牌设计，并且易于搬动，不会影响起居室的整洁和美观。产品将空气处理的功能发挥到极致，将一件产品设计为一件艺术品。

The Dyson Pure Cool purifier fan uses the unique Dyson 360° Glass HEPA filter. This technology captures 99.95% of particles as small as PM0.1, once trapped in the filter, it won't enter your lungs. It projects cleaner, purified air around the room evenly and quietly. Cleaner air then leaves the amplifier loop at a high velocity and is directed over an airfoil-shaped ramp. The product has inherited the design DNA of the line, concise, logical and light of Dyson, which is easy to move, and could be part of the living room. it also takes the air treatment to an extreme extend, successfully turns the industrial product into an art work.

扫一扫查看产品 Pin3D 技术三维效果图
Scanning for the 3D image by Pin3D

海信激光影院
Hisense VIDAA MAX Laser Theater

设计 / 海信工业设计中心
生产 / 青岛海信电器股份有限公司
Design / Hisense ID Center
Manufacture / Qingdao Hisense Electronioцs Co.,Ltd

该产品是全球首款激光影院，设计灵感来源于海面上的帆船。产品克服了现有产品的不足，是一款呈现大画面的激光投影仪产品。产品颠覆当前的液晶显示技术，克服了人眼长时间观看而产生荧光色造成不适感，避免对眼睛的辐射。主机外形采用 3D 切削边， 正面由 16 颗微型 LED 灯组成了“能量环”开机灯效，增添激光感和科技感，同时带有神秘之美。产品在小空间短距离的使用也能有大画面的投影体验，满足用户需求，让用户在家中也能有如身临剧场般的视觉感受。时尚的银色外观与产品功能融合，相得益彰。上部表面为全金属，低调中彰显产品的高端气质。

Inspired by the sails on the sea, this laser theater overcomes the disadvantage, produces a big screen laser projector product which overcomes the discomfort caused by fluorescent phosphor, without any radiation. 16 mini LED lamps like an "energy ring" as an opening light effect, become a highlight of the entire design, the high-tech and laser feeling giving us a mysterious beauty. The stylish silver exterior and product features integration with each other. The upper surface is of all-metal, highlighting the qualities of high-end product.

扫一扫查看产品 Pin3D 技术三维效果图
Scanning for the 3D image by Pin3D

扫一扫查看产品 Pin3D 技术三维效果图
Scanning for the 3D image by Pin3D

探索者
Xplorer V

设计 / 深圳零度智能飞行器有限公司
生产 / 深圳雷柏科技股份有限公司
Design / Shenzhen Zero-tech UAV Limited
Manufacture / Shenzhen Rapoo Technology Co.,Ltd

该产品是一款为全民打造的经济实用的无人机，制造精良。应用先进的技术，使产品可通过智能手机操控，同时拥有优质摄像头。模块化外挂设计，同时支持多款相机，无需工具切换。手机操作，自动跟随，可 360 度环绕自拍，开启全新自拍时代。产品具有精密的三轴陀螺云台及增稳技术，可以高精度多角度控制。产品搭载松下 1400 万像素传感器，高品质成像。云台、电池、飞控中心皆可独立购买和更换，降低用户的整机维护成本。外观设计参考 U2 隐形战机，棱角分明的菱形切面配合炫酷涂装，彰显品位，打造独一无二的未来科幻感。

XIRO is a consuming drone made for all the people with its sophisticated manufacturing, it can be controlled by smart phones. The 3-axis gyroscope and active/automatic stability technology enables high accuracy of angle control. The Panasonic sensor with 14 megapixels achieves high-quality imagery. Pilot can detach or exchange cameras for different purposes without the help of any tools. The costs of purchasing and maintaining has been reduced a lot because of cloud deck, battery and flight control center can be replaced independently. The inspiration of design comes from U2 stealth aircraft. The clean-cut rhombic section design, along with the cool coating, will manifest your taste, creating a unique future sense of sci-fi.

蝙蝠无人机
BAT

设计 / 北京白鲸创享科技有限公司
生产 / 江苏首控制造技术有限公司
Design / Beluga Design
Manufacture / Jiangsu Capital Holding Manufacturing Technology Limited

扫一扫查看产品 Pin3D 技术三维效果图
Scanning for the 3D image by Pin3D

蝙蝠无人机可广泛用于电力巡检、反恐侦查、消防救援、交通指挥以及农业植保等行业的实时探测、目标定位等。产品通过高效智能操控，极大限度地避免危险并及时准确获取信息，同时降低能耗。创新使用 PMI 高强泡沫为芯层结构，最大程度轻量化。整机使用独家专利自主定位充电技术，具有可持续巡航能力。采用自主起降和导航飞行模式，产品更智能化。产品结合蝙蝠的造型设计，采用兰博基尼折纸风格，集合 GPS 主机外壳，由三角面组合而成，形态小巧，有效保护内部电池和电子元件。产品结构件与外罩采用先进复合材料和 3D 打印先进工艺，在国际上处于先进行列，具有极高的经济价值。

The BAT UAV system has been widely applied in power line inspection, anti-terrorism, traffic guidance, disaster relief, agricultural protection, tracking down designated targets, providing real-time inspection and locating targets. This product involves bat-shape outline design with super light-weight and robust carbon fiber structure. The internal filling structure applies PMI high-robustness foam to reach the top level in the function of robustness and light-weight at the same time. Patented charging technique insures the BAT's cruising duration. It is highly intellective. Its system and module have made low cost for maintenance possible. 3D printer technology has been applied in batteries and flight control modules in order to realize fast production. Looking for the design inspiration from the gesture of flying bats, presenting in the origami style like Lamborghini cars, from which the BAT UAV come into being with a distinctive look.

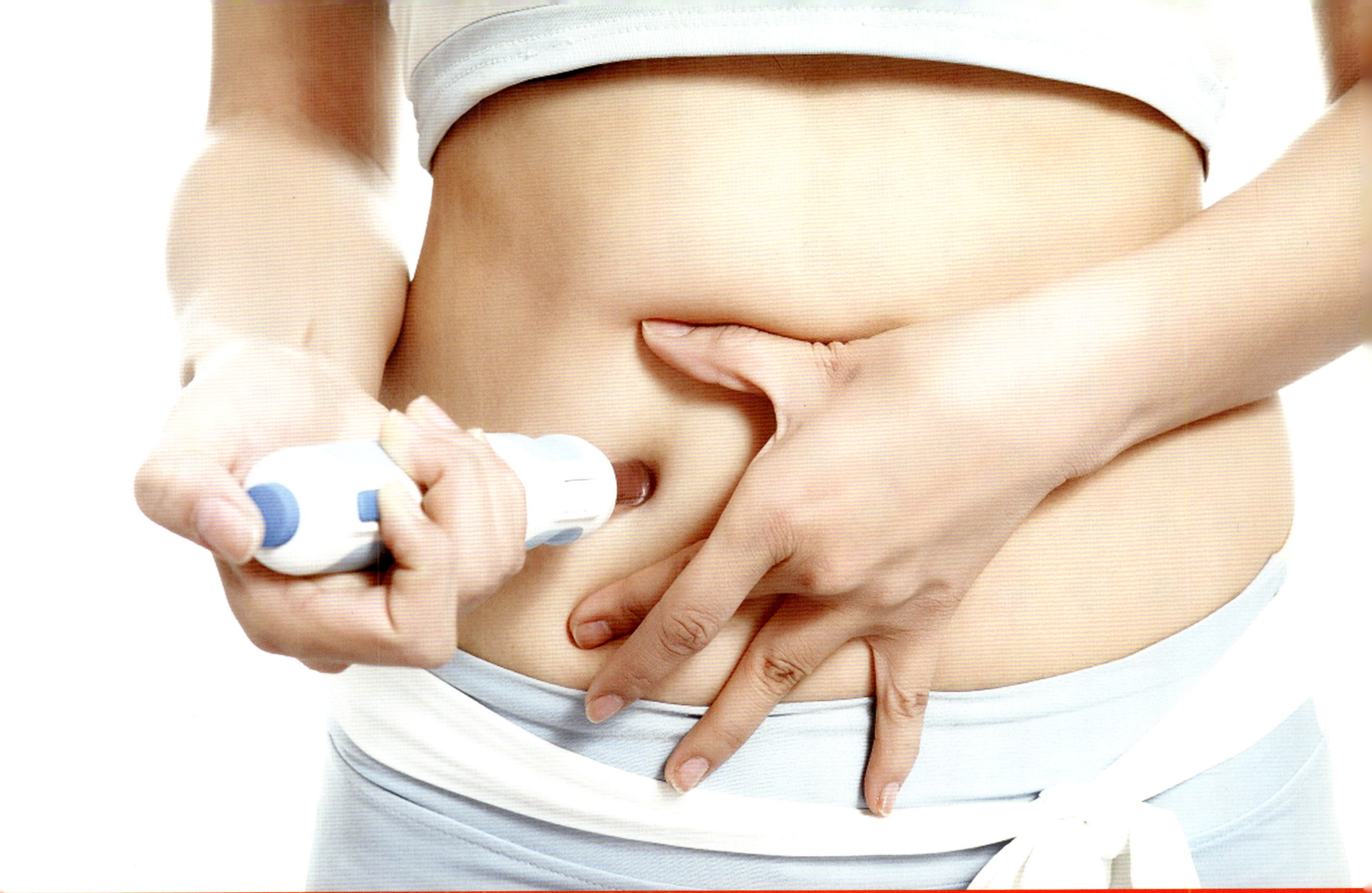

QS-M2 无针注射器
QS-M2 Needle-free Injector

设计 / 陈苏宁
生产 / 北京快舒尔医疗技术有限公司
Design / Chen Suning
Manufacture / Beijing QS Medical Technology Co.,Ltd

扫一扫查看产品 Pin3D 技术三维效果图
Scanning for the 3D image by Pin3D

该产品是目前全球唯一单次灌药多次注射的胰岛素无针注射器，利用机械产生瞬间高压推动药剂经过极细喷嘴，高速穿过皮肤直接弥散到皮下组织，对于每天都要注射胰岛素的糖尿病患者，无针注射器能较好地消除患者对针头的恐惧感，降低刺痛感及感染率，提高胰岛素利用度，缩短起效时间，亦可以避免因长期局部注射而产生的皮肤硬结。材料符合医疗卫生标准并可回收，使用寿命长。圆润造型表现亲和力，摆脱工具感。产品的设计在吸药、调节注射计量、保证注射安全等方面科学、合理、有效，产品的结构设计符合人机工学要求，整体设计品质较高。

With 18 patents the world's sole needle-free injector QS-M2, which is specially designed for injecting insulin into diabetic patients, allows multiple injections after filling the injector only one time for diabetic patients who need multiple insulin injections each day. It uses high pressure instantly generated by machinery to propel the drug through a very tiny nozzle, which then penetrates skin at a high speed to directly disperse the drug solution. Compared with needle injector, QS-M2 eliminates a patient's fear of needles, while minimizing such piercing pain. Moreover, it makes insulin penetrate and instantly disperse throughout skin, thus improving the bioavailability of insulin. The interior of this needle-free injector is mainly made of aluminum and nylon materials, and PC materials make up its exterior. All materials are 100% recyclable and comply with health and hygiene standards. The extraordinary softness of the QS-P is conveyed by its round shapes. The finishing of the body takes a tactile warmth and softness, and also it increases the friction to avoid slipping out.

CHINA RED STAR DESIGN AWARD

Silver Prize

银奖

传祺 GS4
Trumpchi GS4

设计 / 广州汽车集团股份有限公司汽车工程研究院
生产 / 广州汽车集团股份有限公司
Design / Guangzhou Automobile Group Co.,Ltd Automotive Engineering Institute
Manufacture / Guangzhou Automobile Group Motor Co., Ltd

传祺 GS4 定位年轻人专属紧凑级都市 SUV，外形极富形式创新元素，展示了中国机动车设计的新维度。GS4 搭载全新广汽智能车联网系统，实现远程监控车辆数据、启动与熄火、控制空调、诊断及故障信息显示、ECU 升级及标定等。产品搭载传祺第二代 200T 发动机，动力超越 2.0L 自然吸气发动机。产品外观以品牌自身作为设计元素，不仅设计了典型的格栅和引擎盖，还拥有平衡的车身比例和特色的流线外观。产品最大亮点是驾驶室及内饰设计，内部通过合理人机布局实现车内空间最大化，内饰延续了传祺家族展翼式横向设计格局，展示了高超的设计水平和到位的设计细节。

Full of creative elements, the Trumpchi GS4 is a compact urban SUV specially tailored for younger customers, which shows a new dimension in Chinese automotive design. GS4 applies the whole new GAC smart IOV system, could realize the remote monitor of the vehicle data, remote control of start-up and shut-down, AC control, diagnose and display of breakdown, ECU upgrde, etc. Built in the 2nd generation Trumpchi 200T engine, the power is beyond the 2.0L NA engine. The exterior is "branded" with the brand' s own identity not only by designing a typical grill and front hood but also by well balanced proportion and characteristic outer lines. The biggest surprise is the interior and the cockpit-design, it shows a high level of design quality and detailed purity.

Nubia Z9

设计 / 努比亚技术有限公司
生产 / 努比亚技术有限公司
Design / Nubia Technology Co.,Ltd
Manufacture / Nubia Technology Co.,Ltd

此产品是一款优质的智能手机，开创无边框手机交互时代，可通过单手握持及滑动手机边缘完成绝大多数操作。手机边框具有调整屏幕亮度、快速拍照、抓握解锁等功能。产品不仅应用了最新的技术，而且拥有迷人的外观设计，采用5.2寸屏幕以及全球最窄手机宽度。5D弧面玻璃大大提升了屏幕显示的视觉冲击力与触感的流畅度。产品界面设计具有逻辑性并且使操作自然。产品采用无边框设计，体现自由感，满足当代人对无拘无束的生活态度的渴望。产品具有优美的外观设计，并采用精致的工艺技术，使其成为一款上乘的产品。

Nubia Z9 is a high class smart phone. The Arc Refractive Conduction technology created by Nubia has already made a breakthrough in the field of LCD process. The inevitable edges around the LCD panels are visually hidden to create infinite visual effect on the bordered LCD, and allow users to truly get rid of the visual bondage of black edges on traditional smart phones. After combining the world' s narrowest width of 5.2" smart phone, the remarkable 2.5D arc glass (both front and back) creates a smooth contour. The borderless design of Nubia Z9 allows for larger display area on the compact phone body and provides more comfortable hand feel comparing to same or smaller screen smart phones. Borderless reflects that people are yearning for an unrestrained and relaxed attitude towards life and looking for a free lifestyle. Borderless phones bring unrestrained freedom to people. Finally the very well designed proportions and excellent craftsmanship make it a desirable product- a must have.

扫一扫查看产品 Pin3D 技术三维效果图
Scanning for the 3D image by Pin3D

XT680 伸缩臂叉装机
XT680 Telehandler

设计 / 江苏徐州工程机械研究院工业设计中心
生产 / 徐州工程机械集团有限公司
Design / ID Center of Jiangsu Xuzhou Construction Machinery Research
Manufacture / Xuzhou Construction Machinery Group Inc.

扫一扫查看产品 Pin3D 技术三维效果图
Scanning for the 3D image by Pin3D

XT680伸缩臂叉装机采用了多种转向模式和全开启式机罩。产品整机设计紧凑，桥荷分配合理，采用国内首创的全新通透式无骨架玻璃开门的方式，使操作者的视野更开阔，为操作者提供了良好的作业环境。驾驶室及机罩等采用通用化设计，保证多吨位型号通用，减少开发及生产成本。整机造型线条流畅，色彩分割明确，造型仿照人体关节，设计富有力量与肌肉感。产品设计为整体式车架，转弯半径小，机动性能好。整机 80% 采用可回收材质和无铅油漆，降低对环境的污染。发动机机罩上增加曲面压型，使造型与功能完美结合。产品既有力量感又有亲和性，美学品质较高。

This product adopts a variety of steering mode, a fully-open hood, compact structure and reasonable assignment of bridge load. The transparent frameless glass door design, as a noise proof and shock absorbent panoramic vision cab allows a spacious view, providing terrific working environment for operators. Universal design for the cab and hood are the guarantee of the cost reduction. The overall design is full of power and muscular, bionics design is inspired from the human body joint. The adoption of unit frame makes a shorter turning radius and brings good mobility. 80% of the product used the recycled material and lead free paint to reduce the pollution of the environment. Featuring the profiled cover of the cab, the shape and functions are integrated perfectly, the whole product is full of power, yet affinity, is a high level of product of aesthetics.

苏州有轨电车 1 号线
Suzhou Tram Line 1CN

设计 / 法国 MBD 工业设计公司
生产 / 南车南京浦镇车辆有限公司
Design / MBD Design France
Manufacture / CSR Nanjing Puzhen Co.,Ltd

苏州有轨电车 1 号线首次将有轴转向架运用到低地板有轨电车上，大大简化转向架结构，提高车辆运行可靠性，降低车轮磨耗。车轮采用弹性车轮，运行噪音低，舒适性高。产品独创了控制器、控制按钮及超大驾驶视野集成于司机室，易于操作，提高了驾驶安全性。产品探索了有轨电车造型的识别语意，车头设计为笑脸，透露着欢迎乘坐的好客之意。电车车身设计为金色，挡风玻璃为黑色，给人雍容华贵、精致高雅的感受。该产品体现了科技与设计的结合，同时提升了城市形象品质，对我国城市交通系统效率的提高、能源的节省以及民生改善做出了突出贡献。

It is a pioneering design to apply the axle-bogie to 100% low floor tram in China, which has greatly simplified the bogie structure, improves the vehicle running reliability and reduced the abrasion of wheel. The completely-new crash design concept and rapidly exchangeable energy-absorption unit can not only provide sufficient safety for the vehicle but also improve the operation efficiency. The creative design of integration the controller and control buttons onto the driver desk in cab as well as the extra wide driving vision realize convenient interface between man and machine. The vehicle head is designed similar to a smiling face which looks lively and delightful. The golden car body and black windscreen reflects the typical color combination for the luxury industry, which increases the dignity of the car body, giving a sense of elegancy, delicacy and luxury. The combination of science and design is also a promotion the city image.

赞月池茶盘
Praise of Moon Tea Tray Set

设计 / 石大宇
生产 / 北京清庭文创文化发展有限公司
Design / Jeff Dayu Shi
Manufacture / Dragonfly Design Center

该茶盘以棉线与陶锤代替塑料排水管，排水时形成清雅冰柱，解决外观和噪音问题，使造型诗意、雅致。滤水系统由多个圆柱竹条组成，空隙合理，有效过滤，防止阻塞。竹条因水量上下浮动，可提示注水量，又创造错落有致的美感。接水罐设计可拆卸条状提把，方便移动，也可隐藏在内槽中，集美感与功能于一身。产品采用竹子材质，具有中国味，适合应用于茶道中。以竹代木，竹材的清雅与品茗的优雅相呼应，绿色环保。同时，设计细节到位，在倒水的过程中，水流的控制具有创造性，使用中具有趣味性。产品将品茶和设计完美结合，提供奇特的饮茶体验。

By adopting the patented drainage system, where tubular bamboo sticks are arranged in a picturesque order, act as a filter and an indicator of drainage efficiency, the Praise of Moon Tea Tray Set allows more effective tea and water filtering and prevents clogging when tea spillage run through. The handle bar of water container is removable for easy transportation and cleaning, when not in use, can be placed in the inlet for storage. Bamboo is the material most representative of Chinese culture and one of the most environmentally sustainable resources, which perfectly matches the spirit of teaism. The outcome is a magnificent end product with aesthetic appearance and uncompromised functionalities. With this tea tray, tea-making becomes an elegant experience.

“无”衣帽架
Wu

设计 / 周安彬、雷南仕
生产 / 广州高尚生活文化传播有限公司
Design / Zhou Anbin, Lei Nanshi
Manufacture / Gaoshang Living (GuangZhou)Co.,Ltd

“无”是一款运用铣槽工艺，将生产效率、拆装运输、结构美感完美融合的衣帽架。枝与杆的处理让人印象深刻，结构极简单却十分巧妙。产品所用的木材环保，工艺简单，拆装简易，包装合理。铣槽不仅可以作为支架的收纳结构，更成为独特的细节美感。产品主杆分为5段，缩小了包装体积，避免因木棍过长而产生变形。衣帽架的支杆、主杆与底盘可嵌合在一起，最大限度地缩减了包装体积，降低了运输成本。该产品是一件可以走向世界的作品，它将东方手艺人的灵性与当下的时尚完美结合。

The WU coat stand is a perfect combination which adopts milling grooves technique enables a high efficiency work, simple assemble and shipment. The treatment of rod and branch is very impressive, simple but smart. The milling grooves could not only use as the collection structure, but also indicates a special detailed aesthetics. The main rod is divided into 5 parts to avoid the deformation because of the length. A smart collection of branch rod, main rod and chassis could reduce the package, thus, a shipment cost could be reduce. This is a world class work which represent a perfect combination of the spirit of the oriental craftsmen and the current fashion trend.

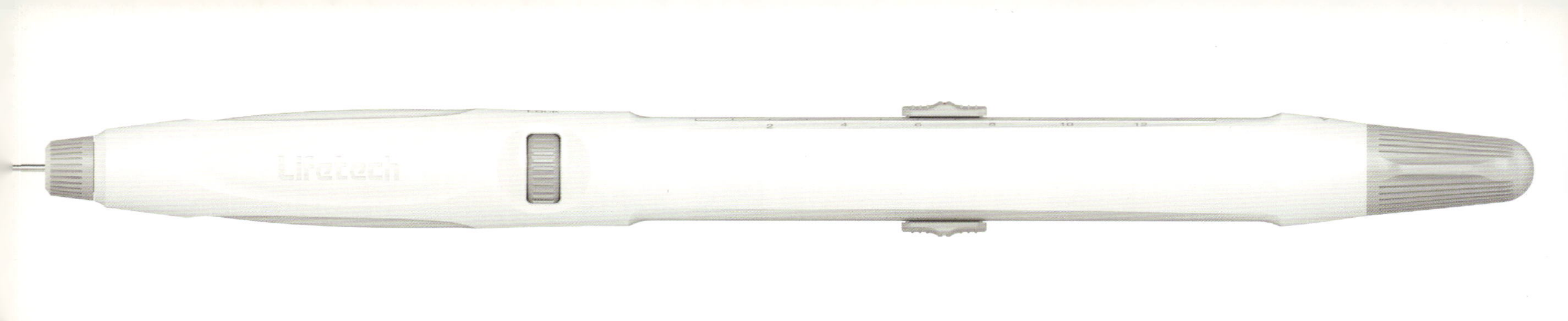

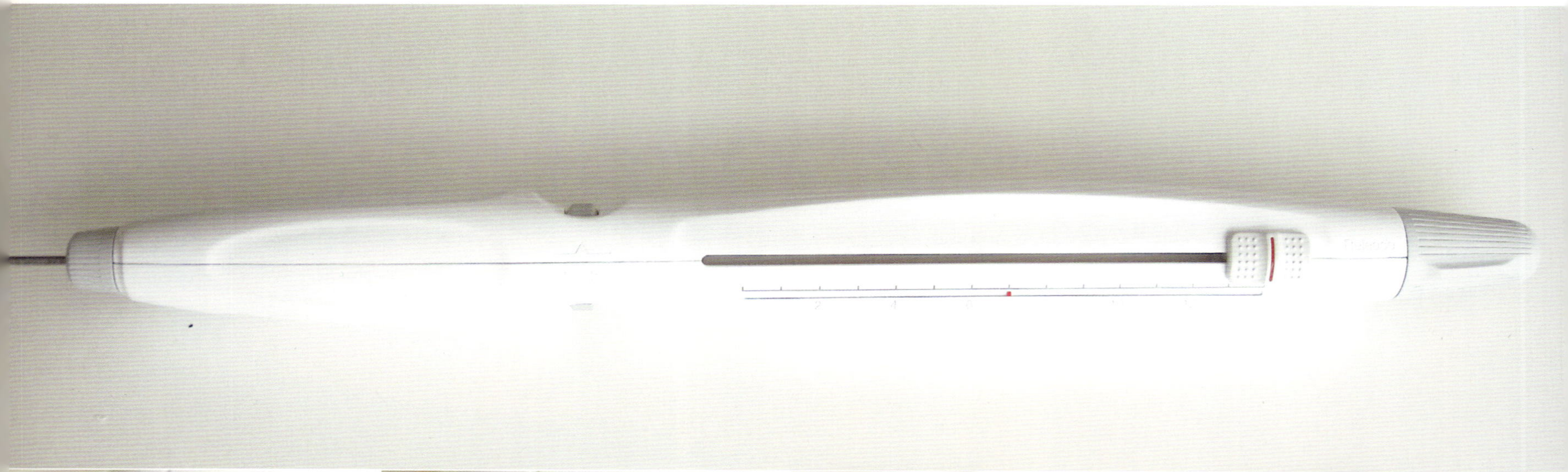

介入医疗器械可吸收封堵器
Absorbable ASD Closure System

设计 / 深圳市四六区工业产品策划有限公司
生产 / 先健科技（深圳）有限公司
Design / April 6th Design Co.,Ltd
Manufacture / Lifetech Scientific(Shenzhen)Co.,Ltd

介入医疗器械可吸收封堵器是全球首款可降解、可吸收材料封堵器。传统封堵器是由不可降解材质制成，其永存人体内会造成并发症。该产品是一个可降解、可吸收植入人体（如心脏）器械。前期可封堵血液异向分流，后期可引导人体自身组织生长，最后在病灶部位完全降解被人体吸收。其在完成“桥梁”作用后可被机体吸收，使缺损完全由自身组织替代，并消除封堵器永久存留体内造成的临床远期并发症和不利影响。外观设计灵感来自有机生物体的自然曲线，并结合人体黄金比例。产品外观没有一颗螺钉，体现医疗产品高精密度的严谨性、宜人性和未来科技感。

The absorbable ASD Closure System is the very first biodegradable and absorbable closure system all over the world. Comparing with the traditional product, it is an implanted equipment which could be biodegradable and absorbable by the human body. In the early stage, the product could block the blood off the incongruous flow. In the late stage, as a bridge, it can lead the body tissue grow spontaneously, and finally be absorbed by the body. This will eliminate the caused related clinical complications and adverse effects in the case of permanent closure maintenance. Product design is based on the organisms’ smoothing line and golden ratio of human body. No screws can be found in the product, which indicates a rigorousness, comfort and future feeling.

定量快开龙头
Quantitative Quick Tap

设计 / 佛山市日丰企业有限公司
生产 / 佛山市日丰企业有限公司
Design / Foshan Rifeng Enterprise Co.,Ltd
Manufacture / Foshan Rifeng Enterprise Co.,Ltd

这是一款功能和美学上完美结合的产品。水龙头的设计采用了简洁并且有逻辑的设计语言，并以满足用户需求为目的。导入了出水预设定量功能，当出水达到预设量，龙头自动关闭，适合为较大容器接水。开关及流量控制把手设计于龙头出水口，用户操作时直接与水接触，避免了洗净的手二次弄脏。控水转轮与产品完美融合，整体完成度非常高。表面处理和几何过度非常讲究。虽然它是一个非电动的水龙头，但却传递出了出色的精准度。该产品的难度在于墙面安装，出口、控制手柄等部件在一件产品上得到完美的处理。

The product is a very appearing combination of functionality and aesthetics. The design of the faucet follows a clear and logic design language and is determined by the user-needs. The preset water quantity function enables the product to automatically shut down when the water reaches the preset amount. The switch is designed at the water outlet to avoid the second pollution by touching it. The control wheel for quantity adjustment is nicely integrated into the entire concept and the overall finish is of superb quality. The treatment of surface finish and geometric transitions is very sophisticated. Although it's a non-electronic faucet it conveys the feelings of outstanding accuracy. The challenge to unify the wall-mount, the outlet and the control knob in one consistent body has been execute perfectly.

FW6108 移动式多功能照明装置
FW6108 Portable Multi-functional Lighting Device

设计 / 海洋王照明科技股份有限公司
生产 / 海洋王照明科技股份有限公司
Design / Ocean King Lighting Technology Co.,Ltd
Manufacture / Ocean King Lighting Technology Co.,Ltd

FW6108 移动式多功能照明装置采用独特的箱式设计，拥有带刹车结构的滚轮装置，可徒手安装和拆卸。产品智慧地满足真实工作中的需要，尤其在自然灾害和事故发生时实用有效，同时也是一款环境友好产品。整体设计非常简洁，易于携带和快速连接。产品采用升降杆结构可增大照明面积，且灯头高度和角度可随意调整。采用开关电源技术，使用微电脑进行智能控制。具有剩余电量查询功能，配置聚光和泛光双灯头，可无极调光。相机云台设计，可取代现场拍照的相机三脚架。同时配置红蓝双色 LED 警示灯，交替闪烁发出警示信号。

FW6108 mobile multi-function lighting device adopts a unique crate design, which is a roller device with brake structure and can be handed assemble and dissasemble. Product wisely meet the real needs of the real working situation, it's particularly practical when natural disasters and accidents happen, meanwhile it's an eco-friendly product. The overall design is very compact, easy to carry and connect. Product utilizes the lift rod structure to enlarge the lighting area, and the cap height and angle can be adjusted freely. Switching power supply technology realizes the computer control. Condenser and floodlight configuration enables the infinite adjustment. The holder is designed as the camera's which could replace the tripod. Red and blue dual color LED alarm are adopted.

門橋躍龍
風儒起代

鴐馳凱飢殼愨釩築糾閔
閆絎訐軒頇紆釬虧鉫貼
鮎覘詁鈷軲鴣鶘鬍結鮚
詰頡擷纈話鴰颳闊捨詒
給貽鮐駘飴颱軹貺說銳
閑鏜絡詻輅[illegible]鉻賀駕駒

方正榜书行
FZ Bang Shu Xing

设计 / 汪文
生产 / 北京北大方正电子有限公司
Design / Wang Wen
Manufacture / Beijing Founder Electronics Co.,Ltd

电脑字库字如何不断创新发展一直是业界关注的问题，此产品在设计上参考了明清两朝科举匾额上的行楷书风，将传统书法与现代字体设计相融合，既有厚重、大气的美感又有细节笔触流动，具有较好的表现力。通过数码相机和电脑辅助设计进行巧妙的飞白处理，是国内第一款有毛笔飞白处理的电脑字体设计。产品实现了笔墨雍容、内韵中正、雄健磅礴、大气灵动的艺术效果。方正榜书行应用范围广泛，适用于商业牌匾、展览、品牌、包装、广告、书籍、电子出版物等，方便、实用、有效。

Founder BangShu is a computer font product that integrates Chinese traditional calligraphy with modern font design. It emphasizes the traditional culture, especially the influence of Chinese calligraphy, which also promotes service ability of cultural innovation for whole society. Bangshu is a calligraphy specifically used for imperial examination tablet in Ming and Qing dynasty. Aesthetic feeling of BangShu pursuits a thick and graceful of the Chinese character strokes. The Founder Bangshu is a combination of traditional calligraphy and modern computer font design. It shows the art effect of natural, special charm, powerful and magnificent, avoid the bored feeling of traditional font to a great extent, it shows great visual effect when being used magnifiedly. Adopting digital camera and computer auxiliary to transform the calligraphy into a computer font makes it a reality to show the ancient calligraphy in computer. This is the very first digital font with brush malapropism skill.

CHINA RED STAR DESIGN AWARD

Best Team Prize

最佳团队奖

联想笔记本设计团队
Lenovo Notebook Design Team

联想笔记本设计团队于 2000 年初成立，成立以来一直承担联想笔记本产品的设计工作。团队由设计、工程、用户体验等多专业人员组成，十几年间，所设计的产品获得超过 40 个国内外奖项，获奖产品包括联想天逸系列、Ideapad 系列、昭阳系列、Yoga 系列等。其中，Yoga 系列产品的创新设计尤为突出，为联想带来的不只是产品设计的创新，更创造了产品品牌及行业内的新形态笔记本电脑模式——Yoga 形态的笔记本。

Lenovo notebook design team founded in early 2000, almost all of the Lenovo notebook product design. The team is a multi-disciplinary team, including of the design, engineering, user experience, etc., in the ten years of its design products have more than 40 domestic and international awards, including the Lenovo Tianyi series, Ideapad series, Zhaoyang series, Yoga series. Especially innovative design of Yoga series that bring not only a product, but also created a new product brand, and inside the industry laptop business mode – Yoga form factor product.

CHINA RED STAR DESIGN AWARD

Best New Designer Prize

最佳新人奖

李若鑫
Li Ruoxin

[大道至简，平淡为归 / Less is more]

1990 年生于四川，2013 年毕业于广西桂林电子科技大学工业设计专业。在校期间，积极参与社会实践，不断自学提高设计水品。毕业后任深圳市想象力产品策划有限公司设计师一职，先后为爱国者、飞利浦、读书郎等企业提供设计服务。设计面覆盖教学、通讯、消费电子等行业。2014 年担任努比亚技术有限公司造型设计师，先后设计 NubiaZ9/Z9MAX/Z9MINI/Nubia 布拉格，产品上市后反向热烈。

Born in 1990 in Sichuan, Li Ruoxin graduated from Guilin University of Electronic Technology, majored in design. He participated in Shenzhen Imagination Design and became a designer, has designed for Aigc, Philips etc brands. Products designed by him are mainly about education, communication and consumer electronics. 2014, He became an designer for Nubia Technology, and designed NubiaZ9/Z9MAX/Z9MINI/Nubia Prague, and the series are popular in the markets.

CHINA RED STAR DESIGN AWARD

Excellent Prize

红星奖

倬茂网络红外摄像机
Infrared Camera Network

设计 / 深圳市感叹号产品设计有限公司
生产 / 倬茂企业股份有限公司
Design / Shenzhen Exclamation Point Pruduct Design Co., Ltd
Manufacture / Zhuo Mao Technology (Shenzhen) Co., Ltd

该产品兼具美感与实用性于一身。产品理念来自于直升飞机，机身悬空，整体喷涂白色，翅膀的地方采用透明 PC 背面丝印蜂窝纹，颠覆了传统摄像机造型。产品机身周身采用铝合金压铸成型，结实耐用并具有防水防尘功能，在室内户外皆可使用。机身所有废料、不良壳料皆可多次重复利用，完美地将环保理念注入了产品本身。

The body is suspended, like a frame for the fighter, sporty, whole body white spray, where the wings on the back of the PC transparent honeycomb screen, elegant fashion, a high degree of recognition in the industry!

康佳 BK929 警务智能手机
KONKA BK929

设计 / 陈万衡
生产 / 深圳康佳通信科技有限公司
Design / Chen Wanheng
Manufacture / Shenzhen KONKA Telecommunications Techology Co., Ltd

该产品从军备中抽取元素，为 IP67 业界最高工业三防等级，可满足各警种在户外、夜晚、雨雾天气等多种复杂条件下执行警务工作。突破性的壳金分离的结构设计，使机身强度较同类型设备增强 3 倍，同时在主壳四角再增加一层防护壳，极大提升防摔防震能力。采用高度可回收的铝金属中框，不含汞的 LCD 显示屏，安全环保。

BK929 using composite staggered design thinking, the extraction of elements from the arms and armor like modeling highlights the equipment configuration and function of the powerful. Equipment side CNC precision manufacturing mechanical texture with the texture of the back of the laser engraving emphasizes the nature of equipment as the product of the police. The different functions of the key design which different sizes and textures, the effective identification of the more abundant details. Rich, line and plane cross turning no matter from any angle observed body can feel rich level and professional equipment sophisticated powerful.

E 动终端
E Mobile Terminal

设计 / 张楠、黄波文
生产 / 福建星网锐捷通讯股份有限公司
Design / Zhang Nan, Huang Bowen
Manufacture / Fujian Star-net Communication Co., Ltd

该产品改变了常规的业务模式，将金融行业柜台的功能整合到一台笔记本电脑里，真正实现移动办公。通过模块化设计来满足各个行业的需求，集成了二代证、指纹仪等功能，并配置外置 3G 天线，解决了户外信号较弱问题。铝壳采用氧化喷砂工艺，塑壳采取细腻的皮纹处理，轻薄便携，根据内部元器件的堆叠，厚度按最小尺寸设计，节省空间。

Portable light, according to the internal components of the stack, according to the thickness of the smallest size design, enough to place the local thickening mode, and then rounded and refinement, such as reducing thin body and makes the body of a hierarchy. Black and silver colors elegant and cool.

智能屏风系统
Smart Screen Systems

设计 / 深圳市柏斯工业设计有限公司
生产 / 深圳市柏斯工业设计有限公司
Design / Shenzhen Perth Industrial Design Co.,Ltd
Manufacture / Shenzhen Perth Industrial Design Co.,Ltd

该系统分为总机和单元机两部分，利用了现代化网络技术实现了无纸化高效率办公方式。单元机与主机相连，接收和显示信息。通过互联网远程控制管理每一个办公卡位人员出勤状况、办公信息，且具备发送公告等功能。外观简洁，背部采用镂空设计。不占用桌面空间，提高办公效率，达到高效的人力资源管理，实现了环保办公的理念。

This design with concise appearance modelling, hale line style, highlight the texture of the metal. Operator hanging on the wall, the design of the back of the hollow out increasing the sense of the future of science and technology, product ChanYuanJi overhead design, convenient power, at the bottom of the USB plug and cables from the external links, high display can clearly see the latest news, also won't take up desktop space, greatly improve the efficiency of office.

智能后视镜行车记录仪
Smart Rearview Mirror Car Driving Recorder

设计 / 深圳捷渡科技有限公司
生产 / 深圳捷渡科技有限公司
Design / Jado Technology Co,Ltd
Manufacture / Jado Technology Co,Ltd

本产品为首款真正实现纯平技术的专车专用产品，低于 1 毫米极窄边框，镜面占比高达 99%，外观时尚简洁，完美保障行车安全。首创悬浮触控菜单，操作更便捷，增强屏幕可见性的同时会根据环境自动调正屏幕亮度，随时保证画面清晰。根据不同车型，配备专车专用支架，确保完美安装。具有一键分享功能，让快乐无处不在。

extremely narrow frame, super flat screen design, simple and generous; electroplating treatment loudspeaker, edge of the lens brushed metal with patch decoration make the product looks more beautiful.

EP404 蜗牛吸盘数据线
EP404 Snail Haptor USB Cable

设计 / 褚明华、申林
生产 / 深圳市洛斐客文化有限公司
Design / Tim Chu, Shuan Shen
Manufacture / Shenzhen Lofree Culture Co.,Ltd

该产品创意来源于硅胶吸盘，通过吸盘元素的设计，让数据线具有更多有趣实用的功能。可以自我卷绕吸附，具有收纳、避免缠绕、便携等特点，还可卷成不同造型为手机起到支撑的作用。解决以往的不便，增加实用的功能，赋予使用的乐趣。采用环保无毒的硅胶材料，易于清洁。可变换设计让用户在使用中去发现不同用法，增加用户与产品的互动。

Creativity is from the silicon sucker, by designing the sucker; the data cable may have more function and bring fun. The product could be self-rotate and absorption, it can be rotated and support the mobile phone with different forms. The eco-friendly silicon material is easy for cleaning, and the changeable design brings different using method.

云电栈
Powerloft

设计 / 深圳市四六区工业产品策划有限公司
生产 / 深圳市赤道极光信息科技有限公司
Design / April 6th Design Co.,Ltd
Manufacture / Shenzhen Equator Aurora Information Tech. Ltd

该产品是全球首创的网络控制无线充电座，一款能显示、可互动的联网终端。用户扫描产品上的二维码可随时了解最新资讯，有利于信息传播。终端控制减少中间生产加工成本，放置公共场合时能够有效减少纸张使用，节能环保。整体采用直线弯折的手法，展现纤细轻巧且流畅的外观。充电头放置两侧方便使用，中空位置放置手机可减少油渍溅污。

This is an online control wireless charging dock, This is a networking terminal that contain a display screen and be able to interact with it. Users recieve information from the QR code display on the screen, the QR code can be changed in seconds, which is providing people to get the latest information immediately. It can reduce the processing expences by using a networking terminal, which is cheaper and faster. The charging lines are sticked in both sides, Curve design at the top of display screen.

小型化卫星信号模拟器
Miniaturization of Satellite Signal Simulator

设计 / 甄大崴
生产 / 航天恒星科技有限公司
Design / Zhen Dawei
Manufacture / Space Star Technology Co., Ltd

该产品是航天恒星独立自主研制的一种小型便携导航信号模拟器，为满足导航设备的闭环测试要求而研发，已经完成了实际工程实现及试验验证。体积小，具有灵活的轨迹仿真功能，可支持复杂的工动态导航信号仿真。表面采用高密度特殊处理，降低了各种资源的浪费，能充分地满足用户研发和测试的需求。

Product modeling in professional as a starting point, the product model combining with its own function, give priority to with black color, suitable for laboratory use environment, buttons and a functional area emphasizes the design, to enhance the operability of the product and beautiful sex. Ultra modern design elements and professional design concept, in order to achieve the hightech,
high-quality design level. Buttons, lights, interface and other details of the product design and the overall building perfect fusion.

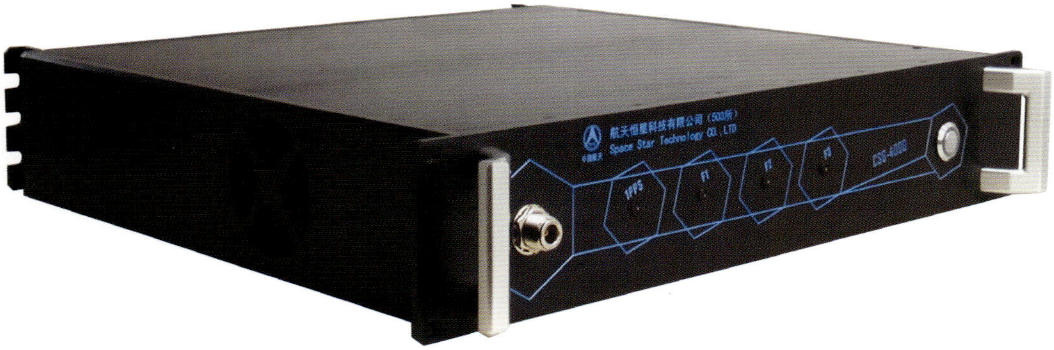

掌静脉认证智能终端
The Palm Meridians Intelligent Terminal Authentication

设计 / 成都拓成工业产品设计有限公司
生产 / 成都芯软件科技发展有限公司
Design / Chengdu Top-Creative Product Design Co.Ltd
Manufacture / Chengdu Cinsoft Technology Development Co.Ltd

该产品利用人体血红蛋白通过静脉时能吸收近红外光的特征，采集手掌皮肤下的静脉影像，并提取作为生物认证特征。采集是 3D 的图像，认证的错误率和失败率都比指纹识别更低，认证方便高效快捷。采用简单易加工制作的造型和工艺，以 ABS 和 PC 环保树脂为基料制作，材料均是可回收的高分子树脂，保证美观的同时又节约了成本。

Palm vein recognition using human hemoglobin can absorb the characteristics of near infrared light when it is absorbed by the human body, and can be used to collect the venous images under the palm skin. W th the other as compared with the fingerprint, iris biometrics, palm vein recognition must be living in the palm of your hand to flow to imaging, put an end to the prosthesis of false identification, and palm vein hidden under the skin, and is not visible to the naked eye, more difficult to copy forgery.

智能行车记录仪
Smart Driving Data Recorder

设计 / 深圳捷渡科技有限公司
生产 / 深圳捷渡科技有限公司
Design / Jado Technology Co.,Ltd
Manufacture / Jado Technology Co.,Ltd

该产品通过方与圆的几何体，进行全新大胆的尝试。采用防抖与碰撞感应技术，有效避免因抖动造成的影像模糊，并在感应到紧急刹车或碰撞时立即启动录影。操控极简，可以完成一键录音、一键回放等工作。可随汽车启动自动开机，汽车熄火自动关机，节能环保。材料采用镁铝合金材质，表面采用晒纹处理，达到了皮革的效果。上市以来销售火爆。

Appearance design: it by square and round geometry, the new bold attempt, in line with the design trend of high-end cars; Lens: made of magnesium alloy material, frosting treatment is better in appearance Surface treatment: texture treatment.

E 人 E 本 T9 商务平板
Business Tablet

设计 / 成都浪尖工业设计有限公司
生产 / 北京壹人壹本信息科技有限公司
Design / Chengdu Artop Industrial Design Co. Ltd
Manufacture / Beijing Ereneben Information Technology Co.,Ltd

该产品为国内首次采用 6 系铝镁合金中框，整机双面覆盖康宁大猩猩玻璃面板，防刮划、耐冲击。外形低调沉稳，典雅大方，专为政商精英设计，可手写处理所有工作。辅以移动办公 3.0 系统，可连通无线投影、无线打印等各种办公设备，随时随地办公。配备 1300 万像素摄像头与双 LED 闪光灯，给用户带来更加畅快的体验。引领数字书写时代。

T9 followed the same, book-inspired design language in the Business Tablet T series, with precisely crafted details in pursue of perfection. A concise yet graceful business style combined with cutting-edge craftsmanship conveys an impression of luxury and elegance.

SIM +蓝牙 SIM 卡读卡器
SIM + Bluetooth SIM Card Reader

设计 / 深圳市嘉兰图设计股份有限公司
生产 / 深圳市嘉兰图设计股份有限公司
Design / Shenzhen Newplan Design Co.,Ltd
Manufacture / Shenzhen Newplan Design Co.,Ltd

该产品是一款针对 iPhone 用户使用的 SIM 卡读卡器，打破 iPhone 只能读取一张 SIM 卡的使用模式，实现 iPhone 手机双卡双待功能，通过蓝牙无线信号与手机配对即可获取读卡器中 SIM 卡的信息。产品可让用户节省身处异地拨打电话的漫游费，同时提供与手机端的双向防丢功能。与信用卡尺寸相近，便于携带。金色材料通过精密的加工工艺，营造出精雕细琢的品质感，让人爱不释手。

SIM+ Bluetooth SIM card reader is specially designed for iPhone users. It breaks the single using mode of one SIM card only within the iPhone and provides the mode of dual SIM dual standby, which could save the roaming charges for users and equip the phone with anti-steal functions. It is easy and simple to handle that users only open the mobile APP and match the Bluetooth wireless signal and mobile phone to read the information from SIM card. The size is similar to a credit card with processor integrated circuit.

能科三防平板
Rugged Tablet PC

设计 / 郑州市浪尖产品设计有限公司

生产 / 能科节能技术股份有限公司

Design / Zhengzhou Artop Design Co.,Ltd

Manufacture / Nancal Energy-Saving Technology Co.,Ltd

该产品为特殊环境使用设备，具有指纹识别、无线射频等功能。造型设计考虑其人机性、及机器的防护性以及带手套操作的特殊性，让使用者在恶劣的使用环境下能高效地处理工作调度和信息控制。壳料大多采用可回收型 PC 及 TPU 原色注塑而成，有较好的手持舒适度并降低对环境的污染。边角均有防护，坚固防摔，已通过 IP 等级标准。

The product is used for special environment, is multi-functional of finger print recognition, and radio frequency identification, etc. Product could be used in unfriendly environment with high efficiency for control and info management. It has passed the IP standard with the professional grade.

三防手机
Dustproof, Shockproof and Waterproof Mobile Phone

设计 / 任敏杰

生产 / 上海数果科技有限公司

Design / Ren Minjie

Manufacture / Shanghai Several Fruit Technology Co.,Ltd

此产品针对特殊环境下的技术人员开发，体现专业可靠的形象特征与产品气质，专业的橙色外机身设计符合了三防人员的身份。壳料采用 PC+ABS 的回收材料原色注塑而成，减少了能源损耗和环境污染。可以在恶劣的环境中使用，如水、沙漠、强力冲击等。整体设计风格采用仿生的设计手法，体现了一种蜘蛛侠式的科技和幽默感。

The professional mobile phones are used for professional grades. The appearance is solid; and the science and technology is better applied. It has the sense of future.

“启” 移动电源
“Switch On” Backup Power Bank

设计 / 潘润松
生产 / 万莱华国际有限公司(香港)
Design / Boby Poon
Manufacture / Manova International Ltd

该产品隐藏电源开关、外壳自然浑然形成电池的保护壳，精巧结构做成清晰的开关手感，容易拆卸分解处理，构造简单降低成本，极致简约，简洁便携，给予消费者优质的使用体验。

This product hides the power switch, the product shell is shaped for the battery, the concise structure brings an easy assemble and disassemble process. The simple and concise design brings consumers a better user experience.

WOW!dea MOCA X7s 多功能便携数据卡
WOW!dea MOCA X7s Multi-functional Portable Data Card

设计 / 北京元隆雅图文化传播股份有限公司
生产 / 北京元隆雅图文化传播股份有限公司
Design / Beijing Yuanlong Yato Culture Dissemination Co., Ltd
Manufacture / Beijing Yuanlong Yato Culture Dissemination Co., Ltd

该产品以“极致简约、超薄便携”作为核心理念，以铝合金作为材质。产品折线设计使外观边缘达到 3 毫米极致超薄，最厚处也仅为 5 毫米，可轻松纳入随身卡包或钱包。通过 OTG 技术，可以轻松为智能手机等提供扩展存储空间。产品可将数码相机等传统数码设备的文档存储至智能手机中，随时随地分享，为用户提供性价比高的移动式数据工具。

Designed with the idea of “simple & slim”, WOW!dea MOCA X7s aims at providing a card-type versatile tool for users in an era of mobile Internet. With a number of proprietary patented technologies, it integrates charger cable, syncing cable, MicroSD (TF)/SD (MMC) data storage card and SIM-eject tool within card-size space 5mm thin and fits easily into your wallet. Relying on the OTG technology, it can easily provide smart mobile terminals with the functions of extended storage space and data backup, and transfer the documents in a traditional digital device like a digital camera to smart mobile terminals for sharing anytime and anywhere through mobile Internet.

多功能光通信工具钳
Multi-tool for Optical Communication

设计 / 烽火通信科技股份有限公司
生产 / 烽火通信科技股份有限公司
Design / Fiberhome Telecommunication Technologies Co.,Ltd
Manufacture / Fiberhome Telecommunication Technologies Co.,Ltd

该产品通过力学设计、材料的应用和表面处理工艺，具备拔光纤和拔光模块的双重功能，完善了操作者的使用体验。采用锌合金压铸件，利于切削，废渣数量少，有利于环境保护与资源节约。关键位置进行切角与圆角的倒角处理，保护操作者。两侧的力臂达到最佳的受力状态，可轻松地将光纤和光模块完好地拔取出来，使操作人员的效率倍增。

The tool has a simple, clearly rhythmical style. Its shape suits the pulling operation excellently. The arm of force is smooth and easy to operate, and the silk-screen design at the rotor is the visual focus. The main tone of the tool is silver gray, which presents high professionalism, with black dotted details showing gradation of colors of the entire product. The key positions of the tool are chamfered to give a sense of affinity. The overall sand blasted surface frees the product from the coldness of a tool and gives richness.

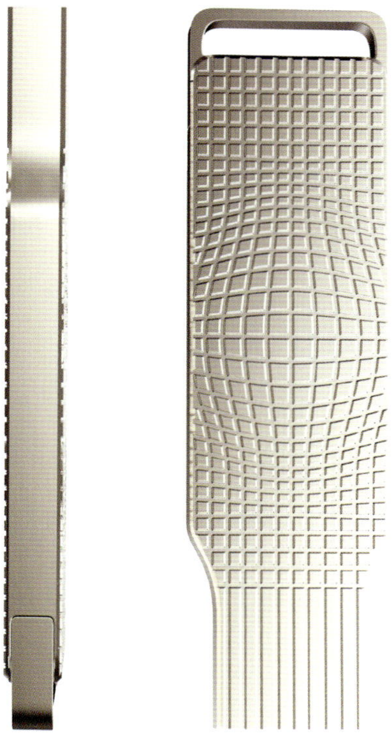

OV U-Net

设计 / 深圳市四六区工业产品策划有限公司
生产 / 深圳市锐仁电子有限公司
Design / April 6th Design Co.,Ltd
Manufacture / Shenzhen Ruiren Electronics Co.,Ltd

这款用金属包裹的 U 盘给人一种经久耐用的感觉。采用“3D 视觉流线”设计，曲面环绕立体线条与金属质感相结合，全金属一体锻造和平面纹理相结合，运用二维空间的线条变化，创造出三维视觉感受。无盖设计解决了使用过程中丢盖的烦恼。产品兼容笔记本电脑、平板电脑、电视和车载音响系统。

The metal alloy makes this flash disk more durable than the plastic one. The pattern design is applying 3D v sual lines to make the flat face look stereoscopic and unique. The whole product is design in integrated forging, combined with the fluently lines on both sides. By using two-dimensional space lines to create a 3D visual feeling, and the no-cover design helps people to get rid of the trouble of losing flash disk all the time.

胸卡工作记录仪
Work Card Recorder

设计 / 郑州市浪尖产品设计有限公司
生产 / 郑州华力信息技术有限公司
Design / Zhengzhou Artop Design Co.,Ltd
Manufacture / Zhengzhou Huali Infomation Technology Co.,Ltd

该产品采取多种佩带方式，后背夹易拆卸，操作便捷。滑动式夹卡，在保证产品整体性时，更方便换卡。轻薄的机身、隐蔽的摄像头和较强的防水等级都凸显产品的高品质。壳料大多采用原色注塑而成，表面蚀纹，能源损耗低。线条硬朗，层次分明，功能结构的密切结合，让产品的专业度与可信度得到淋漓尽致的体现。

This work card record may adopt many adorn way, e.g. back buckle with easy disassemble and operate. The slide clamping is easy to change and could ensure the wholeness of the product. Slim body, hidden camera and water proof demonstrate the high quality. The tough line and hierarchical structure combine with closely with the functional structure is a demonstration of professional service and credibility.

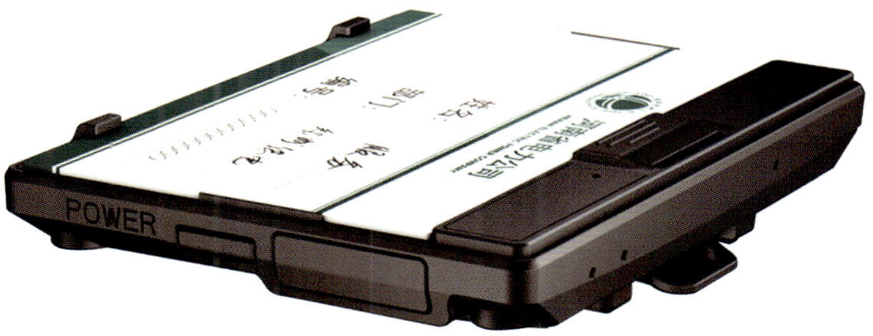

WOW!dea MOCA X8 多功能数据移动电源
WOW!dea MOCA X8 Multi-functional Data Portable Charger

设计 / 北京元隆雅图文化传播股份有限公司
生产 / 北京元隆雅图文化传播股份有限公司
Design / Beijing Yuanlong Yato Culture Dissemination Co., Ltd
Manufacture / Beijing Yuanlong Yato Culture Dissemination Co., Ltd

该产品解决了用户旅途中智能手机等设备数据传输、电量补充的问题。可单手完成该移动电源与通讯设备的连接和使用，轻便简洁，替代繁杂的数据、充电配件，为出行提供便利。该产品通过一机多能通用的高集成化，结合最新主流 OTG 移动设备扩展技术，为用户提供高性价比的移动数据工具，减少相关设备投人，符合安全、环保理念。

Designed with the idea of "simple & slim", WOW!dea MOCA X8 helps users transfer data and charge their smart devices. With a number of proprietary patented technologies, it integrates portable charger, data storage, extended cell phone storage, TF card reader, syncing cable, charging cable, Lightning to Micro USB adapter, and SIM-eject tool into one device. Relying on the OTG technology, it can easily provide smart terminals with extended storage space and data backup.

动捕系统
Perception Neuron

设计 / 灏域联华科技（北京）有限公司
生产 / 北京诺亦腾科技有限公司
Design / OREA Technology（Beijing) Co.,Ltd
Manufacture / Noitom Ltd

该产品为世界上第一套完全无线人体运动捕捉系统，有着全球最小、最轻的无线动作姿态捕捉传感器模块，实现每一个捕捉节点与身体关节的贴合性、不同身体尺寸的兼容性，使设备穿戴、复杂动作变得轻松自然。节能环保，被广泛运用于三维动漫、影视制作、体验式游戏、体育锻炼、机器人等领域。

As a wearable equipment, it covers fields of sensor, sports science, biomechanics and virtual reality at early product research and development stage. With multi-disciplinary crossing and integration technology, it perfectly matches product appearance with human body, making it a function extension of human body. With the design of wireless and attachable bandage, it makes comfortable and natural for product wearing and complex motion.

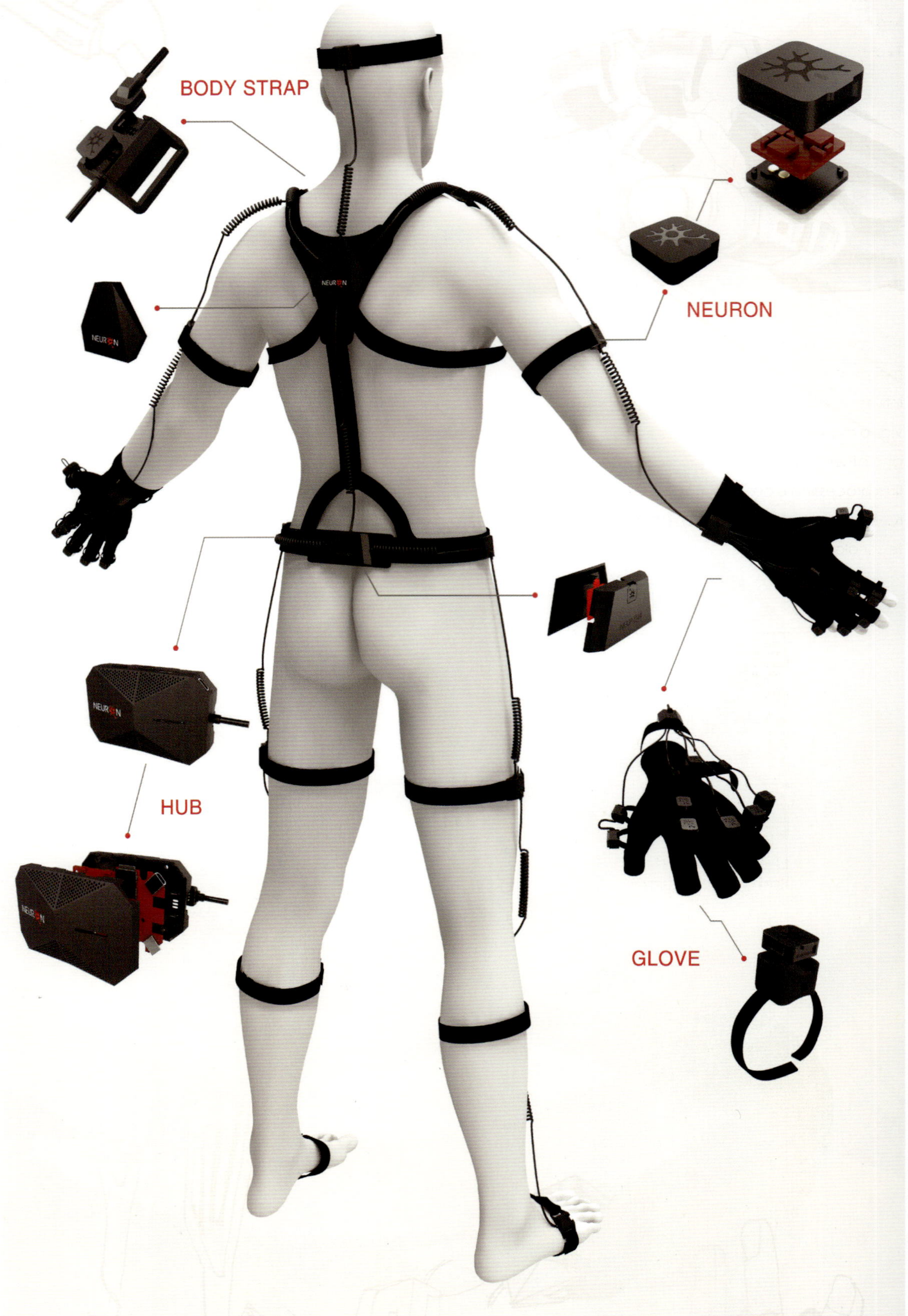

悠宝
Ubox

设计 / 祝正文、陈钟山
生产 / 烽火通信科技股份有限公司
Design / Zhu Zhengwen, Chen Zhongshan
Manufacture / Fiberhome Telecommunication Technologies Co.,Ltd

该产品是以物联网技术为基础，云计算、移动互联网和大数据等新一代信息技术。为用户提供智能网关、视频监控、远程医疗、智能家居业务和其他基于安卓系统的系统应用。外壳采用 0.06 毫米极细纹理，外表面采用最新橡胶漆加配珠光粉，营造出原石效果。攫取了的豆蔻造型，为用户营造出高科技质感的同时带来摒弃和宣泄繁华都市中浓郁的数码气息。

The product is based on the IoT, Cloud computing, mobile internet and big data etc new generation of info technology. Providing the users smart gateway, video monitor, remote medical treatment, smart home and other applications based on Android. 0.06mm fine processing is designed for the appearance to raw gemstone. The cardamun shape is full of sense of technology.

扫一扫查看产品 Pin3D 技术三维效果图
Scanning for the 3D image by Pin3D

旺果儿童手表
Mokeen

设计 / 逸乐工业产品设计（上海）有限公司
生产 / 讯研通信息技术（上海）有限公司
Design / Yiroo Industrial Products Design Shanghai Co., Ltd
Manufacture / Institute Technology (Shanghai)Co.,Ltd

此产品以儿童的眼光寻找和思考，表带采用软性硅胶材质，内部设计有防汗槽，为孩子柔弱的手腕提供舒适的佩戴体验。生命周期长，价格实惠，大大降低了原材料的使用。将通讯放进手表，以沟通与关怀为主线，让家长随时都可以与孩子进行沟通，在找不到孩子的情况下，还可以进行定位追踪，保证孩子安全。

Deesha is a brand for girl. They believe "Every girl is a princess". The designs start from this, seeking and thinking as a little girl, design this children watch. The name is "Love Candy". The designers hope when children wear my watch they can feel their parents' sweet love like candy.

机器人虚拟图文在线包装系统
Robot Virtual Graphic Online Packaging System

设计 / 艾迪普
生产 / 北京东方艾迪普科技发展有限公司
Design / Ideapool
Manufacture / Ideapool.Ltd

该产品创新实现在演播室有限场地里，画面物件根据主持人要求进行动态操作，与人在虚实结合场景中自由穿插走动，实时交互。现场灯光系统均采用 LED 光源，节能环保。设计中融入绘画、电影等视觉设计概念，丰富观众的视觉感受。虚拟物件真实生动，使演播室整合包装设计逐渐成为一门独特的设计艺术种类。产品已有多家电视台成功使用案例。

The product extended the edge of TV packaging theory and embedded entertainment elements into news studios. It perfectly combines designs of construction, decoration, lighting, big screen, multi-screen, real-time packaging, virtual graphic and anchor appearance. With merging art of painting and cinematic design into TV programs, this product significantly improves visual logic / audiences' experience and reaches the state of the art.

中视典全息交互台
Vistandard HoloStation

设计 / 北京天创易造工业设计有限公司
生产 / 北京中视典数字科技有限公司
Design / Exmade Design Consultants Co.,Ltd
Manufacture / Vistandard（Beijing）Digital Technology Co., Ltd

该产品围绕“沁人眼眸，触碰心灵”的设计理念，创新性构筑出双面成像的 3D 新模式。配置 3D 眼镜及智能触控笔，显著提升了 3D 视觉效果，实现了 3D 镜像由“近在咫尺”至“触手可及”的跨越。整体外壳采用塑胶材质，内部框架采用铝合金材质，除保护硬件免受损伤外，具有舒适的操作体验。生产及回收过程均清洁环保。

Vistandard HoloStation has pure appearance, details and highly professional. Overall framework is used metal material with a simple white rendering, fully embodies the product design concept, with a solid stainless steel base which is not only easy to use but easy to clean.

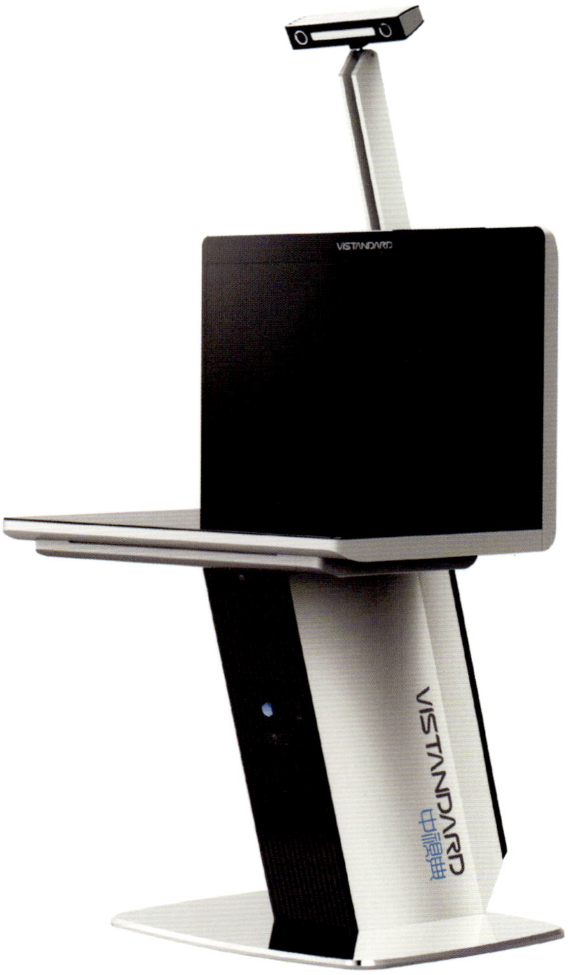

智能穿戴式牵伸康复系统
Intelligent Wearable Drafting Rehabilitation System

设计 / 成都拓成工业产品设计有限公司
生产 / 四川旭康医疗电器有限公司
Design / Chengdu Top-Creative Product Design Co.Ltd
Manufacture / Sichuan Ikcare Medical Electrical Equipment Co.Ltd

该产品在国内首创，采用世界先进的静态进展型牵伸技术，以应力松弛为原理，让患者能够在专业医师的远程指导下完成牵伸训练。充分考虑人机互动，内置的数据记录及传输系统，实现了康复训练从医院到家庭的完美跨越。同时采用高强度塑料，经久耐用。该产品已经受到了来自国内各大医院康复中心及使用者家庭的广泛好评。

Filling a gap in the domestic medical rehabilitation field, the product is adopting the world's advanced static progressive stretching techniques, the product applies stress relaxation principle and contains remote management system. Different from the traditional drawing device and orthosis, it allows you to finish drafting training in remote guidance of professional doctor, easily increase the affected area of the joint activity. In the structural design of the full consideration of human-computer interaction, in genercl, the patient a lone will be able to complete a set of operations.

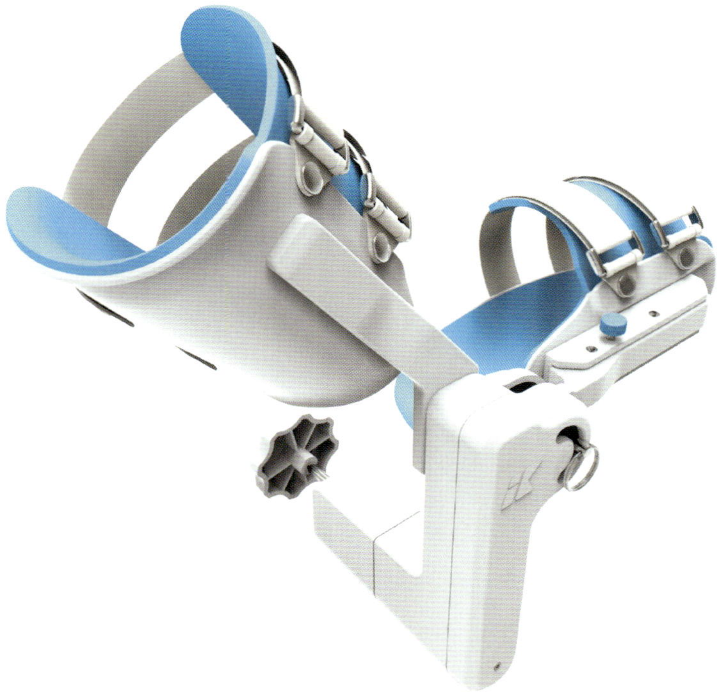

电子铠甲定位鞋
GPS Shoes in Electronic Armour

设计 / 考克（福建）工业设计有限公司
生产 / 福建省莆田市双驰智能信息技术有限公司
Design / Kaoke (Fujian) Industrial Design Co. Ltd
Manufacture / Fujian Province Putian City Shuangchi Intelligent Information Technology Co., Ltd

电子铠甲定位鞋内置蓝牙 GPS 定位系统，可快速定位，防止老人和小孩走失。采用高档鞋材，依据人体力学原理设计，减少走路过程中对人体关节的冲击，有效保护老人和小孩的双足。产品外壳与内胆采用可脱卸式结构，便于更换清洗。外壳采用三角及棱形的支架模块组，TPU 磨砂透明效果与内胆印刷图案相互映衬，具有科技美感。

The case and liner are made of detachable structure for easy replacing and cleaning, which is recyclable. TPU material triangle framework supports the sole, forming the bottom surface of running shoes in one-time injection mould, with Bluetooth GPS buckling mode. Using high-class material and designing based on human mechanics principles, reduce the impacts on the human body joints during walking. It cuts down the risk of joint disease significantly to protect feet effectively and saves costs of health care.

老年智能手杖
Aged Smart Walking Stick

设计 / 北京乐品乐道科技有限公司
生产 / 北京联芯瑞康科技有限公司
Design / Beijing LEAD Technology Co.Ltd
Manufacture / Beijing Leadcore Ruikang Technology Co. Ltd

本产品运用了 GPS 定位、远程监控、手机控制、电子围栏、语音短信等科技成果。通过手机软件，随时掌握老人的出行状况，可设定老人的活动区域并及时发现老人发生的意外。通过老年人手握手杖的习惯进行手掌贴合弧面的造型设计，采用细纹工艺，防滑耐磨。铝合金收缩杆，轻便结实。投入市场后获得极高的市场关注。

Design through the habits and characteristics of stick in the hands of the elderly, fit the palm cambered surface design, not only to hold firmly, it is also need to hold the comfortable, front end slightly larger size, in walking better leveraging and concave in the middle of modeling, using different ways of holding, completely fit the palm and back "pits" and let the fingers more comfortable. Side of the three buttons and a flashlight switch, when holding the stick, the thumb can also easy to operate, hidden type the horn aperture, neither destroys the appearance, and can achieve better waterproof.

iBone 宠物狗关爱智能配件
iBone Dog Care Smart Accessories

设计 / 杭州领跑者工业设计有限公司
生产 / 杭州汪星人科技有限公司
Design / Hangzhou LPZ Industrial Design Co.,Ltd
Manufacture / Hangzhou Wangxing-en Technology Co., Ltd

该产品为一款全方面的智能可穿戴产品，帮助消费者打造全新的与自己爱宠相处模式。可与宠物主人的手机连接，实时监控宠物不同运动状态，还可以分析狗狗情绪变化。防水防抖动，适合宠物不同的运动状态。选材为可回收循环利用的高分子材料，省电环保。表面的可更换面板带来产品色彩的多样性，为宠物主人带来更多的选择空间。

Product design is minimalist style, complete geometric elements constitute the main visual semantic products. The whole rounded outer contour gives communicate science and technology, security, psychological feelings. Minimalist fashion design elements that convey the technical attributes of intelligent products, with the man-machine of fine size, but also allow consumers to have more beauty products Interpretation. Personalized interface icons are displayed, not only demonstrates the brand, but also for pet owners to bring a new visual experience when purchasing products. The surface of the panel can be replaced to bring product diversity of color, to bring more choice to the pet owner.

夹式立体声耳机
Bluetooth Stereo Headset - Clipper

设计 / 深圳市四六区工业产品策划有限公司
生产 / 深圳市万诚通电子有限公司
Design / Apri l6th Design Co.,Ltd
Manufacture / Avantronics Ltd

该产品能让用户连接尚未备有蓝牙功能的家庭影音、电脑或汽车影音，并转换成蓝牙信号传输到蓝芽耳机或扬声器上，实现无线传输播放，用户可以在不同的影音装置上使用无线传输功能。跨界设计理念，让产品与着装融合，使产品像扣子般融入着装中。一字形正面按键设计，更符合人机操作。音量加减号用硅胶材质，加强装饰感。

This audio music receiver can Bluetoothify your wired headphones and home speaker system. If you have a pair of headphones which you just love to use, this gadget comes with a 3.5mm plug, a good solution to turn your favorite Beats, Bose, Sennheiser, Monster, AKG, V Moda, Marshall headphones into wireless headphones. The transboundary design combines the product with dress, weakening the shapes of the product to make it more like a part of the clothes. Straight line button is designed to make it more comfortable and easy to control. The volume button is applied silicon to be a useful decoration.

旗黑家族

FontFamily

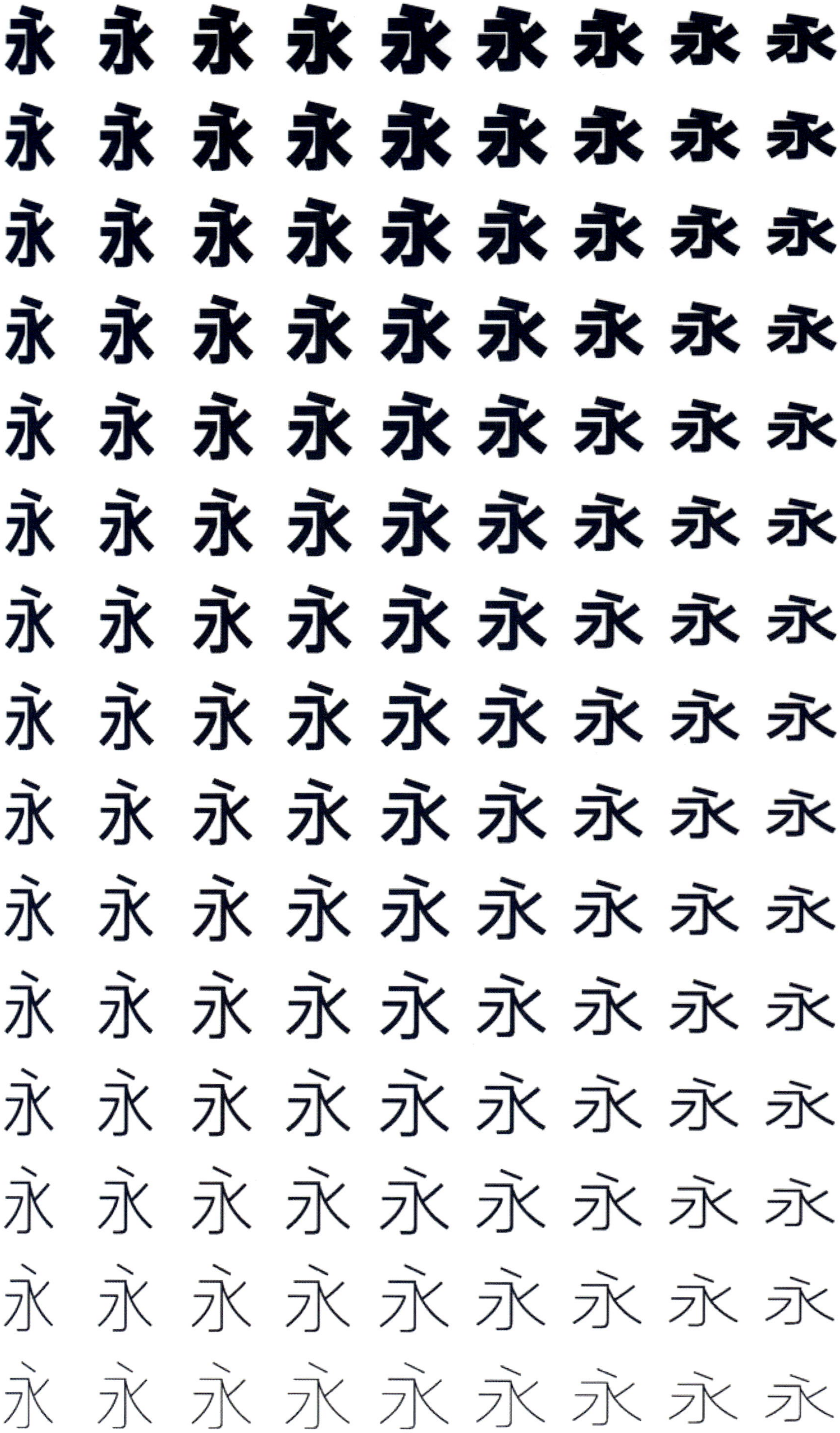

汉仪旗黑系列
HY Qihei

设计 / 北京汉仪科印信息技术有限公司
生产 / 北京汉仪科印信息技术有限公司
Design / Beijing Hanyi Information Technology Co., Ltd
Manufacture / Beijing Hanyi Information Technology Co., Ltd

汉仪旗黑是由三个系列字体（长、方、扁）组成的一个庞大而完整的家族字体，是迄今为止国内具有最大、最丰富字重的家族字体。字体设计劲道有力，具人文风格，避免过大的弧度为阅读所带来的不稳定感，方便视觉障碍者的阅读。通过内白与间距的精细化设计，让文字排版在流畅阅读的前提下，更加舒适通透，减少用户阅读的疲劳感。

Hanyi QiHei is a big sans-serif type family with 15 weights, also containing compressed and condensed sub-families. It is the largest type family in China so far, which is designed to satisfy various needs from clients. No matter in what platforms, QiHei type family has been proved to work perfectly. Customization option also helps corporate clients to achieve their branding image in different situations. In consideration for the readers’ loss of sight, the type designers has put great efforts on function, in order to present texts with high legibility and readability.

乾坤有序，宇宙无疆，星辰密布，
斗柄指航。昼白夜黑，日明月亮，
风驰雪舞，电闪雷响。云腾致雨，
露结晨霜，虹霓霞辉，雾沉雹降。
春生夏长，秋收冬藏，时令应候，
寒来暑往。远古洪荒，海田沧桑，
陆地漂移，板块碰撞。山岳巍峨，
湖泊荡漾，植被旷野，岛撒汪洋。
冰川冻土，沙漠沃壤，木丰树森，
岩多滩广。鸟飞兽走，鳞潜羽翔，
境态和谐，物种安详。形分上下，
道合阴阳，幽冥杳渺，天体着彰。
凝气为精，聚能以场，缩浓而质，
积微显量。化巨幻虚，恍惚成象，
强固凌弱，柔亦制刚。终极必反，
存兴趋亡，色空轮回，动静恒常。
唯实众名，一理万方，父母爹娘，
没齿难忘。兄弟姐妹，危困助帮，
姑姨叔舅，亲戚互访。侄男闺少，
哺育茁壮，夫妻相敬，梦忆糟糠。
隔屋邻舍，遇事谦谅，伯公姬婆，
慈孝赡养。尊朋礼友，仁义君郎，
炎黄二帝，尧舜禅让。禹启世袭，
灭桀商汤，周武伐纣，侯列各邦。
秦皇集权，汉刘楚项，鼎立割据，
乱晋八王。南北对峙，腐朽隋炀，
贞观政要，五代续唐。陈桥兵变，
耻辱靖康，耶律完颜，元建宋僵。
钟离太祖，崇祯吊丧，清军入关，
大臣驻藏。粉碎叛卓，犁域设将，

方正悠黑体
Declare of Founder Youhei

设计 / 仇寅
生产 / 北京北大方正电子有限公司
Design / Qiu Yin
Manufacture / Beijing Founder Electronics Co.,Ltd

此产品属于智慧型设计，以“让文字更亲切，让阅读更舒适”为设计理念。合理调适字面和字距，便于动态性阅读。制定详尽的笔画和部件的制作规范，共有 13 种不同字重，能够保证不同精度的屏幕获得最佳显示效果。摒弃冷酷几何线条，让阅读更舒适，字里行间散发着书法人文之美。字体初步推广以来获得专业人员和用户的广泛好评。

In order to achieve the classical aesthetic sense under new technology, founder YouHei derived beauty from handwriting, abandon cold geometry line, design strokes proper, developing humanistic designing. Meanwhile, meet the function of information transition; improve character legibility and font appearance. Eventually make font more geniality, read more comfortable and give forth the beauty of calligraphy between the lines.

F50LW–B 电热水器
F50LW-B water heater

设计 / 美的集团热水器事业部工业设计部
生产 / 芜湖美的厨卫电器制造有限公司
Design / Industrial Design Department of Water Heater Department of Midea Group
Manufacture / Wuhu Midea Kitchen And Bath Appliances Mfg. Co. Ltd

该产品采用双内胆结构让电热水器显得更薄，用户可以根据用水需求选择双胆或单胆加热，减少在少量使用热水时需要整桶加热而浪费电能损耗的现象。加热快速、内胆自动冲洗避免电热水器长期使用后内胆内沉淀大量铁锈、泥沙、细菌等。动态交互界面突出水温和水量，便于用户快速了解产品运行状态。减少电能消耗、能源消耗与有害物质的排放。

F50LW-B water heater adopts a dual inner tank design for better energy saving. Beside its thin look, the dual inner tank design enables users to select either one or two inner liners to heat up water based on actual water demand, which is more energy and water saving. The automatic washing of inner tanks can avoid the sedimentation of rust and bacteria. The dynamic interface shows water temperature and water level , which facilitates users to quickly understand the running state.

净滤宝
Purification and Filtering Chamber

设计 / 美的集团热水器事业部工业设计部
生产 / 芜湖美的厨卫电器制造有限公司
Design / Industrial Design Department of Water Heater Department of Midea Group
Manufacture / Wuhu Midea Kitchen And Bath Appliances Mfg. Co. Ltd

该产品独创鱼眼 140 度广角滤芯透视系统，无需拆机即可观察滤芯使用寿命情况，及时更换滤芯。无需用电，绿色净氯器，低碳环保。净水除氯效率可达 80%，消除自来水氯气给用户带来的危害。高净水速率，满足市面上绝大多数花洒的用水量。流水型多曲面造型设计模拟水流在空中旋转的动态效果，动静结合，相得益彰。

The purification and filtering chamber adopts an exclusive fisheye 140 degree wide angle perspective system, which enables investigation of the filter condition without disassembly and changing of the filter when necessary. It does not require electricity and is a low-carbon and environmentally friendly product. The efficiency of water dechlorination is up to 80%, which eliminates the health hazard of chlorinated water. Streamlined multi-facet design simulates water flow dynamics, contributing to a perfection of balance.

可以在线买菜的智能冰箱
Smart Fridge which can online shopping

设计 / 惠而浦（中国）工业设计中心
生产 / 惠而浦（中国）股份有限公司
Design / Whirlpool (China) GCD
Manufacture / Whirlpool (China) Co.,Ltd

该产品配以网络智能系统，与超市、用户、企业无缝连接，打造下单购物、货物配送、产品升级、娱乐一体的全新交互系统。独家专利保鲜技术和自带智能显控系统对食品进行周期管理，设置超大两层冷冻区域，满足中国家庭对大容量的冷冻需求，且内置 NANOMIST 水雾发生装置，高效抗菌抗霉。保鲜过程健康环保，不产生有害、有毒物质影响食品安全。

The smart fridge features a user interface and online shopping system, which uses the network smart system to connect with supermarkets for convenient order, delivery, product upgrading and entertainment. It has exclusive patented freshness preservation technology and a smart display system for regular food management. It has two large freezers, which meets family needs for larger freezer space. The NANOMIST frost production device is embedded, which is antibacterial and antifungal. and ensures moisture and freshness preservation. It uses safe and environmentally friendly material, which maintains a safe preservation process without generating any poisonous or hazardous products.

旗舰版空气能热水器
Heat Pump Flagship Edition

设计 / 广东顺德潜龙工业设计有限公司
生产 / 广东芬尼电器有限公司
Design / Chinno Industrial Design Co.,Ltd
Manufacture / Phnix Co.,Ltd

该空气能热水器采用手势交互控制，出水温度可随心掌控。产品具有智能可变容量特点，增强机器扩展性，解决占地大的问题，节能环保。采用创新技术使水温达 75℃，合理混水实现最高出水 430 升，满足需求。钛瓷内胆防腐蚀，板材厚重，承压能力强。独有回水缓流技术，使热水率提高 35%。一体式无痕外观设计，优雅弧线与拉丝面板结合，彰显科技之美。

The brand new heat pump utilizes a new way of interactive gestural control method, and it' s one of our patented technologies. With gently waving your hand, you can choose the temperature easily. Thus we can avoid the problems of push-button and touch-button. With our innovative Technology, the water temperature can reach 75℃ . With the technology of mixing with running water, we can get 430 liters of water when we use, to meet 80% of domestic hot-water needs. The unique technology of backwater deceleration greatly reduces the flow rate through the evacuation of water treatment.

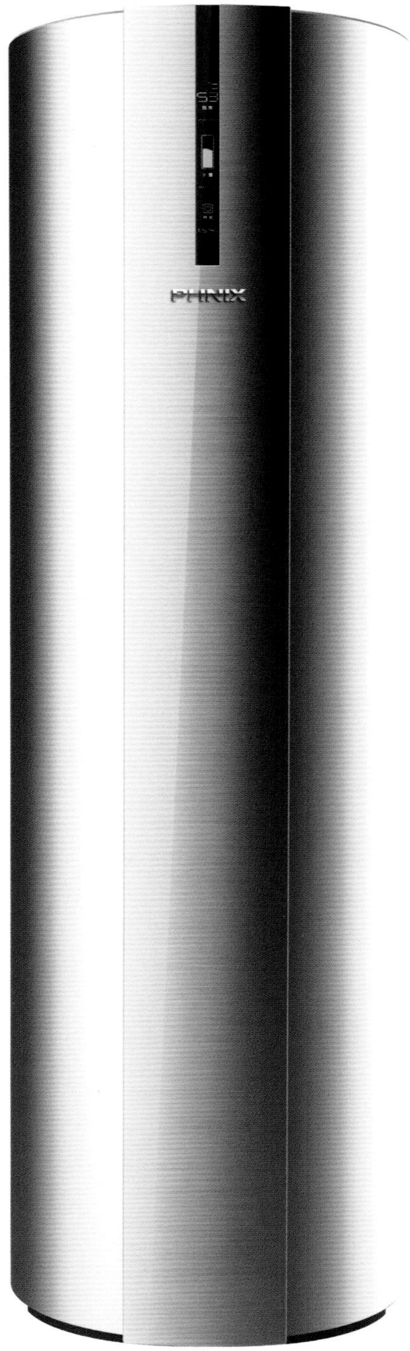

长虹 CHIQ–Q1V 柜机
CHIQ-Q1V

设计 / 四川虹微技术有限公司
生产 / 四川长虹电器股份有限公司
Design / Homwee Technology (Sichuan) Co.,Ltd
Manufacture / Sichuan Changhong Electric Co.,Ltd

该产品是一款柱形柜机空调，空调带摄像头与红外感应，能自动监控房间内人数变化，及时调节温度，达到节能效果。可智能无线网络物联，远程手机操控。 整机采用圆柱形为主体机身，改变传统送风方式，正面长条形出风口使空调工作效率更快，更节省能源。全新的面板分割方式，为后续的同平台新品的开发预留了更大的空间，从根本上节约资源。

The CHIQ-Q1V is a vertical cylinder air conditioning unit with a camera and infrared induction to auto-monitor the number of people in the room and adjust the temperature for energy saving purposes. The digital Wi-Fi connection enables it to be controlled by mobile phone remotely. The cylindrical body changes the traditional wind outlet mode with a much higher efficiency and more energy savings; its new panel design provides a platform for future models.

户外蓝牙音响
Outdoor Bluetooth Stereo

设计 / 深圳市感叹号产品设计有限公司
生产 / 深圳市尊特数码有限公司
Design / Shenzhen Exclamation Point Pruduct Design Co., Ltd
Manufacture / Shenzhen Jonter digital Co.,Ltd

该产品外观时尚独特，2.0 立体声道缔造的声音更加均匀有质地。三面硅胶材质，回扣造型，手持更加舒适。防水结构大大提升了产品在户外使用的持久性。金属后壳与硅胶的巧妙连接提升了产品的档次，也增加了产品牢固性。选用进口环保材料，抗老化性强。通过材质对比，增加了产品层次感，拥有多种颜色搭配，气质高雅。

With a fashionable and unique appearance, the 2.0 stereo sound of the outdoor speaker creates a much better sound. The water proof highly promotes the durability of the outdoor usage. Connection with the metal shell and silicon enhances the product's quality. Echo-friendly material are applied to resistant the aging of products.

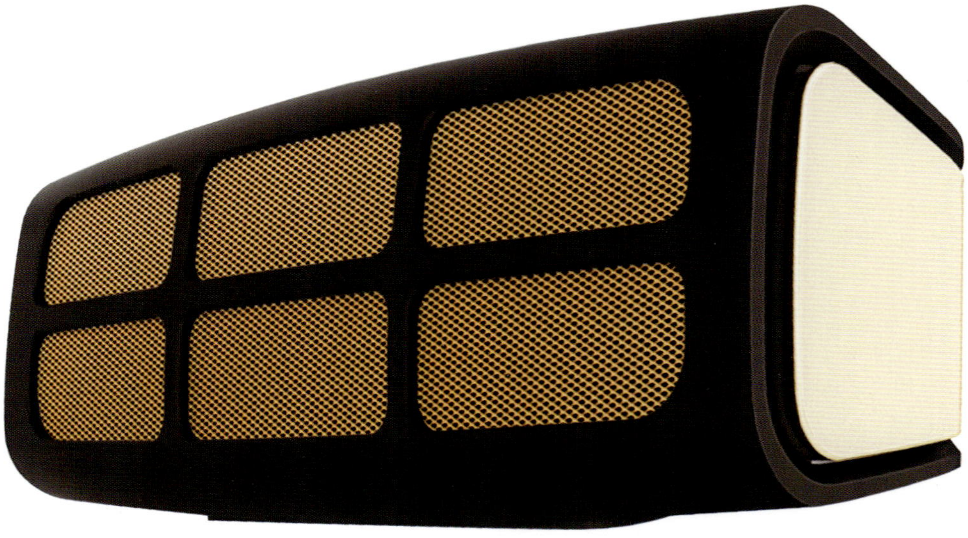

敦拓 磁悬浮蓝牙音箱
Dotop Extension Maglev Bluetooth Speaker

设计 / 深圳市感叹号产品设计有限公司
生产 / 深圳市敦拓电子有限公司
Design / Shenzhen Exclamation Point Pruduct Design Co. Ltd
Manufacture / Shenzhen Dotop Electronics Co. Ltd

该产品将磁悬浮技术与蓝牙音箱完美融合，避免音箱因与桌面等其他物体产生共振，能够将音质的损耗降至最低，保留了音质的纯净。音箱可以飘在空中充电，永不断电，实现了真正的无线充电。外出旅行时可只取下上面的蓝牙音箱，携带方便。凌空悬浮，轻盈自转，外观质感非常强，符合当下流行的审美。

This product is the perfect combination between the magnetic levitation technology and Bluetooth speakers, speakers and other desktop to avoid because objects produce resonance, thus the quality loss is reduced to the minimum, largely retained the purity of tone. Speakers suspended wireless charging technology, the speaker can float in the air charging, never power. The real wireless charging.Travel, Bluetooth speaker, we can only take it easy to carry, utility.Exquisite workmanship, air suspension, light rotation,the metal contains a crystal clear feeling, elegant fashion, free.

Amazing Box Lite 智能家居控制中心
Amazing Box Lite

设计 / 张嘉泳
生产 / 大连华信计算机技术股份有限公司
Design / Mark Cheung
Manufacture / Dalian Hi-Think Computer Technology, Corp.

该产品首次将数字家庭中的智能家居控制中心、数据中心、网络中心三大核心要素有效融为一体，可以为普通家庭提供网络服务、家庭照片。视频等资料的整理存储以及智能家居相关中转控制的服务，切实满足人们对生活品质提升的需求。众筹上市以来，产品凭借强大的功能配以简洁时尚的外观，博得市场一致好评。

The first digital home smart home control center, data center, network center three core elements of an effective integration, The average family can provide network services, organize storage family photos, videos and other information related to transit and smart home control services, effectively meet people's needs to enhance the quality of life. The product, called Amazing BOX lite mini serves family, with its effort to solve main problems of the digital home.

B18 可变形移动电源
B18 Transformable Power Bank

设计 / 深圳市艾狄科技有限公司
生产 / 深圳卡格尔数码科技有限公司
Design / Shenzhen AIDI Technology Co.,Ltd
Manufacture / Shenzhen Cager Digital Technology Co.,Ltd

该产品极大地改进了现有移动电源的不便携性，迷你身材，整机重量 248 克，可随意折叠，改变造型，方便随身携带。分离式的创新结构设计，芯片以及电源分离，以软线作连接，更安全。外壳全部采用硅胶材质制作，手感极佳，充电时可作手机支架：防滑，防水，防摔。独特的外形更增添了潮流感，自上市以来反响极好，热销世界各地。

This product break the rules, change the normal modeling mode, can easily fold to transform its appreance, weight 248 grams, This product use silicone material as shell, which make it a good handfeel. This product seperate structural design, connect the separate chip and power via flexible cord to make it safergreatly improved the non-portability for normal mobile power, it is foldable stuffed small pocket, can be placed flat backpack, can be used for phone holder wihile charging;slip resistance, water resistance, Drop resistance. It has been on the market broken million, an excellent market response, selling all over the world.

极路客 Goluk 智能行车记录仪
Goluk Intelligent Vehicle Traveling Data Recorder

设计 / 深圳洛可可工业设计有限公司
生产 / 北京智趣车联科技有限公司
Design / LKK Design Shenzhen Co.,Ltd
Manufacture / Beijing Mobnote Technology Co.,Ltd

该产品为全球首款支持网络直播的智能行车记录仪，融入了“视频直播”与“社交属性”。内置无线网络连接，为用户提供一键精彩视频抓拍功能，一键分享社交媒体，一键同步行车记录仪与手机，1080P 全高清视频拍摄，无论白天黑夜，清晰捕捉 10 米之内的车牌号码。所有外观材料均为可回收，提高产品生命周期，减少环境污染。

TThis product is the first network intelligent vehicle traveling data recorder in the world with live-video and social features. You can share the video to many SNS platforms including Wechat, Weibo and Goluk' s video square. Goluk is equipped with built-in WIFI connection to provide users with one-button capture function for wonderful moments, one-button social media sharing, and one-button synchronized cell phone and recorder. Goluk supports 1080P full HD video recording,, no matter day and night. All the appearance materials can be recycled, and the luminescent source is environmental LED light, which improves product life cycle and reduces environment pollution.

圣宝 V5 音响
SINGBOX V5 Speaker

设计 / 深圳市感叹号产品设计有限公司
生产 / 东莞市圣宝电子制造有限公司
Design / Shenzhen Exclamation Point Pruduct Design Co., Ltd
Manufacture / Dongguan City Singbox Electronics Manufacturing Co.,Ltd

该产品具有插卡插 U 盘、FM 收音、音频输入、耳机输出、数字按键等功能，还可一键切换录音、一键收藏，使用简单，非常适合中老年人使用。亲肤柔和外壳手感舒适，搭配炫丽动感彩色边框设计，清新典雅，背部类似米奇头像网孔设计，让声音更立体，外观更时尚。侧面与底面形成巧妙的连接，使整个产品的摆放与众不同，更显时尚独特。

This product inserted U disk, FM radio, audio input, output Headset Chinese screen display, digital key, cycle, recording timer switch, several computer speakers and a key switch recording, be equal to anything, a collection of key functions, very suitable for use in the elderlyThe assembly process is simple.Compact body, easy to carry A small rounded body, skin soft shell dear comfortable, with a fabulous dynamic color frame design, fresh and elegant, like Mickey back mesh design, make the sound more solid, more stylish. Cleverly connected to form a side surface and a bottom surface, make the products more fashionable and unique placed out of the ordinary.

旗子 Moretel 智能电话
Qizi Moretel Smart Phone

设计 / 深圳市感叹号产品设计有限公司
生产 / 珠海市齐飞信息技术有限公司
Design / Shenzhen Exclamation Point Pruduct Design Co., Ltd
Manufacture / Zhuhai Qifei Information Technology Co., Ltd

该产品可免费语音视频通话、发信息，拥有超音质音响且具备影音游戏娱乐功能。简洁的扬声孔设计，完全满足喇叭的出音面积。保证无论扬声通话，还是外放音乐，都可以感受到澎湃无毛刺的声音。听筒自带接听按键，使用蓝牙连接，可不受限制地在家中任何地方使用。简约时尚，窄边框设计，优雅电镀装饰件，提升了整个产品的品质感。

This smart phone integrates free audio, video call and message sending. Applying simple style of speakers is a guarantee for speakers and music. Earphone is connected to Bluetooth and enables usage for all the appliances at home with no restrictions. With the simplicity of the slim frame design, this product is full of modernism and quality.

iTvTop 移动网络电视宝
iTvTop Portable TV Box

设计 / 成都浪尖工业设计有限公司
生产 / 深圳清华大学研究院
Design / Chengdu Artop Industrial Design Co.,Ltd
Manufacture / Research Institute of Tsinghua University in Shenzhen

该产品是全球首款 DTMB 移动网络电视宝，可提供人性化智能化的收看新体验。具有 DTMB 移动电视功能、移动电源功能、无线路由功能。产品巧妙的外观设计，可作为手机或平板支架使用，自带 10000 毫安移动电源，用户可随时随地畅享移动数字电视服务。采用铝合金拉伸成型工艺、阳极氧化工艺和塑胶一体成型工艺，工艺成熟简单。铝合金筒状外观，简洁美观。

The first ever DTMB Mobile TV Stick that offers smarter and more user-centered TV viewing experience. Its versatile design can be used as a cellphone or tablet stand. In addition, it comes with a built-in 10000MAh portable power supply which provides user untethered TV viewing experience.This product offers a combination of DTMB TV receiver, portable power supply, wireless router and cellphone/tablet stand. With an app user can enjoy mobile TV viewing experience anytime anywhere.Mature materials are used with no excessive production cost. Recyclable materials are used to minimize pollution. Aluminum extrusion, anodizing, plastic unibody.Aluminum, barrow shaped appearance combined with anodizing process gives it a feeling of quality.

LEBOND 家用冲牙器
LEBOND Teeth Cleaning

设计 / 广州森迪产品设计有限公司
生产 / 力博得电子科技有限公司
Design / Sounded Product Design Co., Ltd
Manufacture / LEBOND Electronics Technology Co.Ltd

该产品设计灵感来源于水滴的形状，棱边处光源照射形成海洋气氛，颠覆了过去洗牙器的传统造型。区别于放置手柄，采用磁性连接，开关无级变速，拥有可伸缩的注水管与 360 度旋转刷头，方便携带，换冲头也十分方便。水箱大小按照严格测试的水量，采用充电插口超声波技术粘合，杜绝漏水问题，减少水资源的浪费。

The design inpiration of this prodct comes from the waterdrop. It's machine body reflection ,feeling like Seasurrounding. Appearance revolution, more beautiful, it has hand shank magnetic coupling, switch stepless adjust, scalable water wire and 360° spin brush.It is convenient to change brush,dustproof waterproof charging，Sonic power Bonding ,no leak, without waste water.

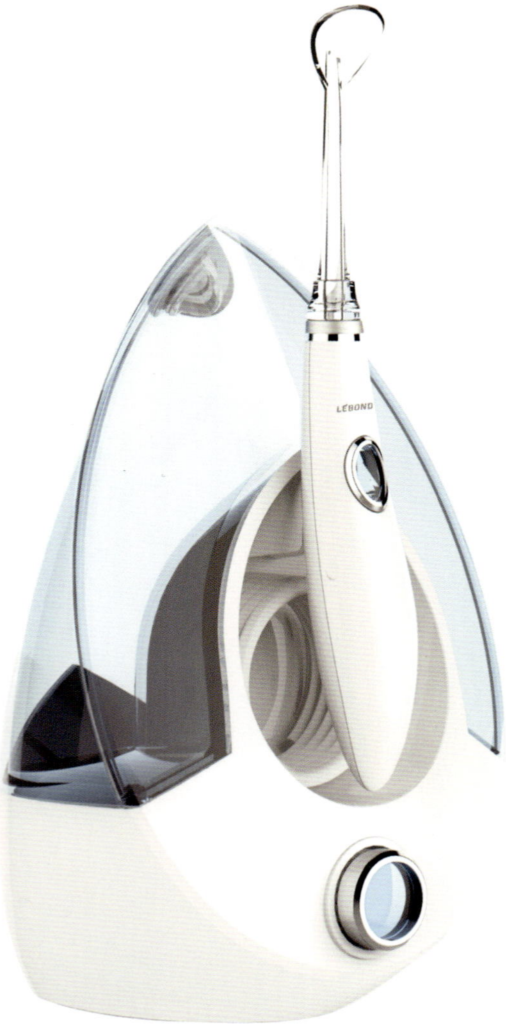

ALLER 箱
ALLER

设计 / 杭州领跑者工业设计有限公司
生产 / 洛克施为空气净化技术（天津）有限公司
Design / Hangzhou LPZ Industrial Design Co. Ltd
Manufacture / Luxsweep Air Purification Technology (Tianjin) Co., Ltd

该产品通过创新设计，首次将成熟的负离子消毒技术应用于儿童玩具消毒领域。采用双极离子隧道技术低温除菌获得多项国际认可，除菌率达 99.93%。材质为环保无毒食品级高强度 PP 材料，轻便环保，可盛放各种类型的玩具。采用一键式除菌设计，15 分钟即可完成除菌，同时具有收纳功能，对于现代家庭具有普遍适用性。

The ALLER box is used for the innovative design, and the mature negative ion disinfection technology is applied to the disinfection of children's toys. It uses advanced iontube bipolar ion tunneling technique to obtain a number of international recognized low temperature sterilization, sterilization rate of 99.93%. Box the advanced hot runner injection of various molding, material for environmental protection non-toxic food grade high strength PP materials by design of one key sterilization, 15 minutes to complete sterilization.This product can bloom all types of toys.

Smart Care 智能家居套装
Smart Care

设计 / 上海艺凯设计有限公司
生产 / 海尔
Design / GK Design Shanghai Inc
Manufacture / Haier

该套装由五个产品组成，通过手机软件可随时随地掌握家里的情况，实现对家用电器和电子产品的无线控制。一旦探测到活动，即可打开或关闭所有设备。减少了家庭过度购买硬件设备而造成的电子硬件垃圾的过度替代及浪费。圆形作为统一的造型元素贯穿于整个套系，哑光的材质和饱满的弧面使整套产品感觉柔和而又可靠，富有亲和力，与现代家居环境相融合。

SmartCare is the wisdom of life open platform most newly hatched intelligent Home Furnishing suit which consists of five components. The APP lets users to grasp the situation at home whenever you want, it achieves the wireless control of household appliances and electronic products. Circular, as a universal design element, runs through the whole series. Matte material and the curve of the product surface makes people feel soft and reliable, and ccn be easily integrated into the modern Home Furnishing environment.

扫一扫查看产品 Pin3D 技术三维效果图
Scanning for the 3D image by Pin3D

神妈奶瓶
Smamoo Milk Bottle

设计 / 杭州领跑者工业设计有限公司
生产 / 山东麦格信息技术有限公司
Design / Shan Dong Moogeek Informction Technology Co.,Ltd
Manufacture / Shan Dong Mooggeek Information Techenology CO.,LTD

该产品致力于利用互联网大数据，为新生儿父母提供科学喂养系统支持。通过恒温、浓度检测等模块，实现对喂奶温度和冲泡温度的调节和转换。能够分析出每次喂奶后宝宝的饮用量，吸收的营养成分及其含量，形成自己宝宝的数据。采用无线充电技术，使用户学习与使用轻松便捷，解决了在旅途、夜间等情况下喂奶的问题。

The commitment to the use of the Internet data and provide scientific feeding system support for parents of newborn. Products by constant temperature and concentration detection, gravity detection, temperature detection module, realize to feeding temperature and brewing temperature of conditioning and conversion, according to the information of different brands of milk powder to adjust the corresponding brewing temperature. And can analyze the baby after each feeding, the amount of drinking, absorption of nutrients and its content.Using a wireless charging technology, users to learn and use easily, such as travel, to solve the midnight multiple user pain points.

扫一扫查看产品 Pin3D 技术三维效果图
Scanning for the 3D image by Pin3D

AR–F40I501 电饭煲
AR-F40I501 Rice Cooker

设计 / 龙域设计
生产 / 浙江爱仕达生活电器有限公司
Design / Loe Design
Manufacture / Zhejiang ASD Household Equipment Co.,Ltd

该产品采用电磁加热原理。内锅采用精铁锻造工艺，底部独有的水动力波纹设计配合磁感线圈起到均匀加热的作用。设有双破泡机构，可以做到持续沸腾而不溢锅，煮出松软香甜的高品质。方型结构并采用顶部操作，具有便捷的触控开关和 LED 灯控效果。采用清洁可回收材料，与食物接触部分皆为食品级素材，保证了使用者的健康饮食。

This product uses electromagnetic heating. The pot adopts iron forging process, the unique hydrodynamic corrugated design of the bottom of the pot with magnetic induction coil has the effect of uniform heating. At the same time, it has double broken bubble mechanism that can keeping boiling without overflowing. The top has a convenient touch switch and LED lighting control.Electromagnetic heating, the unique hydrodynamic corrugated design and double broken bubble mechanism improve the cooking quality. Our products use clean and recyclable materials, the parts contact with foods can meet the requirements of the EU LFGB-food grade material.

海尔 IH 电磁电饭煲 HRC–IFZ502 咖色
Haier IH Electric Cooker HRC-IFZ502 Brown

设计 / 苏州海歌电器科技有限公司
生产 / 海尔生活家电
Design / Suzhou Haige Electrical Technology Co.,Ltd
Manufacture / Haier's Household Appliances

该产品采用 IH 环绕 3D 立体加热，使热量直透米芯，将营养全面释放。海尔智能芯 T–sweet 甜化技术，让食材更加入味。欧米茄精钢厚釜内胆，五层材质复合而成。具有 LCD 大屏幕，外观时尚，触摸控制。十大材料功能选择，可拆卸内盖，特有预约记忆功能。24 小时预约，省电环保。

This product has IH around 3 d heat, big circulation boiling, straight through heat meters core, nutrient release more comprehensive, ingredients serving platter!10 material selection function, can remove the cover, unique booking memory function.Haier intelligent core T - sweet sweet technology, sweet glutinous rice full Q.To make an appointment for 24 hours, save electricity environmental protection.The omega thick stainless steel kettle tank, five layer composite material.LCD big screen, fashionable appearance, touch control, fashion decorative panel.

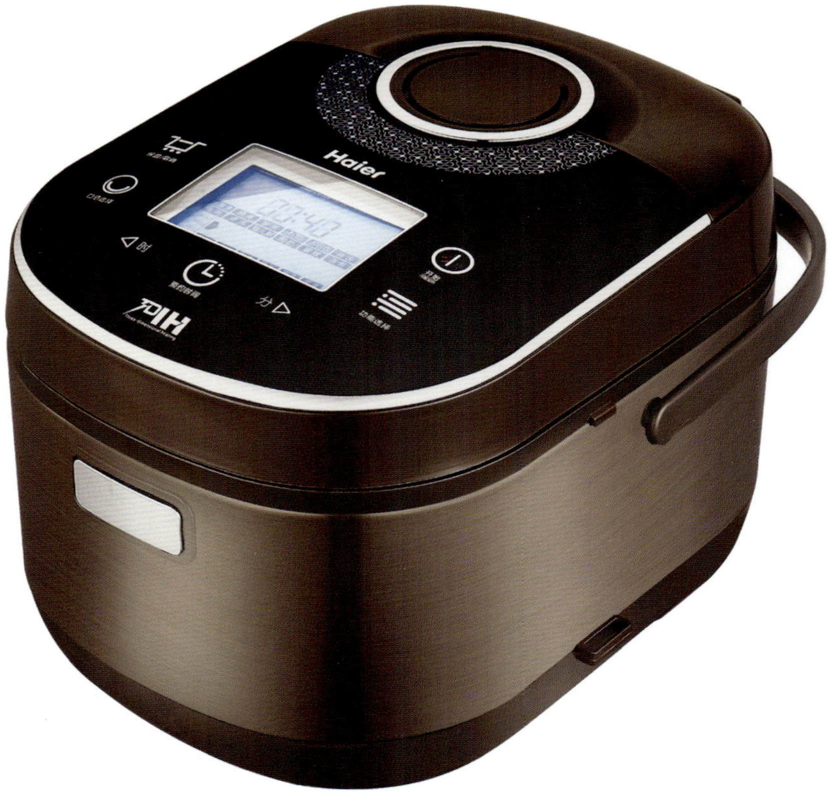

胚芽米机
Germ Rice Machine

设计 / 韩永利
生产 / 北京心觉工业设计有限责任公司
Design / Han Yongli
Manufacture / Beijing Sense Industrial Design Co.Ltd

该产品其特征在于壳体以及滤筒，其设置在壳体内，可将生产出来的胚芽米的麸皮过滤去除。滤筒的底部设置不是网状结构，这样就可以在生产胚芽米过程中保留下胚芽米中产生的碎米以及一些碰落的胚芽，达到了保持培养米的留胚率的目的。提倡现磨现吃的食米方式，即时加工保证最佳口感。整机风格突出，色彩搭配协调，功能和外观完美兼顾。

The characteristics of this product lies in the shell and a filter cartridge, which is arranged in the shell body, the filter cylinder is an opening on the upper end of the first accommodating groove, side wall is of the mesh structure can remove the production of rice germ bran filtering and, filter cartridge is arranged at the bottom of the not reticulate structure, so that you can keep in germ rice broken rice and some touch of germ in the embryo rice production process, keep it in the rice germ without being filtered out, also reached the rice culture of embryo rate, the purpose of keeping. Advocate now grinding eat rice, using rice germing machine grinding out fresh embryo rice, instant processing to ensure the best taste.The volume is small but very strong, the overal style prominent, color coordination, balance function and perfect appearance, is indeed a rare design excellent.

AP–F50I104 电压力锅
AP-F50I104 Electric Pressure Cooker

设计 / 龙域设计
生产 / 浙江爱仕达生活电器有限公司
Design / Loe Design
Manufacture / Zhejiang ASD Household Equipment Co.,Ltd

该产品采用小家电业界顶级 IMD 大面板，操作界面为顶置式触摸控制模式，不用低身弯腰就能轻松操作，特别适合正在怀孕的准妈妈和视力下降的中老年人操作。锅盖上面设有笑脸形状自动排气孔，可全自动电脑排气，精确控制排气时间、排气量，即便是不会做饭的使用者也能做出美味可口的饭菜。与食物接触部分全部符合食品卫生标准，安全环保。

The product uses the best IMD panel, with the top-mounted touch control mode,without bending and operate easily,especially for being pregnant mothers and the vision loss elderly.Top lid with a "smiley face shape" automatic vent, IH electric pressure cooker uses fire heating technology with intelligent regulator design, fully automatic computer exhaust, precise control of exhaust time, even if you can also make a delicious meal. The parts contact with food conform to food hygiene standards, using imported food-grade silicone,safe and effective,ecofriendly.

Pulse 无线音乐智能灯
Pulse LED Wireless Speaker

设计 / 浙江生辉照明有限公司
生产 / 浙江生辉照明有限公司
Design / Zhejiang Shenghui Lighting Co.,Ltd
Manufacture / Zhejiang Shenghui Lighting Co.,Ltd

该产品可安装在普通灯座上，内置蓝牙技术，可在智能手机或平板电脑上安装相应软件来遥控此灯具，使之播放音乐与调整亮度。通过蓝牙技术，1 个主灯最多可支持 7 个副灯。光源使用LED 技术，具有25000小时的使用寿命，节能环保。压铸铝及双层金属烤漆表面，弧线形纹理扩大散热表面积。造型时尚美观，三种颜色可供选择，自上市以来销售火爆。

This smart Pulse bulb can be assembled on common base, with bluetooth inside, the user can control this bulb via the relative App installed on smart phone or pad. To get the music and switch the light as well. By bluetooth, 1 master light manages 7 satellite lights.It use LED technology for it's illuminant, with 25,000 Hrs lifetime performs energy saving and environmental protecting. Die-casting aluminum and double-layer metal baking finish face. The product, has Candy Apple, Neutral White and Pewter 3 options for choice, which owns fashion appearance and technology.

咪库 感温调奶棒
Milq Temp-Sensing Mixer

设计 / 李伟湛、杨先英
生产 / 重庆伟立仕科技有限公司
Design / Li Weizhan, Yang Xianying
Manufacture / Wellness Tech

该产品是一款精确智能感温调奶棒产品，可精确测量并提示温度，为婴幼儿调奶及温热母乳提供精确控制温度、科学添加益生菌、快速降温的方法。采用安全食品级材料，人性化温度提示的设计创新特点。实时显示温度，充分调奶，快速降温，可适合任意尺寸的奶瓶。具有临时放置收纳、USB 充电接口功能，小尺寸轻量化方便出行携带。

This prodcut is a milk stick product with precise intelligent temperature sensing, accurate measurement and prompt the temperature range of the stirring rod, to provide a precise temperature control, scientific added probiotics, rapid cooling method for infant milk and warm the milk. The product has the safety food grade material,the humanity temperature prompt design innovation characteristic.Real-time display of temperature, fully adjustable milk, rapid cooling.Real-time display of temperature, fully adjustable milk, rapid cooling; lightweight and easy to use, suitable for any size of bottle; base can be used for products using the process of temporary placement of storage; USB charging interface, with wide applicability; small size, lightweight convenience carry.

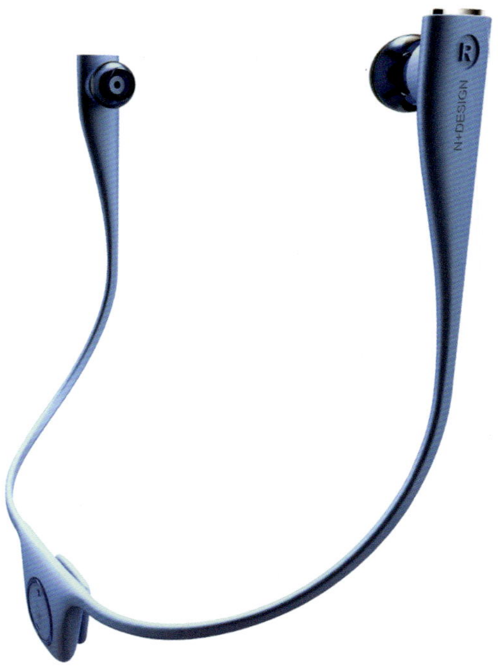

N 智能运动耳机
N Plus Intelligent Motion Headphones

设计 / 深圳市恩佳产品策划有限公司
生产 / 深圳市恩佳产品策划有限公司
Design / Shenzhen Nplus Product Planning Co.,Ltd
Manufacture / Shenzhen Nplus Product Planning Co.,Ltd

该耳机顶端内置磁铁，可将耳机对吸成项圈状，演变出前挂、后挂等佩戴方式，更灵活地满足了人们的使用习惯。模块处自带呼吸灯，夹至衣领处，夜跑时可警示后方车辆。底部中控处内置传感器，通过手机软件实时监控颈椎健康。由金属按钮与整体硅胶构成，硅胶很好地起到了运动耳机的三防效果，佩戴轻巧、舒适的同时减少对环境的污染。

The magnets are built in the top of the headphones, headphones can be changed to a necklace. Users can wear it in front or back side; it will satisfy people's habits more flexibly. There is a breathing lamp in the module. Users can clip it to collar, the lamp will warn vehicles behind when running at night.It can do real-time monitoring for cervical health through APPmove the Bluetooth module.The headset' s material consists of metal button and the overall silica gel, silica gel played an important role for the 3-proofs.It is more approachable, and can also reduce the pollution to the environment.

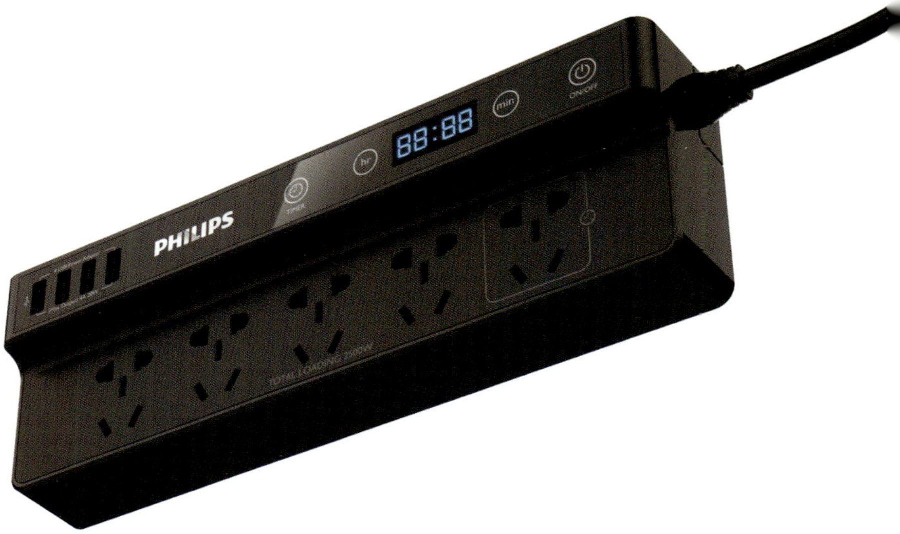

智能湿水牛皮纸包装机
Water Soluble Kraft Paper Packer

设计 / 宁波市法诺工业产品设计有限公司
生产 / 宁波赛美达环保科技有限公司
Design / Ningbo FANUO Industrial Product Design Co. Ltd
Manufacture / Ningbo Media Environmental Technology Co., Ltd

该产品可设置选择全自动、半自动、手动及脚踏等多种模式工作，一台机器工作效率相当于四个工人工效率之和。所使用胶纸为 100% 环保、100% 可回收利用的牛皮胶纸。自动记忆出纸功能与光感应功能配合，可使其工作效率在原先基础上再提高 50% ~ 200%，效率最大化，为人们打包提供了一种高效环保的包装新模式，并已获得多项发明及实用新型专利受理。

The machine set automatic, semi-autcmatic, manual, foot work and other working models, so that its work efficiency is equivalent to the sum of four artificial.This machine uses 100% green 100% recyclable Kraft tape, the raw material is two 35g paper and starch glue, the glue will produce viscous, when been heated.The macnine has auto print memory and light sensor function, When it step into auto memory molds, Work efficiency can be increased by 50% to 200%.The appearance is concise and easy, Has the sense of science and technology.The product has won a lot of inventive and utility model patent.

智能插座
Smart Socket

设计 / 深圳市想象力产品策划有限公司
生产 / 深圳市昊达电子有限公司
Design / Imagination Design Co.,Ltd
Manufacture / Shenzhen Holdtec Eletronics.Co.,ltd

该产品是一款安全、节能的智能插座。除具备常规 220V 交流供电配置外，还提供 5V 直流 USB 输出。提供 USB 接口方便用户给各类数码产品充电的需求，具备过压、过载、过流、防雷击、防静电五大保护功能。拥有智能定时关闭功能，当插座处于通电状态时，插座的定时孔位将在设置时长后自动关闭。开关机及定时功能采用触摸方式设计用触摸操作，更为简洁流畅。

This product is a safe and energy-efficient smart socket. It isn't only equipped with the routine 220V alternating-current generating device, but also provides with the 5V direct-current USB output. This product also has five protective functions, which respectively are against overvoltage, overload, overcurrent, lightning strike and static electricity. The socket has the function of the intelligent timer switch-off. When the socket is in conducting state, the timer hole site will shut automatically followed with the setting of the time duration period.The designe adapt the touch-based operation, which are made to be more concise and smooth.

蓝牙触控键盘
Bluetooth Touch Keyboard

设计 / 深圳雷柏科技股份有限公司
生产 / 深圳雷柏科技股份有限公司
Design / Shenzhen Rapoo Technology Co.,Ltd
Manufacture / Shenzhen Rapoo Technology Co.,Ltd

该产品为一款超薄的蓝牙触控键盘，最薄处仅 4.3 毫米。触控板提供多达 15 种的触摸手势，用户在日常使用过程中，可以免去伸手点击屏幕定位的麻烦，直接通过触控板来对光标进行操作，一块键盘，即可执行用户所有命令。造型小巧典雅，搭配铝合金材质底盖让这款蓝牙触控键盘为用户带来强烈的视觉冲击感。

This is an ultra-slim Bluetooth touch keyboard E6700 whose thinnest part of the body is only 4.3mm.The touchpad provides as many as 15 kinds of touch gestures so that users can avoid being bothered to click the screen to locate in the process of daily use, but operate the cursor directly through the touchpad, therefore, a keyboard is enough to perform all the commands of the users. Exquisite and elegant shape design.The material of bottom cover is aluminium alloy,shows an irresistible visual enjoyment.

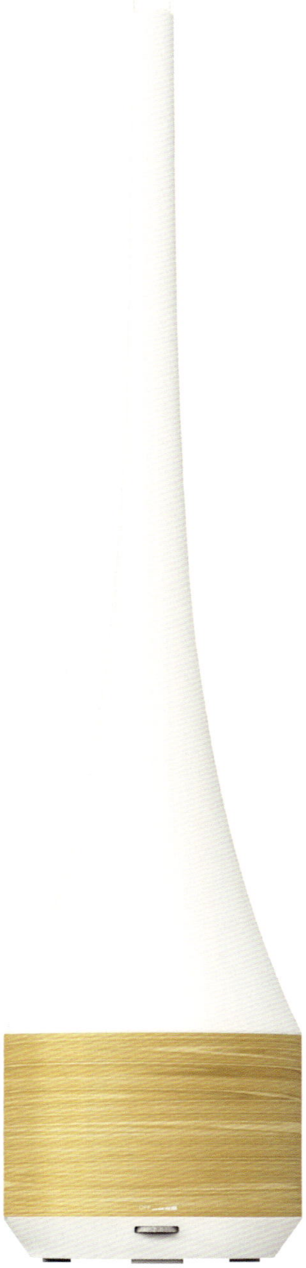

加湿器
Humidifier

设计 / 联创工业设计中心
生产 / 深圳市联创科技集团有限公司
Design / Lianchuang Industry Design Center
Manufacture / Shenzhen Lianchuang Technology Group Co., Ltd

该产品采用先进的集成式机芯，一体模块式设计，通过超声波高频震荡将水震荡成水雾，利用风机产生的气流扩散到室内达到调节室内湿度的目的，同时具有暖加湿功能，冬季也可使用。所占空间小，雾量大小根据用户需要自由可调，出雾口可 360 度转动，缺水后会自动报警。产品灵感来源于生活中花瓶的造型，给用户带来全新的使用感受。

Using ultrasonic high frequency to let water quit from surface, become natural mist and spread with the airflow which produced by the fan to adjust the indoor's humidity. Also has warm mist function, can be used in winter.small size, adjustable mist volume, 360° rotation nozzle, easy to adjust mist direction. Together with water scarcity protection, automatically alarm when there is not enough water in the tank, safe to use.The new design comes from the division of original simple structure, disposed elaborately on details, so that the product is harmonious with highlights and bring a brand new feeling to customers.

智能音箱灯
Intelligent Speaker Lights

设计 / 深圳市想象力产品策划有限公司
生产 / 深圳市乐百川科技有限公司
Design / Imagination Design Co.,ltd
Manufacture / Betrue Technology Co.,Ltd

该产品是一款跨功能的设计产品，结合音乐、多彩灯光、免提通话、与时钟功能，并融合多种控制方式，包括智能手机软件孔控制，触拍感应及按键控制。凸显音乐与灯光的融合，让使用者在聆听音乐舒缓心情的同时还能在柔和灯光所营造的氛围下温暖身心。采用的材料全部为可降解与回收的环保材料，设计简约且具有标志性。

Intelligent Speaker lights is a cross-functional product design, combined with music and colorful lights, speakerphone, and a clock function, and integration of a variety of control methods, including smart APP aperture control, touch sensors and keys to control shot.Fusion of music and lights，allows users to listen to music soothing mood and unwind in the warm atmosphere created by soft lighting, touch voices.Intelligent speaker lights does the absolute environmental protection, the material is biodegradable and recycling environmental protection material, no harm to the environment.

蓝牙户外音箱
Bluetooth Outdoor Speaker

设计 / 深圳雷柏科技股份有限公司
生产 / 深圳雷柏科技股份有限公司
Design / Shenzhen Rapoo Technology Co.,Ltd
Manufacture / Shenzhen Rapoo Technology Co.,Ltd

该产品为具有三防特性的蓝牙户外音箱，外表面多彩硅胶设计，柔软耐磨。蓝牙 4.1 技术、NFC 快速连接技术，连接轻松完成。柱形外形，网孔均匀分布，享受 360 度全方位震撼音频享受。特殊的防水喇叭，弹性极好的硅胶边框及精密的结构，使音箱具有强大的防水、防尘、抗摔性能，适应更艰苦的环境。内置大容量锂电池，一次充电长时间使用，环保高效。

Silicone materials with many colors provides the comfort and waer resistance. Bluetooth 4.1 technology and NFC technology provide simple and convenient connection. Cylindrical shape with uniform mesh distribution provides 360 degrees high-quality stereo sound.Splash-proof, dust-proof and shock-proof functions ensure the speaker can work well at many environments.The built-in lithium-ion battery is charged via charging cable and lasts for long time with a single charge.

扫一扫查看产品 Pin3D 技术三维效果图
Scanning for the 3D image by Pin3D

Core V21 平躺式机壳
Core V21 Case

设计 / TT Design
生产 / 曜越科技股份有限公司
Design / TT Design
Manufacture / Thermaltake Technology Co.,Ltd

该产品前置 200 毫米超大静音风扇，后方预留 140 毫米风扇安装空间，拥有绝佳散热效能及高度扩充性，可直立或横向放置主机板的机箱，玩家可依自己喜好调整。堆叠组合模式设计提供弹性规划内装以达到极致散热和最佳效能表现，适合各类型 PC 玩家打造出符合自己理想的水冷或气冷超频系统。金属制造，可回收，对环境影响低。

This product has a 200mm fan on the front panel,and it offers an endless stackable and flexible thermal solution. It allows externally-modular upgrades for enthusiasts to create dual systems. Designed for use in either a vertical or horizontal orientation on the motherboard, users can customize the chassis for the best viewing presentation. Optimized Ventilation With its exceptional cooling ability, the Core V21 offers various mounting points to support all types of cooling systems, including DIY/AIO liquid-cooling systems and air-cooling units.The product made by metal, recyclable,has low impact on the environment.

弓—控制保护开关
Bow - Control Protection Switch

设计 / 温州左岸品牌设计推广有限公司
生产 / 德力西电气有限公司
Design / Leftbank Design
Manufacture / Delixi Electric Co., Ltd

该产品打破传统产品呆板、冰冷、硬朗的形态，采取弓形元素设计，集成了传统的断路器、接触器等主要功能，可启动延时、过压及欠压保护等保护措施，有效提高产品附加值和安全性，提升了产品档次。产品采用模块化结构形式，方便组装拆卸。由环保材料制作而成，减少对环境的影响。

This prodcut integrates traditional circuit breakers, contactors, overload relays, starters, isolators, motor integrated protection, etc. The main functionWith a start-up delay, overvoltage and undervoltage protection, inverse time overload long delay protection, under current protection, phase unbalance protection, stall protection functionImprove value-added products, improve product quality.Using environmentally friendly materials, reduce the impact on the environment. Modular structure. Easy assembly disassembly.To break the traditional products dull,cold, tough shape, take the bow element design, the overall shape is more simple, the atmosphere, but also has characteristics of a high degree of recognition, convey the tension, stable and reliable.

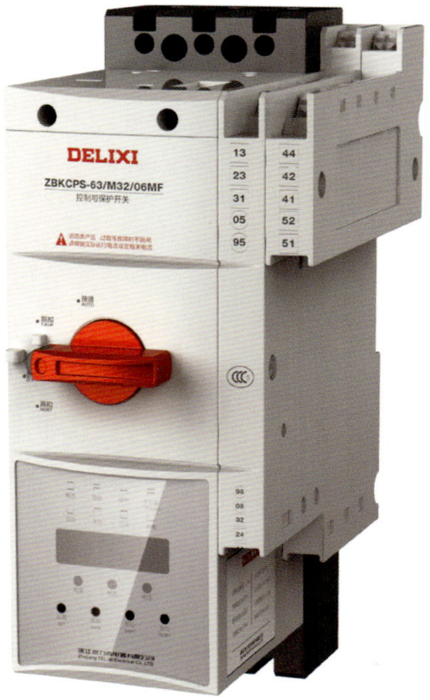

Up Box 3D 打印机
Tiertime Up Box 3D Printer

设计 / 北京洛可可科技有限公司
生产 / 北京太尔时代科技有限公司
Design / LKK Design Beijing Co..Ltd
Manufacture / Beijing Tiertime Technology Co.,Ltd

该产品内置空气过滤器和 LED 照明系统，是准专业级桌面 3D 打印设备。拥有无需人工操作的全自动校准平台。提供多种打印模式，包括节省材料的非实体打印模式，减少材料成本。打破传统打印机规整的“方盒子”，侧边略微倾斜的边角设计使产品既富有品质感又蕴藏极大的鲜活力。

The 3D printer built the air weapon and LED lighting systems, is a quasi-professional class desktop 3D printing device. It is an all automatic calibration platform.Built-in trays integrated design, allows users to operate it easier. It offers a variety of printing modes, including a non-solid printing mode to save material and reduce material costs. Using a dark metallic paint with a high-gloss black frame could enhance quality feel.In the main color of deep black and gray background, a highly recognizable features asymmetrical bright ribbon embellishment breaking the traditional square box printer structured feel. Plus side slightly inclined corner design, the product contains both rich and great sense of quality fresh force.

iEagle—智能航拍无人机
iEagle-Intelligent aerial drones

设计 / 深圳市鼎典工业产品设计有限公司
生产 / 深圳市艾特航空科技股份有限公司
Design / Shenzhen Designdo Industrial Design Co., Ltd
Manufacture / Shenzhen Art-tech R/C Hobby Co., Ltd

该产品配有高效率的驱动电机，飞行姿态、续航能力等都位于行业顶端，一体化机身设计保证雨雪天气畅飞无阻。可以搭载手机和平板电脑，让用户享受第一视角的乐趣，一键返航等功能使初次体验的用户也能快速掌握飞行方法，手动和全自动飞行模式的随意切换更是令操作过程更智能。上市以来，深受航拍爱好者、商业拍摄、摄影爱好者、航模爱好者的喜爱。

iEagle-Intelligent aerial drones is the perfect combination of technology and art, designers on the basis of aerodynamics sculptural beauty products. Fly with freedom and speed just like an eagle .It is easy to fly stable,safe. Integrated designed fuselage,make sure the safe flight in rainy and snowy weather.It configured with high efficient esc,and PAC new technical system. Adopt the golden section on the design of aircraft and controller,make them looked more harmonious and attractive. It show technology-advanced and professional.

长虹“T”空间客厅鲜品区
T-space Living-room Refrigerator

设计 / 四川虹微技术有限公司
生产 / 四川长虹电器股份有限公司
Design / Homwee Technology (Sichuan) Co., Ltd
Manufacture / Sichuan Changhong Electric Co.,Ltd

该款冰箱受书架造型启发，整体厚度仅有 53 厘米，在业界首创纤薄外观，同时能有效利用客厅空间，不会显得笨重不美观。创造了一个全新的产品概念，即作为家庭的第二台冰箱放置于客厅。三门对开冰箱，较大的左门后面涵盖两个空间：上方为酒品区，下方为臻品区，右上方的门体对应着的是常用区。采用可避免冷气流失的门中门结构，节约能源。

Its unique bookshelf-inspired, slim body is new in the industry and allows an efficient use of living-room space without being as obtrusive as a traditional refrigerator. T-space is a new product concept, specifically designed as the home' s second refrigerator to be placed in the living-room.This is a 3-door refrigerator. The larger left door includes the wine-cooler area at the top (where the door is transparent) and the boutique items area at the bottom. The right-top door corresponds to the commonly used items area and it features an energy-saving double-door construction. The right-bottom door is the tea area (freezer).The right-top door corresponds to the commonly used items area and it features an energy-saving double-door construction.

德意吸油烟机 CXW-230-HK2086
DE&E Hood CXW-230-HK2086

设计 / 飞鱼设计（杭州）有限公司
生产 / 浙江德意厨具有限公司
Design / Feish Design (Hangzhou) Co.,LTD
Manufacture / DE&E Appliances Co., LTD

该产品独创的穹顶式吸油烟机结合了欧式油烟机与塔形机的优势，与传统欧式油烟机相比拢烟区域面积多 30% 以上。创新研发的风压智能补强系统，自动感应公共烟道压力变化，彻底解决高层住宅公共烟道拥堵及油烟倒灌的问题，并有效降低噪音至 53 分贝，开创清新舒适的厨房环境空间。由一体成型的不锈钢压制而成，把未来科技自然融入到最新厨房环境中。

This prodcut's innovation range hood combines both advantages of continental smoke meters and pyramid shaped range hood which hcs a super deeply smoking cabin that the area is more than 30% than traditional range hoods.The latest innovative research and development of smart wind pressure system with wideband adaptive motor auto-induced the pressure changes in the public flue to adjust the turbine speed.With the low-noise impeller of hypersonic fights, all innovative research and development are want to give the users a comfortable and fresh kitchen environments.In the visual experience, it comfortable and naturclly bring the future technology into the latest whole kitchen environment.

魅厨套系
N+ Series

设计 / 北京圣宝地工业设计有限公司
生产 / 华帝股份有限公司
Design / CBD Group Corp.
Manufacture / Vatti Corporation Limited

该套系由烤箱、电蒸箱、微波炉、消毒柜组成。烤箱拥有 11 档智能控制，进行 3D 立体烘焙。电蒸箱的感应式按钮智能控制系统与隐藏式自动供水系统是产品的设计亮点。微波炉具有微波加烧烤的组合功能。消毒柜可三重全效杀菌，并采用“一键安心”快捷键设计，防辐射、防泄漏、防烫伤。整套产品智能控制，使用简洁，并加入对儿童的保护设计，使用更加安全放心。

This product has four parts: Oven, Electric steamer, Microwave oven and Disinfection cabinets. The oven has intelligent control 11,3D baking Steamer. The electric steamer is built-in water tank drain.The microwave + Grill function.Disinfection cabinets: triple effective sterilization; dual core layered sterilization, energy efficient; triple anti-radiation, leak-proof, scald protection; "one-click peace of mind" shortcut key design firm rail designIntelligent control, use more concise; child-protection design.Entire series appearance not only high-end atmosphere, while both comfort.

美的436L法式四门系列冰箱(BCD-436WGPZM/BCD-436WTZM)
Midea 436L French-door Refrigerator(BCD-436WGPZM/BCD-436WTZM)

设计 / 合肥美的电冰箱有限公司
生产 / 合肥美的电冰箱有限公司
Design / Hefei Midea Refrigerator Co., Ltd
Manufacture / Hefei Midea Refrigerator Co., Ltd

该产品通过速冷抽屉的设计，使温度快速冷却，满足快节奏的生活中对于快速冷却的需求。保湿抽屉通过滤膜技术锁定水分来保证整个间室高保湿的环境，延长食物的新鲜时间。可以存放横向尺寸较宽的食品，金属背板设计及雷达感温精确控温保证间室温度的均匀，防止温度的波动造成食物的变质，令生活方式更为便捷和健康。

The rear air duct of freezer can sustain the uniformity of freezing air for the whole chamber, so as to prevent food damage due to temperature fluctuation; meanwhile, the design of fast cooling drawer can quickly lower temperature, satisfying the demands of modern fast-paced life for fast freezing; the moisturizing drawer forms an integral sealed space by silicon filter membrane cover board, which can lock moisture content by filter membrane technology to ensure the high moisturizing environment and prolong the freshness time of foods.The layout of refrigerating space allows consumers to store the foods with a large horizontal size.

长虹五门智能冰箱
BCD-370WP9B Smart Refrigerator

设计 / 四川虹微技术有限公司
生产 / 四川长虹电器股份有限公司
Design / Homwee Technology (Sichuan) Co., Ltd
Manufacture / Sichuan Changhong Electric Co.,Ltd

该产品通过增加一个额外的独立抽屉，让用户可以在一个更加节能的家电上享受更专业的食品存储。可通过无线网络连接到互联网，使用智能手机便可直接控制冰箱。冷藏、软冷冻或深冷速冻功能可满足不同用户的需求。额外设计四个可以移动的密封盒，方便食品分类并防止串味。外观优雅、高品质感，可很好地融入现代厨房环境，无界钢化玻璃搁架设计体现出家居化和高品质感。

By adding one extra drawer, users can enjoy more specialized food storage in a higher energy-efficient appliance.The smart refrigerator is connected to the internet via Wi-Fi; this means users can control the appliance from a smartphone. It can fast deep-freeze food and better preserve its nutrients. At the same time, it can match the needs of different users, as it can be utilized as fridge, soft freezer or deep freezer. The two drawers at the bottom are the deep-freezer.The refrigerator comes with four sealed movable boxes (two big and two small) that provide convenience and easy classifying of different types of food.The frameless glass front gives an elegant, quality feel to the BCD-370WP9B smart refrigerator, and enables it to blend perfectly into a modern kitchen environment.The borderless glass shelves convey a furniture-like, high-quality image.

燃气灶 S902B
Gas Stove S902B

设计 / 宁波欧琳厨具有限公司
生产 / 宁波欧琳厨具有限公司
Design / Ningbo Oulin Kitchen Utensils Co., Ltd
Manufacture / Ningbo Oulin Kitchen Utensils Co., Ltd

该产品采用三自主专利三引射管燃烧器，大大增强一次空气引射能力，燃烧充分。适合中式烹饪，满足了用户对大火力的需求，同时采用的电池更换提醒、0 秒启动功能，极大地方便了用户的使用。大尺寸承液盘与钢化玻璃黑白色经典搭配，极大保护钢化玻璃灶面受热冲击爆裂的概率。铸铁一次成型锅架，带夜光指示旋钮，彰显产品高端大气。

This gas stove’ s self-owned patent triple injecting pipes burner enables the thermal power reaches 4.7KW which is suitable for Chinese way of cooking and meets the needs of great thermal power, and the adopted functions such as batter replacement warning and zero second starting greatly facilitates the operation.The one-piece liquid bearing plate design and the one-time forming burner mounting hole solve the quick installment during production, one-time forming cast iron pot rack with luminous rotary knob highlighting the dignity of the product.

家用智能榨油机
Intelligent Household Oil Press

设计 / 深圳洛可可工业设计有限公司
生产 / 深圳得力人电器有限公司
Design / LKK Design Shenzhen Co., Ltd
Manufacture / Shen Zhen Deliren Electric Appliances Co.,Ltd

该产品将榨油步骤简化为翻盖式，简易的操作一键智能启动、运用螺旋式镗杆挤压原理，使用食品级 306 不锈钢压铸工艺，油和渣高精度分离，可以达到 95% 以上出油率。榨油后的原料还可以加入奶油和鸡蛋制作糕点，最大程度节省成本。秉承“设计改变生活”的理念，让用户体验设计带来的简单、实用、乐趣和幸福感。

Intelligent Household Oil press,simplifies the oil steps to flip, the simple operation of the one-key smart start, using the principle of spiral boring bar extrusion, using food grade 306 stainless steel die casting technology, oil and residue separation has high precision,can reach more than 95% yield efficiency.After the oil raw materials can also add cream and egg pastry Maximum cost savings.Adhering to the concept of Design changes life, the oil press gives considerations to every detail in the design of appearance,function,cleaning and storage,allowing users to have experience for the simplicity,practicability,fun and happiness.

苏泊尔全景视窗电饭煲
Supor Panoramic Windows Rice Cooker

设计 / 宁波浪尖工业产品造型设计有限公司
生产 / 浙江苏泊尔股份有限公司
Design / Ningbo Artop Design Co., Ltd
Manufacture / Zhejiang SUPOR Limited by Share Ltd

苏泊尔全景视窗电饭煲采用超大创新钢化玻璃火力视窗，可视化烹饪便于掌握煮饭状态，同时防烫抗压。产品使用大图标操作面板，方便老人识别和操作。创新球形厚釜火旋风内胆，提升米饭口感。产品采用塑胶注塑和不锈钢，易清洁，抗油污。面板采用 IMD 材料，高端时尚，便于清洁。产品整体圆润小巧，融合厨房环境。

The Supor electronic cooker adopts the panoramic window enables the cooker to see the cooking state. Large size of the operation panel enables elders to operate. The thick and spherical gallbladder of electric cooker improves the taste of the rice. Adopting mainly plastic injection molding and stainless steel, it is easy to clean and resistant the oil. The panel is IMD. Following the principle of design of ""easy""With Round ,small and Japanese style,it is easy to blend kitchen environment.

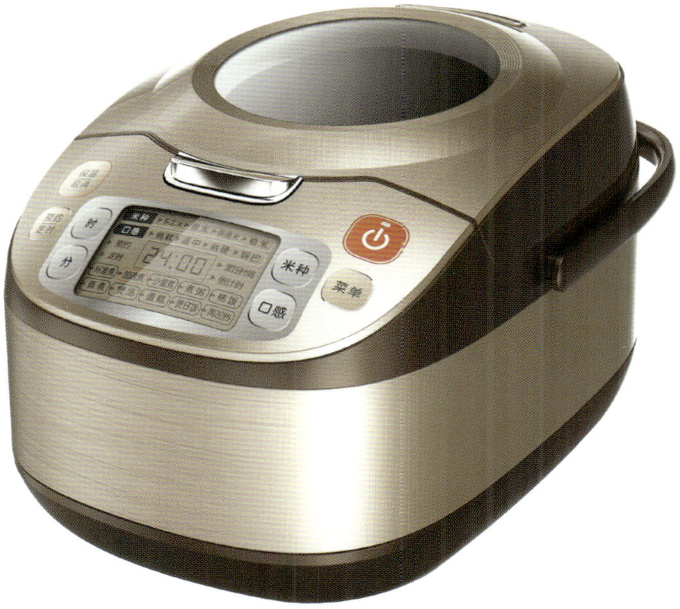

CXW–220–TJ20 吸油烟机
CXW-220-TJ20

设计 / 帅康集团
生产 / 帅康集团
Design / sacon
Manufacture / sacon

该产品平整一体化设计，关闭时整体大平板，方便厨房清洁擦洗。触摸式控制，杜绝油烟倾入，易操作易擦洗。防碰撞设计，在人的高度范围以内没有直角设计，下边沿的钝角加合适倒角的方式更大程度避免了碰撞可能带来的伤害。独创的自适应换气功能，确保烹饪结束后厨房空气环境的全面更新，消除异味残留，同时还能最大程度地节约能源。

The humanized design closer to people life, reflects hood practicality. Integration design, large glass panel and the whole big flat leads easy to clean. Touch control prevent ampblack seeps into the hood, which is easy to clean. The prevent collision design has no orthogonal in the height of people, the obtuse angle in below edge to avoid collision. Intelligent Air Flow function ensures the kitchen environment is refreshed after cooking, as well as the elimination peculiar smell, also save energy.

乐凡空气炸锅
Lefan Air Fryer

设计 / 青鸟工业设计有限公司
生产 / 广东顺德乐凡电器有限公司
Design / Bird Industrial Design
Manufacture / Guangdong Shunde Lefan Electrical Appliances co., Ltd

此款空气炸锅利用世界先进的高速空气循环技术，只用空气不用油或少用油烹饪，不产生大量油烟，降低脂量 80%，同时适宜的温度可保证食物营养不流失。快速循环热空气和烤箱部件形成独特结合，以快速便捷的方式煎炸食物，与传统煎炸方式相比减少气味和蒸汽，易于清洁，安全经济。外观简洁大方，色彩与功能结合，深受消费者喜爱。

This high speed air circulation technology of the air circulation fry pot could reduces 80% fat quantity of the French Fries than the traditional one, Rapid cycling warm air and a unique combination of oven widget allows you to fry all kinds of delicious food in a quick and convenient way. Concise and easy appearance, loved by consumers of all ages, the combination of color and function also favored by users.

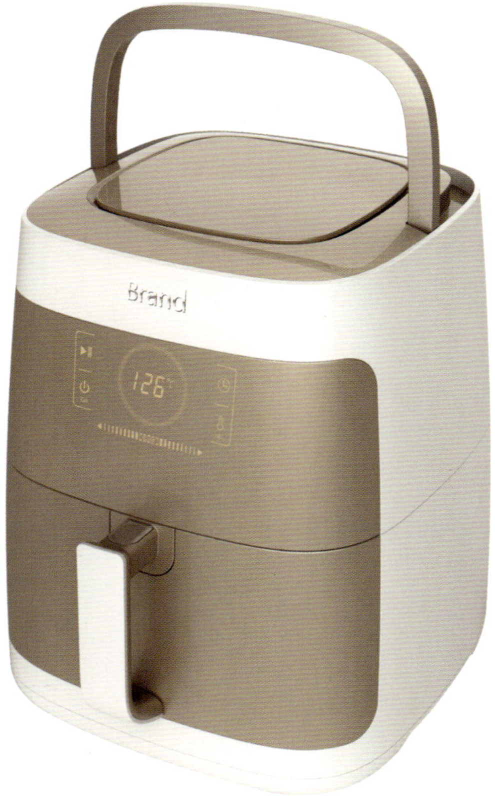

球釜电饭煲
Rice Cooker

设计 / 马汉、张胜兰
生产 / 浙江苏泊尔家电制造有限公司
Design / Ma Han,Zhang Shenglan
Manufacture / Zhejiang Supor Electrical Appliances Manufacturing Co.,Ltd

球釜电饭煲具备 IH 电磁环绕加热系统及全触摸人机操作界面，同时设计精致紧凑。产品拥有 SUPOR 电饭煲米饭专家的核心价值球形厚釜内胆。产品体积小，功能强大，全触摸界面带给消费者更舒适的体验。产品易清洁，易收纳。正片采用 IMD 操作界面，更具耐用性。产品省去多余装饰件，结构简洁。减少不锈钢煲身的使用比例，更灵巧。

We observed that the kitchen of consumers more and more crowded, streamline the product dimension is imperative.This exquisite compact products have a combination of IH surrounded by electromagnetic heating system and the touch of the man-machine interface.The spherical thick kettle bladder is a core value in SUPOR electric cooker rice expert.Small but powerful, all touch interface brings consumers more comfortable experience. Positive IMD operation interface, more lasting durability.Dispense redundant decoration, the parts are present in the most concise way.In this design we reduce the use of stainless steel pot body proportion, make the product look more smart, pot and pan wave design in modern make the product more comfortable.

启智 A9 集成灶
Integrated Stove JC-A9

设计 / 浙江森歌电器有限公司
生产 / 浙江森歌电器有限公司
Design / Zhejiang Seng Electronic Appliance Co.,Ltd
Manufacture / Zhejiang Seng Electronic Appliance Co.,Ltd

该集成灶采用生物智能感应系统和技术。滑屏变频控制风速大小，时尚简单。烟灶智能联动，信号可同步传递至控制单元。虹吸式风机系统采用向下排烟方式，提升排风量和风压。采用冷凝式净化系统和全铝质材料拢烟板，降低负压风道内温度，实现油烟分离。台面前部采用弧面造型，不积液、导流快。采用超大尺寸无缝整体拉伸通体承液盘，防止汤汁流淌。

The integration oven adopts biological smart sensor technology. The sliding screen wind speed adjustment applied to wind speed control. While opening the cooker switch, synchronization signal is transmitted to the control unit, issued a directive to start the fan system. The arc slider hidden type air suction is opened to form a coating type smoke collecting structure, which effectively increase the smoke collecting effect.The oversize seamless one stretch compound table is arc shape on front control area, which has the characteristics of no effusion, quick diversion, could effectively prevent soup liquid flow into the inside of the stove.

智盒—青芒 智能网络机顶盒
Family Entertainment Center

设计 / 深圳智我科技有限公司
生产 / 深圳雷柏科技股份有限公司
Design / Shenzhen Zivoo Technology Co.,Ltd
Manufacture / Shenzhen Rapoo Technology Co.,Ltd

该产品首创触摸 + 按键的操控方式，兼顾实体按键手感与多样触摸交互。采用智能语音识别操控，告别繁琐操控，让用户体验到人工智能的魅力。应用商场提供海量应用，操作顺畅。还可结合定制的麦克风，让用户在家也能体验优良的 K 歌效果。多种靓丽的色彩搭配新型外观，增加用户的选择空间。

The pioneering control and operation method combining touching and pressing keys balances the hand feeling of pressing physical keys and the multiple touch interactions. The control and operation system of intellectual speech recognition enables users to get rid of complex control and operation. Application stores provide a large number of applications for users' options. KTV function and zivoo customized microphone can let users experience the good effect of KTV at home. The young and beautiful colors, and the new appearance are rare in the industry.

飞利浦专业级行车记录仪 ADR810
Philips ADR810 Driving Recorder

设计 / 上海木马工业产品设计有限公司
生产 / 飞利浦中国投资有限公司上海研发中心
Design / Shanghai Moma Industrial Product Design Co.,Ltd
Manufacture / Philips(China) Investment Co., Ltd

飞利浦专业级行车记录仪产品采用 6400 超高感光度，拥有单反级超级夜视功能、超大 156 度广角、保障安全的一键录像功能和瞌睡提醒功能。记录仪可配合车载架悬挂，无毒、稳定性强。使用以水为介质的环保型水性金属漆，符合行业标准。采用内置锂电池，减少污染。外观材料采用 ABS+PC 高性能树脂材料，在暴晒下不会变形。造型简约，线条流畅，黑色为主，机身轻巧。

ADR810 professional vehicle traveling data recorder has a super night vision capabilities, large 156 ° wide angle, the patented "one-click video recording" as well as "sleepy reminder" to ensure the vehicle safety. Nontoxic, nonflammable, stability, with water as the medium of environmentally friendly water-based metallic paint, the targets are reached and exceeded the national and industry standards, using the built-in lithium battery, reducing battery pollution.Appearance of materials using ABS+PC materials, such materials take into account the product does not deform in auto exposure environment.

智能血糖仪—魔镜
Magic Mirror

设计 / 上海木马工业产品设计有限公司
生产 / 上海康之元信息技术有限公司
Design / Shanghai Moma Industrial Product Design Co.,Ltd
Manufacture / Sybercare Technologies Inc.

该产品为一款为中年女性量身定制的实时血糖监测仪，运用了特殊的镜面涂层设计，营造出与女性化妆品气质相当的形态感觉。不仅使用步骤简单方便，同时也便于随身携带，可将血糖数据实时同步到智能设备上。简洁的设计元素，去除了不必要的部件，数据能够清晰地显示在设备屏幕上。时尚、轻奢的设计风格，为使用者提供舒适和方便的体验。

This blood glucose meter is specially designed for woman,We create a fashion trend and low-key luxury style of the product. The Magic Mirror reduce the anxiety of the user because of the detection of the blood sugar, and provide comfortable and easy psychological experience for the user.The intelligent blood sugar can collect data accurately, and easy to use. It can synchronize data with intelligent device.The blood glucose meter uses simple and stylish design elements for the high-end middle aged women to track and monitor the blood sugar valve in real time, and it removes unnecessary parts.

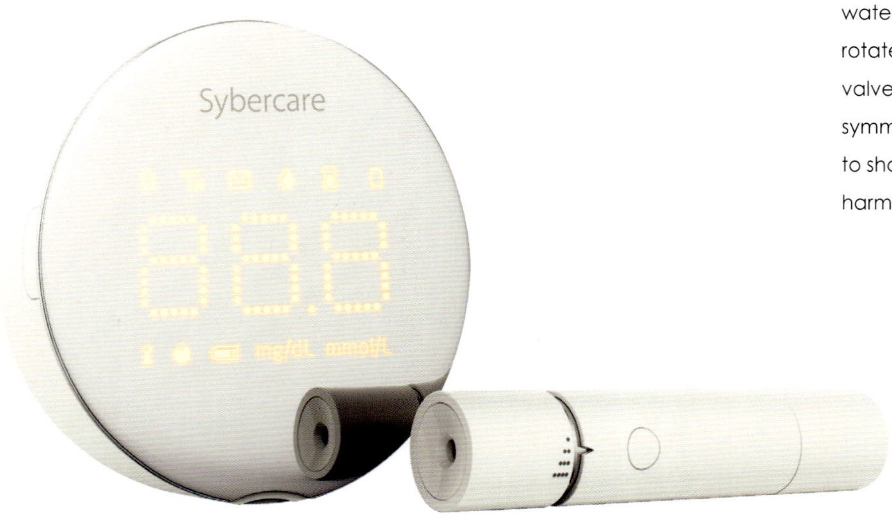

软水机“融”
Water Softeners, "Harmony"

设计 / 贾雪峰、李文锋
生产 / 上海开能环保设备股份有限公司
Design / Justin, Li Wenfeng
Manufacture / Canature

该产品采用逆流再生技术，更加节盐省水，运行更高效。旋转式加盐口设计，造型具有操作的引导性更方便快捷，尤其是在橱下安装时节省空间。独家漏水报警、缺盐报警和余氯杀菌技术让使用更安全智能。采用对称设计，通过曲面线条的变化让产品凸现简洁美感，同时局部点缀高亮度色彩醒目时尚，让产品层次更加丰富。

The water softner machine adopts the “up flow regeneration” technology to save salt and water, make it high efficiency. Ensured high efficiency and advanced function save material. The unique cabinet body design to fix the inside tank, reduced the traditional mid cover, easy to assemble, cambered design is to ensure the strength of the cabinet body and to avoid shaped after water and salt filled during using. Adopting innovation rotated cover structure, obvious identification, and insert valve, extremely saving space. The product adopts symmetric design language, the curve and lines changes to show it nice design, simple circle bring soft and harmony.

三点式蓝牙音箱
Sound Pipe V1s

设计 / 杭州凸凹工业设计有限公司
生产 / 杭州凸凹工业设计有限公司
Design / Tao Design
Manufacture / Tao Design

该音箱将鲜亮色彩、时尚外观与便捷操作相结合。发声单元位于音箱上侧，使声域通过 v 形以三点式有效分配，声场更开阔，层次感和空间感更强。产品采用 v 形柱状结构，管状深声腔配合喇叭，声音圆润饱满，表现力强。根据高音与低音不同规律，上扬的高音喇叭加强高音区品质，底部低音孔与桌面形成共振，强化厚重感。多种颜色与金属镀层展现混搭美感。

The Seamless V shape looks more delicate, rise design makes the sound unit is arranged in the sound box on the side, tessitura by V shape design to three points in the form of effective distribution, making the sound field more open, and brings the sense of hierarchy and a stronger space feeling . V shaped cylincrical structure, 1.9 inches tubular deep cavity seamlessly with 1.7 inch loudspeaker unit is effective with the cavity structure, showing a mellow and full tone, and enhcnce the sound expressive force.

“三角鲑”蒸汽地拖
Sea Purse

设计 / 杭州凸凹工业设计有限公司
生产 / 杭州凸凹工业设计有限公司
Design / Tao Design
Manufacture / Tao Design

该蒸汽地拖采用三角鲑式设计，可清洁卫生死角。产品推拉轻便，操作简单。使用一体式大容量透明可视水箱，一键式极简操作，加热速度快，清洁能力强。产品占地面积小，收纳方便。清水便可清洁，适合各类地板使用。清洁布可循环使用，绿色环保。“三角鲑”运用环保型 ABS（合成树脂），根据人体工学原理打造手柄和绕线、水箱设计，提供健康简约生活方式。

The steam cleaner bionic design of the sea purse could clean floor without any blind corner. It’ s easy to pull and push, very easy to operate. The adoption of the one-piece big transparent container makes the operation easier. Eco-friendly ABS is adopted, the ergonomics design enables people a simple way to use and pack.

除螨吸尘一体机
Sterilizing&Handheld&Stick Cleaner Integrated Machine

设计 / 吕知轩、姜鸿胤
生产 / 苏州欧奈电器科技有限公司
Design / Super, John
Manufacture / Ounai Electric.Co.,LTD

该产品集除螨功能和手持吸尘器、推杆吸尘器三功能于一体，通过拍打、吸尘、杀菌，避免螨虫细菌引发疾病。产品可调节角度和增加延长管、手柄，省时省力，操作轻便。吸尘通道设置传感器，检测颗粒物含量，通过声音和灯光警示含量超标。产品除螨快速，除尘轻松，安全环保，营造健康环境。采用电镀件、透明件与 ABS（合成树脂）材料相结合，增加层次感。

The new UV Sterilizing cleaner could not only adjusts the product working angle enabling consumers an easier and convenient way of operation, but also extends the tube and handle to increase the product working radius. Besides, the product sets up dust & germ particle concentration sensor on suction airflow pipe to check the consistence content of dust & germ particle in suction airflow pipe, when the consistence are out of limit, the product will give a voice alarm or light alarm, then tell consumer to increase the sterilizing time on this place.

悦 me 智能机顶盒
Yue me Smart Set-top Box

设计 / 上海木马工业产品设计有限公司
生产 / 中国电信集团公司智能家居业务运营中心
Design / Shanghai Moma Industrial Product Design Co.,Ltd
Manufacture / China Telecom Corporation Smart Home Business Operation Center

悦 me 智能机顶盒是中国电信自主知识产权产品，提供即插即用的影音娱乐、民生应用、健康医疗、在线购物等多种家庭信息化服务。统一外观及配置，建立品牌形象，便于统一运营。统一系统接口与技术标准，加快推出新产品。产品开发声控遥控器和全键盘遥控器。产品具待机模式，降低耗电量。采用光毛面对比和柔触感橡胶漆增加手感，体现简单、智能、乐玩理念。

Yue me the depth of customization set-top box to the strategic importance of China Telecom. will help enhance the user perception, but also easy to form a national centralized unified operational advantage; another uniform system interfaces and technical standards, to speed up the progress of application development. Yue me set-top box market, to provide users plug and play audio and video entertainment, people' s livelihood and applications, health care, video games, online shopping, and other family information service.

家用智能机器人
Smart Home Robot

设计 / 北京智加问道科技有限公司
生产 / 北京家度科技有限公司
Design / ZCO Design Co., Ltd
Manufacture / Beijing Jiadu Technology Co., Ltd

该产品将古代儿童虎头头饰与现代墨镜时尚元素相结合，是一款以家庭娱乐为应用场景，实现智能行走避障、远程视频通话监控、在线娱乐教育及云数据处理分析的智能家庭机器人。机器人以 ROS（机器人软件平台），Linux 操作系统，Arduino 电子原型平台，Android 操作系统技术为依托，整合云计算与传感器技术，创造智能电子互动平台。产品采用可回收医用级塑料和金属，原色注塑。外型线条简约流畅，富生命感，温暖可爱。

This robot realizes functions with avoiding barrier, remote video call monitoring, online entertainment education and cloud data processing, is a combination of the ancient children headdress tiger with the modern sunglasses. Based on the ROS, Linux, Arduino and Android technology, the robot is an integration of the cloud computing and sensor technology. The product is using recycled medical grade plastics and metals.

怡兰全屋净水机
Yilan House Water Purifier

设计 / 宁波浪尖工业产品造型设计有限公司
生产 / 福建怡兰净水科技有限公司
Design / NingBo Artop Design Co., Ltd
Manufacture / Fujian Yilan Water Technology Co., Ltd

该净水机可用怡兰 ePad 平板电脑监测数据和使用状态，实现用水过程全程监控，提供智能管家式服务。前置过滤采用工业机滤罐，实现大水量的别墅分质供水。产品可定制，滤芯和滤壳可自行更换，满足不同需求。整机采用不锈钢和钣金材料，可回收利用。采用钣金折弯焊接工艺，加工简单，成本低。产品线条硬朗，层次分明，造型与功能结合，具有专业感。

This product is using smart Elan ePad Tablet PC set Android operating system can provide effective predicted data and test reference, as well as provide accurate test result and real-time operating state to realize the computer monitor of using water, providing "smart butler service" for user. The sheet metal bending welding, simple process and low cost; sheet metal and stainless steel shows its specialty as well.

无线吸尘除螨机
Wireless Dust Mites Machine

设计 / 吕知轩
生产 / 苏州欧奈电器科技有限公司
Design / Super
Manufacture / Ounai Electric.Co.,LTD

该产品将除螨功能和手持吸尘器合二为一，解决拆线、插电、拖拽等麻烦， 通过拍打、吸尘、杀菌等，避免螨虫细菌引发疾病。手持吸尘器可取出单独使用，具有延长接管功能，方便清理。产品寿命长，运行稳定。使用电镀件、透明件与 ABS 合成树脂材料相结合，增加层次感，材料无污染易于回收。优美曲线给人舒适感，灯效与电镀件增加科技感，设计与功能完美结合。

The rechargeable dust mite killer &Vacuum cleaner well solved the issues of repeating plug, cording management etc. and it is also a 2-in-1 design of dust mite killing and handy Vacuum cleaner, solved the issues of current machines in the market which can' t be used as a separate vacuum cleaner. As the handy Vacuum cleaner could be taken out as a separate machine and match extension tube to extent the cleaning radius. Dust mate cleaner and Handy Vac in unit design which match perfect, curve lines make the design more visible and comfortable.

UCON 智能遥控器
UCON Smart Remote

设计 / UCON Design Team
生产 / 南京悦控智能科技有限公司
Design / UCON Design Team
Manufacture / Yuekong Intelligence Co.,Ltd

该产品是一款统一管理家电的智能遥控器，将信息技术平民化、家居化，集成无限网络、蓝牙、红外等于一体，简化沟通成本。产品具备自定义快捷键和模式切换功能，适配不同电器。具备防丢功能，可一键找回。产品待机时间长，可放在底座上充电。手机软件有近 10000 种设备数据，可远程预约开启电器。功能按键区、屏幕显示区、底座控制区采用模块化设计，风格简洁纯净。

This is a smart remote control integrates WiFi, Bluetooth, a variety of infrared communication protocol, to create in the hands of the family remote control core, greatly simplifying the cost of communication between users and devices. UCON retained the most streamlined key, and at the same time it has a custom shortcut keys and mode switching function, to fit the normal operation of the electrical appliances are different, the houseful appliance, a hand control.

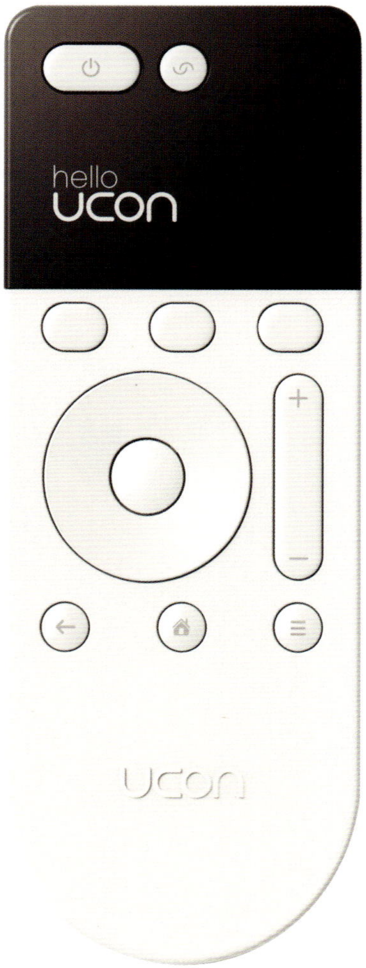

震撼者 3D 7.1 全景立体环绕声电竞耳机
Shock 3D 7.1 Virtualized Surround Gaming Headset

设计 / TTdesign
生产 / Thermaltake
Design / TT Design
Manufacture / Thermaltake

该产品首次把声音结合延迟与变化所制作出环绕的效果运用至电子竞技游戏上，拥有创新的LED红光自发性律动功能，其发光模式会依循音乐节奏与旋律以及不同类型的游戏属性，以快慢频率作呼吸式的发光，充分符合使用者当下律动情境。罩式大尺寸复合材质蛋白皮革耳套，能随时提供最佳的长时间配戴舒适度与绝佳包覆感。

The SHOCK 3D 7.1 headset offers users true in-game immersion via enhanced 3D virtualized surround sound. LED accents further add to the gaming atmosphere of the headset.3D 7.1 virtualized surround sounds offers a fully immersive experience in-game. The LED lighting pattern reacts to the sound of your music or game, to enhance the overall experience.Twelve environmental sound effects accessible by software, allow users to further tune the sound.A bendable and pivotable microphone allows for easy access to necessary voice communications within games.

中兴超简遥控器
ZTE Super Simple Handset

设计 / 中兴通讯股份有限公司
生产 / 中兴通讯股份有限公司
Design / Zte Corporation
Manufacture / Zte Corporation

中兴超简遥控器具有三个特点：超薄超轻设计；方向键内外圈斜面设计，导向更加精确，使用更加省力；整体造型简洁时尚，大曲线设计使未来感强。产品按键以及按键图标设计简洁易懂，适合每个家庭成员。产品所采用的材料和工艺都符合国际标准，绿色环保。产品通过欧盟《RoHS 指令》要求，采用超轻材料，实现轻薄效果。

The product has the following three characteristics, the slim and light weight design, the arrow keys has an inside and outside bevel design which makes the direct more accurate. The overall shape is concise and fashion, the big curve design gives a sense of future. Buttons and icons are all designed simple and easy to use. The ultralight material and other materials are all eco-friendly material.

竹构一月影环形灯
O Light

设计 / 杭州凸凹工业设计有限公司
生产 / 杭州凸凹工业设计有限公司
Design / Tao Design
Manufacture / Tao Design

此款环形灯将环保材质、时尚外观、便捷操作相融合。采用竹子制造，天然环保，回归自然，坚持“简单、美感、实用”的原则，创造出时尚环保产品。摒弃传统小夜灯多余装饰，环形设计增加趣味性，以传统拨动式按键给人不同的使用体验。竹壳经过高温蒸煮和碳化工艺处理，清新健康。环形灯表面经过精心打磨，保留天然纹理，极具美感。整体呈现简约大方的风格。

This is an eco-friendly stylish "Ring" Lamp with convenient operation. Made of bamboo, it's adhering the principle of compact, aesthetical and practical to make this fashionable product. Abandon the toggle redundant decoration, "ring" itself brings a fun way of operation. After the high temperature and carbonizing process, the bamboo shell goes fresh and healthy. The surface is carefully polished and made to retain the natural texture of bamboo. The overall design brings people a sense of freshness, makes people return to the nature.

军规级抗震防水移动硬盘
Armor A65 /Armor A65M

设计 / 钟健志、吴家祯
生产 / 广颖电通股份有限公司
Design / Chien-Chih Chung, Chia-Chen Wu
Manufacture / Silicon Power Computer & Communications Inc

产品是一款 2.5 寸移动硬盘，设计灵感来自船身流线造型，让使用者感受休闲旅游趣味。产品采用三层防护设计，有效保护硬盘内部数据，并提供防水、防尘、防震之三大防护功能，提高防护等级，延长使用寿命。隐藏式带线设计，让线材随硬盘携带而不增加体积。产品以降低 PET 塑料使用量和节省包装材料和运费为目标，较少资源，并可回收再利用。

Armor A65 is a 2.5-inch portable hard drive. The conception of its design was originated from the streamline shape of a ship, which let the users intuitively think of products as relating to “water” and further feel leisure and tourist interest. Adopts a three-layer design to effectively protect the internal data of hard drive disc (HDD), A65 is the first portable hard drive which provides the protection of waterproof, dustproof, and shockproof. A65 offer a all-around protection to prolong the life span of itself effectively. Products fully comply with all safety regulations and standards.

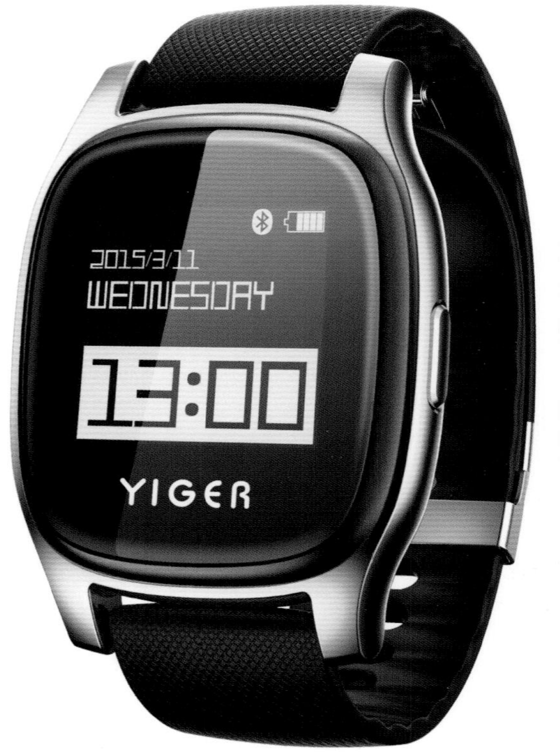

逸格智能手表
Yiger Up

设计 / 深圳意臣工业设计有限公司
生产 / 深圳市宏电技术股份有限公司
Design / Innozen Product Design Co.,Ltd
Manufacture / Hongdian Corporation

该产品是一款健康智能手表，通过传感器监测活动数据和生理数据，可识别并记录运动状态，拥有睡眠监测和日常状态监测功能，给用户提供运动建议和生活指导。产品细分不同场景监测数据，更专业。使各项监测指标间建立关联，健康指导更全面。皮肤电阻传感器应用于对个人活力状态的监测，独一无二。无线充电技术、触屏操作及记忆 LCD 屏，更具科技感。

Yiger is a wearable health smart watch, recognizes and records the sports status by identifying and recording contains motion state, the real-time heart rate and sleep monitoring, condition monitoring functions such as daily, science of sports health advice to users, reasonable work and rest life guidance, to help users in work and life. The application of the wireless charging technology, touch screen operation, and don’ t need to light up the Memory of the LCD screen will make watch more sense of science and technology.

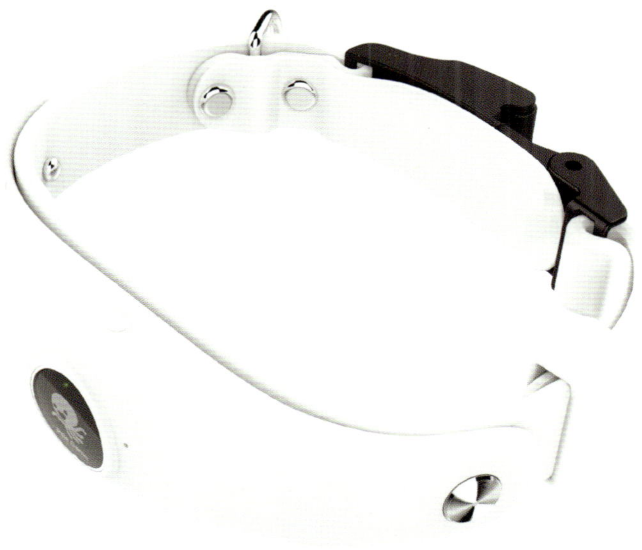

数码宠物定位器
GPS Pet Tracker

设计 / 深圳市浪尖设计有限公司
生产 / 郑州派乐数码科技有限公司
Design / Shenzhen Artop Design Co., Ltd
Manufacture / Polegame Inc.

采用大胆创新的结构方式和项圈硅胶内部注尼龙带的工艺，使得产品既美观又舒适，适合任意大小的宠物佩戴。产品强大又丰富的功能保障用户更安心地带宠物进行户外活动，有效防止宠物的丢失。具有轨迹查询、越界警告、定位跟踪等主要功能。每次向手机端发送的定位信息都会自动保存至云端，可以随时查看当天任意时段的移动轨迹。

This is a real-time GPS pet tracker that creatively integrates flexible glue with nylon fiber on material, to solve the problem of over soft or tough touch. It is designed to attach to any size of collar so users can keep track of their pets wherever they go, making sure they always get home safe. With the tracker can monitor pets' activity and record adventures on a smart phone or computer. In addition, the users can get texts alerts from mobile phone APP so will know right away if their pets get lost.

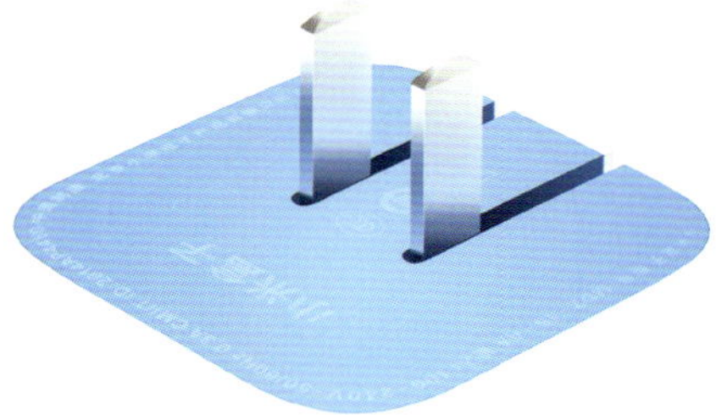

小米小盒子
MI Box Mini

设计 / 沈希洁
生产 / 小米科技有限责任公司
Design / Shen Xijie
Manufacture / Xiaomi Inc.

MI Box Mini 是微型全高清网络机顶盒。超小的机身具备了强大的移动性，便于旅途携带。运行安卓系统并支持 Dolby DTS，搭载强劲 4 核 CPU，4+2 核 GPU，让视频、游戏都变得极其流畅。超过 14 万小时正版内容，实时更新。采用电源直插设计，整机只有一个 HDMI 接口，前所未有地提升了产品的易用性。配备蓝牙遥控器，操控绝无死角。

The MI Box Mini is by far the world's smallest online VOD set-top box that can render HD videos in up to 1080p. Mini's super tiny pocket friendly design brings true mobility to an online VOD set-top box. The included remote control uses BLT low energy Bluetooth technology so that it doesn't have any operational blind spot. It's powered with a Cortex-A7 quad-core CPU and a blazing fast 4+2 core GPU, giving you an ultra-smooth video watching and gaming experience. The only connectivity interface is HDMI, reducing its complexity and enhancing ease of use.

对开门冰箱 BCD-630WPDGB（鎏金黑）
Side-by-side Refrigerator BCD-630WPDGB (Intangible Pomp)

设计 / 李琦、崔北艳
生产 / 合肥晶弘电器有限公司
Design / Richie Lee, Julia Cui
Manufacture / Hefei Kinghome Electrical Co.,Ltd

该冰箱采用双循环系统，冷藏和冷冻室独立分割，避免食物串味，也可将冷藏室关闭，节能环保。表面采用电镀玫瑰金色，与黑色面板搭配显高贵典雅。轻触式吧台，轻松开启，拿取便捷。采用ECO节能模式，自动记录分析饮食作息习惯，提供最佳节能方案。钢化玻璃面板手感细腻，不锈蚀、不褪色。产品电脑控温，立体斜角送风，控温精确。

This refrigerator adopts double circulation system could make the fridge compartments separate from freezer to avoid the smell mixture, also can close the fridge part to save energy. Exclusive rose golden makes the product noble and elegant. The ECO energy saving mode recognize automatically and memorize frequency of user open & close the door, record and analyze user's diet habit. The computer control temperature could accurately sets the proper temperature to store foods at random, bevel angle air supply makes temperature inside cabinet more even.

无霜冷藏冷冻箱
Frost-free Refrigerator

设计 / 杭州领跑者工业设计有限公司
生产 / 杭州华日电冰箱股份有限公司
Desigr / Hangzhou LPZ Industrial Design Co. Ltd
Manufacture / Hangzhou Huari Refrigerator Co., Ltd

无霜冷藏冷冻箱创新地将操作区域设计在冰箱把手位置，集中整合交互行为，通过不同材质和色彩区分，降低操作频率，设计极简，功能至上。产品体积合理，适合居家空间，同时更省电。把手模块以注塑工艺成型，与钣金壳体无缝配合。产品采用优异的拼焊工艺和精细的钣金折弯，打造出一款集美学和功能为一体的经典之作。

Products abandon cumbersome functional definition, innovatively designed operating area in the refrigerator opening and closing of the handle position, will focus on the integration of interactive behavior, and separated by zor es of different materials and colors to reduce the user's operating frequency. The fridge occupies a reasonable space and the daily run and the daily is more reasonable, more convenient to use. Fine sheet metal bending, welding process to ensure the product as a whole compact body beautiful presentation.

樱花“都市时尚系列”烟炉一体化设计
Range Hood

设计 / 上海木马工业产品设计有限公司
生产 / 樱花工业设计中心
Design / Shanghai Moma Industrial Product Design Co.,Ltd
Manufacture / Shanghai Tweis Information Technology Co., Ltd

樱花“都市时尚系列”烟炉一体化设计采用统一的面板与汤盘尺寸，方便实用。创新可翻转炉架，适应不同种类锅具的摆放需求，减少材料浪费。燃气灶与电磁灶组合，满足多种烹饪需求。产品使用数字显示的独特交互体验，同时采用上提式旋钮操作方式和独特镜面反射模块。采用能源钣金冲压和不锈钢拉丝处理。黑色亚克力和圆角处理，使产品简洁大气。

The product has adopted a untied size of the panel and soup plate, practical and easy to use. The new reversal rack makes it adapt to a variety of pans. The combination of gas cooker and electrical cocker meets different cooking needs. The universal digital screen brings new interaction experience. It is designed with a unique specular reflection module. The combination of gas cooker and electrical cooker meets different cooking needs, and maximize the use of energy.

老板 5900 油烟机
Robam 5900 Range Hood

设计 / 杭州老板电器股份有限公司
生产 / 杭州老板电器股份有限公司
Design / Hangzhou Robam Applicances Co., Ltd
Manufacture / Hangzhou Robam Applicances Co., Ltd

此款油烟机拥有出色吸油烟效果。挡烟板采用电动翻转方式，科技感十足。滤油网采用电腐蚀工艺和菱形网孔设计，有效过滤油烟，减少对核心部件的损害，利用磁铁固定，不需工具可拆卸清洗。产品拥有大风量，同时有效控制噪声。挡烟板设置防夹手提醒功能，保证安全。主体使用黑色玻璃，易擦洗。操控系统采用电容触摸按键，操作简单。

Robam-5900 is positioned as the most premium range hood. It has the best smoke in-taking effect. The smoke deflector uses electrical rolling design, which is very innovative. The oil net is fixed by magnet, which can be removed and cleaned without using other tools. Meanwhile the product's noise is well controlled. The smoke deflector set clamping hands caution reminder to ensure the safety of users. The operation system is capacitive touch-key which is simple to use, and cooperate very well with appearance.

海信多门冰箱
Hisense Multi-door Refrigerator

设计 / 海信工业设计中心
生产 / 海信容声（广东）冰箱有限公司
Design / Hisense Industrial Design Center
Manufacture / Hisense Ronshen (Guangdong) Co., Ltd

该多门冰箱外观融入家居设计精髓，兼具传统法式冰箱和对开门冰箱的优点，技术承袭海信冰箱领先技术，独创三温区独立循环系统，满足消费者扩大冷藏空间和分类细化冷冻室和温室的需求。产品采用变频低噪、立体送风系统和立体照明系统，降低能耗和噪声。玻璃面板四周圆角切割，增加亲和力。采用无边框粘贴玻璃设计，运用玻璃异形加工工艺，灵动精致。

The appearance of the product integrates the essence of home design, and the functions perfectly combines the advantages of traditional French refrigerator and side-by-side combination refrigerator and technologically inherits Hisense's international leading technology. Moreover, it creates unique three-zone independent circulatory system, meeting the dual consumers' needs of space expansion of cold storage and the detailed classification of freezer and variable storage. Contrast crystal clear glass white glass panels to delicate and restrained sleek matte black handle, black and white, light and dark, creating great contrast visual impact.

易清洁燃气灶
Easy-cleaning Gas Stove

设计 / 广东顺德东方麦田工业设计有限公司
生产 / 广东万家乐燃气具有限公司
Design / East-innovation Shunde GD Co.,Ltd
Manufacture / Guangdong Macro Gas Appliance Co.,Ltd

产品采用创新的无接水盘设计，油污无处可藏，一抹即可，锅支架与燃烧器巧妙固定，区别通常的锅支架设计与固定方式。旋钮采用了 60 度斜角设计，与通常 90 度直角的旋钮设计不同，抹布可以深入旋钮底部进行清洁，使得油污无处可藏，清洁变得非常轻松简单，是一款更适合中国家庭使用的产品。

This gas stove has the creative non-water box design, leaving no place for greasy dirt to hide. The skillfully fixation of pot support and burner makes it different from the ordinary design of pot support and the method of fixation of it. The rotary knob adopts the 60° slanting angle, different from the ordinary rotary knob design at right angle. In such way, the duster cloth can reach the bottom of the rotary knob.

小天鹅比佛利滚筒洗衣机
Little Swan Beverly Front-loading Washing Machine

设计 / 无锡小天鹅股份有限公司工业设计团队
生产 / 无锡小天鹅股份有限公司
Design / Wuxi Little Swan Company Limited ID Team
Manufacture / Wuxi Little Swan Company Limited

该产品是有良好用户体验的滚筒洗衣机，具有感知洗涤液自动投放功能和全触摸彩色显示屏，并加入强劲新型水流。产品可根据衣服多少判定用水量、洗涤剂量和洗涤时间，省时、省电和静音。全触摸彩屏更方便掌握使用方式和设置洗衣程序。副显示屏可在较远距离掌握洗涤状态。抽屉盒扣以手用按键取代，门圈采用无螺钉焊接，简洁精致。产品可用手机操控。

Being as a better user-experienced washing machine, this product can calculate the time according to the quantity of clothes. Comparing with ordinary motor, BLDC motor is more powerful which can adjust the output power and dispense the detergent according to the amount. The full- color touch screen can also richer interface design and integrated design, making it easier for consumers understand and master the use, and can help the users to quickly set up the washing program. The drawer box is simplified by using buckle to be the replacement of the push button. Door ring design also adopts screw-free welding.

JBL Control X Wireless

设计 / 哈曼设计团队
生产 / 哈曼国际
Design / Harman Design Center
Manufacture / Harman International Industries

该产品是电池供电的无线立体声扬声器，可同时使用 4 个扬声器创造更广阔的声场。可通过蓝牙串流音乐，或使用输入接口播放音乐。扬声器之间无需互联电缆或电线连接，摆脱发射器或线缆连接限制。高效率波导技术提供卓越的声场成像和细节。扬声器耐用、富有现代气息，适应家庭、宿舍、营业场所或公园、海滩等室内外场合应用，单次充电可使用 4 小时。

This portable Bluetooth speaker pair outputs immersive stereo sound without any wires or cables between each speaker. If you require a wider soundstage, simply add an additional pair of Control X Wireless speakers (sold separately) for simultaneous playback on up to 4 speakers. The JBL Control X Wireless is a battery-powered wireless stereo speaker pair. Each speaker is rechargeable and can be used for up to 4 hours without a charge. The JBL Control X Wireless speakers offer a rugged, contemporary design for indoors or on-the-go. These durable speakers were built to bring out the best in your music no matter the space.

JBL Grip 100 / JBL Grip 200

设计 / 哈曼设计团队
生产 / 哈曼国际
Design / Harman Design Center
Manufacture / Harman International Industries

通过大量调研，并在运动员的帮助下进行产品的设计工作，使 JBL Grip 符合人体工学的设计，除确保稳固贴合双耳外，还提供舒适的佩戴感，无论骑行在崎岖的道路上，还是进行高难度动作时都能够确保不会滑动掉落。独特的整合式线夹系统让用户可以通过不同的方式佩戴耳机。JBL Grip 200 还配有一个话筒和按钮，用于处理通话和控制音乐。

Through extensive consumer insights, the JBL Grip was designed in collaboration with action sport athletes to insure innovative design and functionality to meet the consumer needs. The result is a durable, sport headphone with proven ergonomics that never hurt and never fall out, while allowing the athlete to maintain awareness of surroundings. The ergonomic design of the JBL Grip provides a highly secure yet comfortable fit that stays in place during the most intense rides and tricks. The unique, integrated cord pinch system allows the earphones to be worn in a number of different configurations. The JBL Grip 200 also includes a microphone and button for phone calls and music control.

JBL Trip

设计 / 哈曼设计团队
生产 / 哈曼国际
Design / Harman Design Center
Manufacture / Harman International Industries

JBL Trip 是第一款便携式车载蓝牙免提设备。可拆卸夹具使产品可挂扣到汽车的遮阳板，也方便携带至其他场所。产品搭载了哈曼的专利降噪技术，在噪声环境下也能清晰通话。产品可通过蓝牙无线发送导航和 ADAS（高级驾驶辅助系统）应用，进行语音提示。采用环保包装和无毒材料，维修方便，可循环利用。采用 ABS + TPE 双注塑技术，给人柔软磨砂触感，同时可保护扬声器。

JBL Trip is the first portable in vehicle Bluetooth hands free kit in the market. With the well designed detachable clamp. It can be clipped to your car’ s sun visor, or can even be taken to your hotel room, kitchen or office without interrupting your music or phone call. HARMAN’ s exclusive Voice Cancellation technology allows for crystal clear phone calls in the vehicle even with road and wind noise in traffic. JBL Trip uses ABS + TPE double injection to give rugged and soft touch feeling while protect the speaker at the same time. Using JBL’ s icon design language: integrates with vehicle interiors; Modern, functional, expensive-looking.

Harman Kardon Onyx Studio 2

设计 / 哈曼设计团队
生产 / 哈曼国际
Design / Harman Design Center
Manufacture / Harman International Industries

该产品是智能设备的终极声音伴侣，通过 4 个有源扬声器和双无源辐射器让优美声音时刻萦绕在身旁。精致的外观掩藏了内在丰富的无线技术，方便用户即时访问周围任何启用蓝牙的设备和高品质声音。时尚、迷人、别具一格的外形，将 Harman Kardon 备受赞誉的设计风格融入到生活之中。柔软触觉和金属质感的结合既时髦又不失温馨。

Harman Kardon's Onyx Studio 2 provides the ultimate sound companion to your smart devices, delivering room-enriching sound through its 4 powered speakers and dual passive radiators. Its sophisticated appearance camouflages its wealth of wireless technologies inside allowing for instant access to any of your Bluetooth-enabled devices and quality sound all around. With Bluetooth connectivity, it delivers quality sound stemmed from you smart devices. The integrated rechargeable battery can have up to 5 hours play time, giving you convenience of playing music anywhere at your home.

和而泰电炖锅
HET Electric Cooker

设计 / 宁波浪尖工业产品造型设计有限公司
生产 / 深圳和而泰智能控制股份有限公司
Design / NingBo Artop Design Co., Ltd
Manufacture / Shenzhen Het intelligent control Co., Ltd

这是一款实现手机网络互联的智能电炖锅，创新地采用陶瓷材料，通过手机软件控制，能够精确定制使用者的口味，可实现蒸炖一体的烹饪方式。通过后台大数据分析，为每位用户健康私人定制，全新的体验与操作方式，增加用户的使用频率。整体外观以传统的蒸笼为元素，盖子把手设计与锅盖相融合，风格统一，用户可轻松体验生态健康“轻奢华”生活。

This is an intellectual electric cooker which can be connected to mobile phone. Everyone's taste can be custom-made accurately by app. It can realize steamed and stew unify. By analyzing big data, it could customized for every user's taste. The overall appearance's element is Chinese traditional steamer. The handle design is well integrated with the cover, to achieve the style unified.

车载净化器
Car Air Purifier

设计 / 广东顺德东方麦田工业设计有限公司
生产 / 广东顺德博兰尼电器实业有限公司
Design / East-innovation Shunde GD Co.,Ltd
Manufacture / Bolani

该产品采用创新性塔式螺旋结构，易拆装，360 度全面净化无死角。小巧灵动，采用整体成型工艺，成本低。金属机身，无二次喷涂，无污染。机身一体成型拉丝金属外观，与车内环境高度融合。

Innovative tower-type helical structure is easy to assemble and disassemble, 360° no blind spot. The overall shape is small and exquisite. The metal body, without secondary spray and decrease the pollution. The adoption of helical structure and unibody of machine body conveys a stylish appearance, and can integrated with the inner environment of the cars.

壁挂式空气能热水器
Wall-mounted Air Energy Water Heater

设计 / 广东顺德东方麦田工业设计有限公司
生产 / 广东万家乐燃气具有限公司
Design / East-innovation Shunde GD Co.,Ltd
Manufacture / Guangdong Macro Gas Appliance Co.,Ltd

采用空气能与电热结合的热水器，专为大户型房屋结构的消费用户设计，满足用水需求。在产生热水的同时，能产生冷气供给厨房。使用节能省电钣金和塑料结合，通过外观优化产品内部技术结构，使产品更协调，与家居环境匹配。

This is a water heater which combines air energy and electric heating. It is specially designed to satisfy requirements of water use for large houses. It can generate cool air for kitchen, while producing hot water. Save energy and electricity. Combination of metal plates and plastics makes the product brilliantly match with household environment by means of optimizing the inner technological structure of the product.

油烟机 CXW-200-IF6
Range Hood CXW-200-IF6

设计 / 宁波欧琳厨具有限公司
生产 / 宁波欧琳厨具有限公司
Design / Ningbo Oulin Kitchen Utensils Co.,Ltd
Manufacture / Ningbo Oulin Kitchen Utensils Co.,Ltd

该产品采用最新研发的油烟动态分离装置，自动油烟分离，大大减少了油烟对大气的污染。低功率节能电机，吸力大，噪音小，能耗低。可智能延时，一键 3 分钟自动延时，扫除余烟享美味。外型时尚新颖，采用钢化黑玻璃与不锈钢相结合，时尚美观具有强烈的视觉冲击效果，给厨房带来更多的艺术气息。

Adopting the latest dynamic oil fume separation technology, the range hood reduces the pollution of the air dramatically. This product adopts energy-saving technology with the low power motor, the “dual-core impeller” and “static volute” with large suction, small noise and low energy consumption. Intelligent one key for 3-minute automatic time delay is to clear away the remaining fume.

小天鹅比佛利全自动洗衣
Little Swan Beverly Top-loading Washing Machine

设计 / 无锡小天鹅股份有限公司工业设计团队
生产 / 无锡小天鹅股份有限公司
Design / Wuxi Little Swan Company Limited ID Team
Manufacture / Wuxi Little Swan Company Limited

产品采用 iAdd 自动投放技术，对每一次洗涤，都能自动测算衣物重量，兼顾洗涤水量，精细到一点一滴，确保衣物洁净无残留。智能感温系统可智能感觉环境温度，智能调整洗涤时间，节省能源。首创一键开门技术，只要轻轻按一下按键门盖自动打开，彻底解放双手。全新的水魔方水流使得衣物更加洁净，可提高衣物洗净效果与均匀度，提高漂净率。

Using iAdd automatic delivery technology，every wash can automatically measure the weight of laundry, taking into account the amount of wash water, fine to bit by bit, to ensure that the clothes clean and free of residue. The intelligent temperature system could adjust the temperature according to the environment. The innovative one-press opening technology can free your hands.

商用跑步机
Commercial Treadmill

设计 / 北京艾德沃工业设计有限公司
生产 / 山东大胡子运动器材有限公司
Design / Beijing IDW Industrlal Design Co.,Ltd
Manufacture / Shandong Dahuzi Fitness Equipment Co.,Ltd

该产品增加18.5寸安卓触摸屏系统，于跑步运动中将人体、机器的特征全面显示，同时具有很强的娱乐功能，在锻炼中增加娱乐性。独特的动态响应的驱动系统实现互动式速度调整、互动式地形调整、模拟不同的跑步环境。心电监护系统则会时时关注身体情况。硬朗的造型打破跑步机行业以多有的流线、动感造型特点，体现出健身器材刚毅、利落的特点。

The treadmill, with its 18.5 inches Android touch screen, could display the comprehensive characteristics of the human body, also is full of entertainment while running. The unique dynamic response driving system realizes the interaction of speed adjustment as well as the terrain adjustment, simulating the different running environment. ECG monitor system is monitoring the body condition.

弘宜森合空气净化器
HOYI Air Purifier

设计 / Andre Santos、张雯
生产 / 弘宜森合（北京）科技有限公司
Design / Andre Santos, Zhang Wen
Manufacture / Hoyi Technology, Inc

该空气净化器在内部实现了 7 层过滤，具备更加优异的净化过滤性能。由底层 360 度吸纳污染空气，顶部 360 度出风，由下而上的底部进风和垂直风道的设计，更快速地让洁净空气扩散室内每个角落。净化器带有 PM2.5、温度、湿度传感器，能够实时监测周围环境数据并通过机器显示界面以数值形式反馈给用户。基于互联网，手机手机软件可远程操控，智能监控、收集与统计环境空气。

Air purifier have 7 different layers of filter inside, which makes it outstanding from the other average purifier with 3-5 layers of filter. The polluted air would be efficiently absorbed in the bottom part from 360 degree. In the top, purified air can also be diffused from 360 degree more rapid to every corner of the room. Monitoring and feedback The air purifier are equipped with PM2.5 sensors, temperature sensors, humidity sensors, which can monitor get all the data from surround environment in real-time.

威力“极光”系列喷淋自洁桶波轮洗衣机
Aurora Series Spray Self-Clean Washing Machine

设计 / 青鸟工业设计有限公司
生产 / 中山东菱威力电器有限公司
Design / Bird Industrial Design
Manufacture / Zhongshan Dolim Electric Power Co.,Ltd

该款洗衣机特有喷淋装置，每次脱水的过程中内桶高速旋转，同时 360 度喷淋，冲洗内桶外壁的残留杂质，长久保持内外桶的健康环境。全新的立体晶钻不锈钢内桶与鲨鱼鳍高筋波轮设计，能形成立体的洗衣水流带动衣物，形成对衣物的全面护理。与普通洗衣机相比，具有抗菌防霉的作用。

With the special spray device of the washing machine, the product could wash the inside and out of the barrel completely with the 360 degree spray to maintain clean and healthy. The solid crystal in stainless steel barrels of the shark fin high wave wheel design could form a whole new 3D flow to drive the clothing and to form a comprehensive care of the clothes.

F6.6—15AQ1 电热水器
F6.6-15AQ1 Water Heater

设计 / 美的集团热水器事业部工业设计部
生产 / 芜湖美的厨卫电器制造有限公司
Design / Industrial Design Department of Water Heater Department of Midea Group
Manufacture / Wuhu Midea Kitchen and Bath Appliances Mfg. Co.,Ltd

该产品为全球首套厨房用智能活水电热水器。首创智能遥控器，远程遥控、信息自反馈等。专利电子排水系统，排出内胆中沉积的细菌、重金属、三氯甲烷等有害物质，有效避免了对水质造成的二次污染。通过智能遥控器进行温度调节、开关机以及一键排水等操作，实现人与机器的无界限交互。采用先进的高光蒸汽注塑工艺，环保可回收材料，减少污染。

F6.6-15AQ1 water heater is the world' s first kitchen smart running water heater with various features of smart touch control, remote control and auto information feedback. With the patented electronic drainage system, it enables the expulsion of hazardous substances such as bacteria, heavy metal and trichloromethane accumulated in pipelines so as to effectively prevent secondary pollution to water. The smart remote controller can be used to adjust water temperature, power on and off and one-key water drainage, which enhances human machine interaction. It applies advanced high-gloss steam injection moulding processes and uses environmentally friendly recyclable material, which reduces environmental pollution.

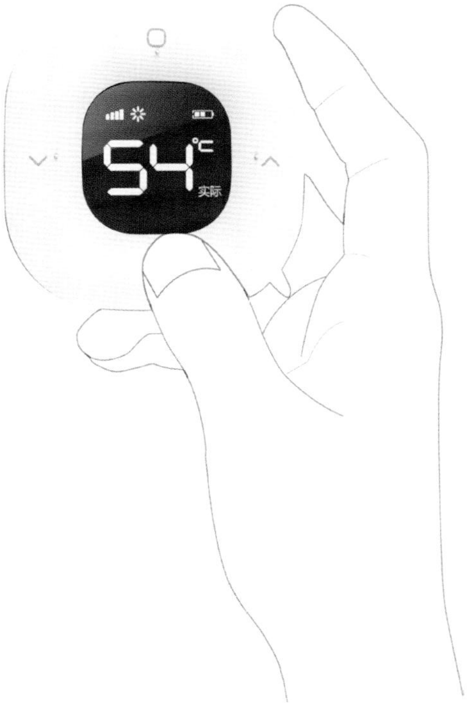

双面对横式取暖器
Balance Type Heater

设计 / 吉明静、马小康
生产 / 广东美的环境电器制造有限公司
Design / Ji Mingjing, Ma Xiaokang
Manufacture / Guangdong Midea Environmental Appliances MFG Co.,Ltd

独创双面对横式外观，体现了产品双面发热的功能特性，可使热量导流更加快速、均匀，在工作过程中可兼顾更多的人。使用场景中不论在那个角度都可展现完美产品视角。采用轻触的操作方式，更可通过无线网络配合美的智能家居手机软件，实现与手机无缝对接。双对称出风控的设计不但体现了功能的强大也显示出产品不俗的美感。

Original double face horizontal and symmetrical appearance reflects the character of it double-faced heat function, which can satisfy more people' s needs in working..Any point of view can show perfect product vision. Adopted touch operation mode and matched the Midea smart APP through WIFI, it can achieve seamless connection with the phone and then control your life. Double heating can make heat flowing more quickly and evenly, which warmth can be shared by family members together.

miniJ 滚筒洗衣机
miniJ Washing Machine

设计 / 杭州奥格工业设计有限公司
生产 / 宁波吉德电器有限公司
Design / AUG Design Co.,Ltd. (Hangzhou)
Manufacture / Ningbo Jide Electrical Appliance Co.,Ltd

紧凑而又具备全功能的小型滚筒洗衣机具有创造性的设计，是目前市场最小的滚筒洗衣机。为了适应现在的城市居住空间特点，重新设计全部产品结构。专为年轻人特别是年轻父母设计，适合家庭作为辅助洗衣使用，针对婴幼儿也有专用的洗涤模式。在功能全面，交互充分考虑到了年轻人群的使用习惯和特点。产品上市后，目前在新渠道和众筹渠道受到用户的热烈回应。

In order to adapt to the current characteristics of urban living space, this is a completely redesigned washing machine for Chinese market. Creative design with a compact and full-featured small drum shape is for young people and young parents design, suitable for home use as an auxiliary laundry, specially consider for infants and young children have special washing mode. Since the clear positioning of the target people, the product wins quite a positive response from the market.

北鼎电水壶 K206
Buydeem K206

设计 / 张默晗、钟文金
生产 / 深圳市北鼎科技有限公司
Design / George Mohan Zhang, Zhong Wenjin
Manufacture / Buydeem Technology (Shenzhen) Co.,Ltd

北鼎电水壶采用第二代聚能双劲芯，独创 FAST 智敏精控技术精准调整火力。提壶采用暂停自动记忆技术、冷水识别沸腾技术、缺水自动断电技术，三大功能一键操作，使用便捷。可记忆专属沸点，解决高原烹煮问题。盖中盖设计，烹煮更灵活。细密不锈钢茶篮设计，有效过滤茶渣。产品使用德国肖特玻璃，纯净通透，抗酸耐腐蚀，环保耐用。

The second generation electronic water pot adopts the original FAST intelligent control technology makes the control more precise. The operation becomes much easier as we have technology of automatically memory and suspend when lift kettle from power base, and automatically resume when put down the kettle on power base. This glass is pure and transparent, can stand shock heating and chilling and can also stand acidity and corrosion.

不用弯腰看火燃气灶
Gas stove, no need to lean over for observing the fire

设计 / 赵磊
生产 / 广东顺德东方麦田工业设计有限公司
Design / Zhao Lei
Manufacture / East-innovation Shunde GD Co.,Ltd

该产品可实现不用弯腰低头即可调节火力，可在同一炉架上下翻转，兼容平底锅与尖底锅的功能。且符合大众消费水平，便于清洁，防止锈蚀。采用黑色黑晶玻璃，整体简洁大气，符合大众审美。

This product's special function is to adjust the fire without bending down, and could be applied on the same oven to the pan and V-bottom wok. It adopts the black crystal glass to fulfill shape of concise and grace, is in accordance of the public aesthetics.

全自动吸油烟机
Automatic Range Hood

设计 / 广东顺德东方麦田工业设计有限公司
生产 / 广东万家乐燃气具有限公司
Design / East-innovation Shunde GD Co.,Ltd
Manufacture / Guangdong Macro Gas Appliance Co.,Ltd

产品可自动识别油烟大小，调节吸风量，减少用户操作，且节能环保，符合大众消费的要求。产品采用不锈钢焊接，便于清洁，可防止锈蚀。使用黑晶玻璃，简洁大气，且符合大众审美。

This product could automatically identify scale of cooking fume and adjust the aspirating capacity. Operation procedures are reduced to fit the demand of the public, energy saving could meet the general consumers' need. The whole body is welding with stainless steel which is easy to be cleaned. The black crystal glass is adopted to convey the compactness and grace.

小米插线板
MI Power Strip

设计 / 贺嘉、宋世琦
生产 / 青米（北京）科技有限公司
Design / He Jia, Song Shiqi
Manufacture / QingMi (Beijing) Technology Co.,Ltd

该产品是具备 3 个国标组合孔与 3 个具有智能快充功能的 USB 接口的插线板，在符合国标要求下，采用锡磷青铜一体化铜带，结构布局紧凑，比同等产品尺寸小 50%。对十几年不变的过载保护开关重新设计。USB 充电接口内置自动识别芯片，自动分配功率，具备 2A 快充功能。82% 的电量转化率，相比大多数充电器更节能。

Under Chinese national standards, its internal structure is compactly laid out, and the tin-phosphor copper strip is designed into an integrated one, making its size 50% smaller than the competing ones of the same configuration, for which we also altered the design and structure of the overload protection switch that remain unchanged for decades. Inside the strip, a built-in smart chip automatically distributes power to 3 USB ports. It supports 2A fast charging for smart phones & tablets with a 20uA protective threshold value for electric leakage. With conversion efficiency at 82%, it is more energy-saving than most of the conventional chargers.

小米体重秤
MI Body Scale

设计 / 姜婧
生产 / 安徽华米信息科技有限公司
Design / Jiang Jing
Manufacture / Huami Inc.

独有光线感应器，可自动调整灯光至眼睛最舒服的亮度。为提升整体的精度能力，重写了传统电子体重秤的计量算法，同时使用三种计算方式，在短时间内抓取更多细节数据，使测量结果更准确，误差值低于同类产品一倍以上。用户可随时通过小米运动手机软件查看数据、身体变化的曲线记录，还可以根据 BMI（身体质量指数），进行健身计划与饮食调整。产品还可对称重记录存储，最多可达 800 条。还可自动识别家中成员，实现全家共享。

By uniquely using a light sensor, MI smart scale is able to adjust the display's brightness to an appropriate level automatically under different lighting situation, make sure reads on the display can be seen very clearly while contribute to energy conservation. The user can view the data and the curve records of body changes anytime and anywhere through the APP in order to see their process of transformation clearly and perform fitness program and diet adjustment based on BMI.

小米盒子增强版
MI Box Pro

设计 / 程兆鹏
生产 / 歌尔声学股份有限公司
Design / Cheng Zhaopeng
Manufacture / GoerTek Electronics

小米盒子增强版是一款支持 4K 超高清播放的互联网电视盒，其拥有丰富的内容资源及应用，用户可通过产品在电视上免费收看数量众多的正版授权高清电影、电视剧、综艺节目、动漫等内容。小米盒子增强版采用互联网直接销售模式，省去了中间商、店面租赁等费用。硬朗且富有张力的曲线，勾勒出产品简洁大方的外形。

The MI Box Pro is an internet set-top box supports 4K playback, it contains countless videos and applications, which allows users to find and watch their favorite movies, TV dramas, variety shows and animations. The MI Box Pro measures 101 mm around the widest points and 19.5 mm around the thickest points, the overall size is 5% smaller than the last generation, which reflects an extreme compact design. The simplicity design and the contrast between polished and mat black surface give it a pristine look.

小米手环
MI Band

设计 / 王涛
生产 / 安徽华米信息科技有限公司
Design / Wang Tao
Manufacture / HUAMI INC.

产品采用军用传感器，可记录每天的运动数据，并进行睡眠监测，自动睡眠状态识别，无需手动切换，通过数据监测，可以了解每晚的深度睡眠时间和浅度睡眠时间。同时具有手环绑定身份，免密码解锁手机、手机来电提醒等功能。可与手机通过低功耗蓝牙（BLE）实时连接，将运动与睡眠数据同步至 APP 端。APP 端可以记录全年运动数据，并提供健康建议。用户还可分享数据到微信、QQ 或微博。

The wristband adopts a military sensor to track the motion data on a daily basis and monitor sleep, record sleep status without manual change. It is a pedometer, a sleep monitor, a missing call reminder as well as a smart alarm that can be used to unlock a smart phone. By simultaneously connected with the phone via BLE, motion and sleeping data are synchronized to App, which can offer personalized health suggestions based on your annual motion data it recorded.

母婴体重秤
Weight Scale for Mother and Baby

设计 / 中山市涅磐产品设计有限公司
生产 / 广东乐心医疗电子股份有限公司
Design / Zhongshan Nirvana Design Co.,Ltd
Manufacture / Guangdong Transtek Medical Electronics Co.,Ltd

首创抱婴测重模式，专为妈妈及宝宝设计，抱着宝宝称体重，察觉宝宝最细微的体重变化。防滑防侧翻，安全轻松。超薄秤体设计，背光源显示效果。采用智能“SENSE ON”技术，实现自动开机和关机功能的创新，让用户无需开机动作，上秤即显重量，方便、快捷，而且能在环境温度任意改变的情况下仍然保证称重准确。

Specially designed for moms and babies, this scale is anti-skid and anti-rollover, enable to weigh the baby while holding in mom’s arms. The ultra-thin scale has a back light to display. “Sense on” technology could realize the auto-turn up and auto-turn down. By standing on the scale, weight is displayed and easy to read.

拉卡拉支付卡表
Payment Watch

设计 / 义乌市浪尖工业设计有限公司
生产 / 拉卡拉集团
Design / Yiwu Artop Design Co.,Ltd
Manufacture / Lakala Payment Co.,Ltd

穿戴式刷卡器从便携移动支付，改善传统生活方式的理念出发，具有一卡通、支付功能，还有睡眠、计步、久坐提醒等智能手表的功能，亦可作为普通手表使用。整机采用可回收循环利用的环保材料。拥有圆润的表盘，金属装饰件与之搭配，更具现代感和时尚感。内部的纹路优雅连贯，更有助于排除腕部汗液，使其很好地适应运动佩戴。

In consideration of the portable mobile payment and the improvement of traditional lifestyle, this innovative wearable swipe was born. It is not only a watch, but also a smart watch consisted of several functions such as slumber, step calculation, sedentary remaining and so on. It also has the functions of one card solution and payment. The perfect cooperation between a round dial and metal decoration can make it more modern and stylish.

创维 _G9200 电视
Skyworth_G9200 TV

设计 / 深圳创维—RGB 电子有限公司工业设计研究院创新设计中心
生产 / 深圳创维—RGB 电子有限公司
Design / Skyworth -RGB Electronics Co., Industrial Design Innovation Design Center and Research Institute
Manufacture / Skyworth-RGB Electronics Co.,LTD

超轻薄 4K 极清 LED 电视，薄至 7.5 毫米轻至 15 千克，采用全球位数最高的 soc 64 位电视芯片，独立可拆卸 soundbar 音箱，在达到完美音效的同时也为用户提供了多种使用形式。并解决了以往超薄电视音效不佳的问题，给用户带了完美的视听享受，让产品能够适用于各种场景，还可通过蓝牙一键唤醒 soudbar 音响，轻松播放手机或平板电脑上的音乐。至今国内外共计销售 12568 台。

This 4K LED TV is ultra slim and light (7.5mm/15kg). SOC 64 bit TV chip is used. The independent and removable soundbar provides users with perfect sound effect and multiple using methods. The independent soundbar overcomes the previous poor sound effect. Its removability offers many ways to use in different scenarios. It can be turned on by Bluetooth to play music from phone or pad. Since its launch in Feb 2015, 12,568 sets have been sold.

NR 系列空气净化器
NR Series Air Purifier

设计 / 李三新、袁志强
生产 / 广东美的制冷设备有限公司
Design / Li Sanxin, Yuan Zhiqiang
Manufacture / GD Midea Air-Conditionging Equipment Co.,Ltd

全新的设计理念，使用简单，极简的外观及结构设计，巴黎卢浮宫风格的出风格栅设计，几何形的造型元素。零件减到最少以减少模具及生产工人的数量，无其他浮华的工艺处理，紧凑的产品设计使空间得到高效利用，单位面积可以运输更多的产品。超低的成本的同时实现了产品的高品位。

The air purifier adopts a simplicity concept of design, from the appearance to the structure. The parts are reduced as few as possible so as to reduce the amounts of the moulds and production workers; there is no other flashy technology processing; impact product design enables the spaces to be effectively utilized, and unit area can transport more products, Which focuses on usability, touch, texture and proper prices without depending on excessive decoration.

AKG Y23U

设计 / 哈曼设计团队
生产 / 哈曼国际
Design / Harman Design Center
Manufacture / Harman International Industries

最小巧的入耳式耳机，却拥有 AKG 获奖无数的录音棚音质。彷如羽毛般轻盈，加上超舒适的佩戴感，以致于让用户忘记了它的存在。采用高性能的 5.8 毫米驱动器以推动 AKG 品质的声音，并搭配一键式通用线控 / 话筒，充分诠释以小见大。极致小巧的身形和轻盈的材料，打造出彷如无物的佩戴感。夺目、超轻盈设计，四色可选。

The smallest in-ear headphone featuring AKG' s award-winning, studio quality sound. You' ll take them everywhere you go – largely because you won' t even remember you' re wearing them. With high-performance, 5.8mm drivers, their ability to deliver AKG-quality sound is the biggest feature about the smallest headphones we make with additional 1 button universal microphone/ remote. RoHS and EuP compliant. Extremely small and using light weight materials, customers will forget that they are wearing them. Big sound in a small package with 5.8mm drivers. Attractive, ultra-lightweight design, available in four colors. Super-soft ear tips are supplied in four comfortable sizes for a superior fit.

逸曦发烧友入耳式耳机
ECCI Hi-Fi In-ear Headset

设计 / 深圳洛可可工业设计有限公司
生产 / 逸曦电子科技有限公司
Design / LKK Design Shenzhen Co.,Ltd
Manufacture / ECCI Electronic Technology Co.,Ltd

该产品的设计方案采用简约仿生化的设计思路，提取天鹅浮游水面的形体语言，将其艺术化和美感化，满足入门级音乐发烧友对产品独特个性化的消费需求。在佩戴方式上，使用新型化的绕耳式，加强耳机的稳固性，简化佩戴流程方便使用，让消费者长时间佩戴使用也不会产生不适感。满足亚洲人耳型佩戴使用。

The design idea of ECCI Hi-Fi In-ear Headset is bionic. It exacts water swan floating body language, and makes it artistic and beautiful, which can meet the personal consumer demand of entry-level music enthusiasts. As the wearing ways, it used newly over-ear style to simplify the wear processes, which makes the users easy-used and soft though they wear it for a long time. In consideration of the Asia' s need, the headset will be stable whether you are sitting or running, the headset will match your ear perfectly.

JBL Everest Headphones

设计 / 哈曼设计团队
生产 / 哈曼国际
Design / Harman Design Center
Manufacture / Harman International Industries

这款无线耳机融入了Exclusive NXTGen降噪和Enviro Aware等多种技术，性能至臻至强。Exclusive Next Gen降噪技术能减少外界影响，而JBL的新功能enviroAWARE则让用户能够掌握身边的情况。传奇的JBL Pro Audio，加上能按照耳杯佩戴位置自动进行调整的TruNote自动校准功能，可使用户抛开世事烦嚣，沉浸在个人的音乐世界之中。

Everest NXT wireless headphones allow you to be immersed and energized by your music like never before. With features ranging from Exclusive NXTGen Noise Cancelling Technology to enviroAWARE Technology, it's the ultimate feature package for wireless. With Legendary JBL Pro Audio and TruNote Auto Calibration that automatically calibrates sound based on how earcups fit around your ears.

扫一扫查看产品 Pin3D 技术三维效果图
Scanning for the 3D image by Pin3D

联想双耳无线胶囊耳机
Lenovo Earphone 900

设计 / 联想设计与用户体验中心
生产 / 联想
Design / Lenovo
Manufacture / Lenovo

联想双耳无线胶囊耳机是一款隐藏式的微型耳机，蓝牙双耳无线技术，旨在打造更舒适，音质更好的立体声蓝牙耳机。让使用者从传统的耳机线中彻底解脱出来，无连接线束缚的使用体验，享受更好的无线体验。可在多场合应用，且具备便捷充电功能，携带方便。

Lenovo wireless earphone 900 is an out of sight Bluetooth earphone, designed to be comfortable and high sound quality for two ear wireless Bluetooth earphone. Be adaptive into wire free user experience is easy to charging and carrying. It is a new development direction of Bluetooth earphone. Before this one, there are only one-ear Bluetooth earphone and two-ear sport Bluetooth earphone in current market. This product belongs to a wearable device. It is mainly made by harmless material for human and environment.

天府通公交手环
Tian Fu Tong Bus Bracelet

设计 / 彭戈、孙智宇
生产 / 成都莫比智能科技有限公司
Design / Peng Ge, Sunny
Manufacture / Chengdu Mobi Intelligence Co.,Ltd

产品流线的造型灵感来自于莫比乌斯环，几条棱线交替环绕，给人一种无线延伸地感觉。产品能有效的监测佩戴者的健康状况，具有 3D 体感技术，能玩体感游戏，同时具有无线射频技术，具有一卡通支付功能。兼具睡眠监测、一卡通支付、智能闹钟、运动跟踪、体感游戏、丢失告警、门禁钥匙、支付密盾八大功能。

The inspiration of the streamline modelling for this product is from Mobius, With technology of three-dimension somatosensory, RFID (Radio Frequency Identification) and all-purpose pass, this product can effectively detect one' s health status. It brings the users the unique experience of interaction, motion sensing games, sleep monitor, online one-card payment, smart alarm clock, motion tracking, motion sensing game, loss of single, and payment of secret shield.

血压计 XY-211
Mobile Health Blood Pressure Terminal

设计 / 杭州奥格工业设计有限公司
生产 / 浙江铭众医疗器械有限公司
Design / AUG Design Co.,Ltd (Hangzhou)
Manufacture / Zhejiang Medzone Medical Devices Co., Ltd(Hangzhou)

这是一款为东方家庭特意优化的血压计，通过和手机 APP 的链接，更方便地让不同家庭成员测量并记录各自的血压数据。老年用户可以和子女远程共享自己的健康数据，在现代社会中维护传统的东方孝道和亲情。同时，数据的积累和跟踪，可以让用户即刻在后台得到医生的关注和意见推送。产品的设计语言来源于玉石，安静、自然、圆通。

This is a sphygmomanometer specially designed for oriental families, connecting with mobile phone and App, it can conveniently used by family members to record blood pressure respectively. Elderly people could share data with their children, children also could maintain the relationship through such detail to fulfill their filial duty. By the tracking and accumulation of the data, users can get advice from the doctors as well.

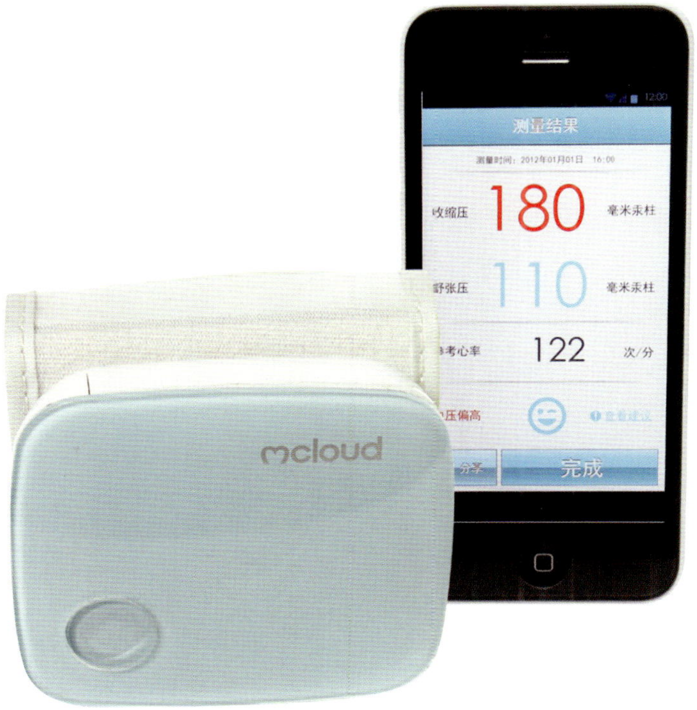

联想 Yoga 遥控鼠标
Lenovo Yoga Remote Mouse

设计 / 设计与用户体验
生产 / 联想
Design / Lenovo
Manufacture / Lenovo

独特的可翻转设计，使鼠标在不同使用场景中具备不同的使用模式。外壳由半透明材料制成，背部搭载可触控的电子墨水屏，给用户带来全新的交互体验。双模无线连接技术，让用户不再为线材和接口而烦恼。超薄的设计理念（厚度仅为 13.5 毫米），器件都经过精心设计与摆放，方便用户出行携带。采用触控板替代传统滚轮，且遥控模式具备多媒体控制以及演示控制功能，用户与 PC 的交互更加方便有趣。

With the unique rotation mechanism design, mouse in different user scenario have different use mode. Mouse made of translucent materials. Touch control screen with colorful multi-layers smart ink on the mouse' s reverse side. It will give user a new interactive experience. Dual-mode wireless technology let users no longer worry about wire and lack of port. Ultra slim design (the mouse thickness is 13.5 mm) ,the component is highly design-driven , it is portable for user to bring it everywhere.

单手直饮运动水瓶
Sports Flask

设计 / 朱熙超、张斌
生产 / 上海思乐得不锈钢制品有限公司
Design / Zhu Xichao, Zhang Bin
Manufacture / Shanghai Solid Stainless Steel Products Co.,Ltd

单手直饮运动水瓶专为户外骑行和跑步而设计，人性化的外观与结构设计，创新性的单手打开方式，使用者在骑车和跑步的时候可以轻松地用一只手打开并饮用，让使用者更好的体验运动的快感。采用 SUS304 不锈钢为主要瓶身材料，同时内部精密电解，可有效抑菌。整个产品线条简洁而富有张力，似三刀两斧劈砍而成，比例协调，契合运动产品的特质。

Sports drink flask with one hand straight outdoor riding and running specially designed for humane appearance and structural design, innovative way to open with one hand, the user can better experience the thrill of sports. The entire product line is concise and full of tension, like Mito two ax cut made in proportion and density has caused.

儿童益智餐具
baby training tableware

设计 / 周龙
生产 / 浙江瑞翔婴童用品有限公司
Design / Aaron
Manufacture / Zhejiang Reshine Babycare Co.,Ltd

该产品碗耳上"C" "X"图案与勺叉相呼应，培养宝宝区分左右和配对能力，训练大脑发育。符合人机的软胶把手，设计触感舒适，碗耳软胶设计便于修整黏附在勺内的辅食，喂养过程中，家长无须自己用嘴巴整形食物，干净卫生。碗盖暗藏勺叉收纳空间，方便携带干净卫生。搭配双面吸盘，给宝宝独立进食的自由。外形圆润浑厚顺滑，浑厚胖感，Q感十足。

The "C" and "X" pattern on bowl ear match with spoon and fork so can practice baby how to make difference with left and right and improve matching capability to have a positive effect on baby brain development . The lid bowl has the space to store the spoon and fork, easy to carry and clean.

魔盒健身车
M—BOX

设计 / 浙江金棒运动用品有限公司
生产 / 浙江金棒运动用品有限公司
Design / Zhejiang Jinbang Sports Equipment Co.,Ltd
Manufacture / Joybold Sports

这是一辆健身车，车体完全折叠后形成一个盒子状，可轻松收纳在房间各个角落，也可作为一件家居艺术品放置在家中，达到健身与居家装饰的完美融合。采用环保皮革坐垫，运行时噪声低至 25 分贝，使用过程利用磁场作用产生阻力，绿色环保，无污染。全车内置式折叠系统，可折叠成一个盒状，重量轻至 16.9 千克。

This is a sports car, but also a Home Furnishing life art. The body is folded into a box shape, can be easily store at every corner of the room. The whole car built-in folding system can be folded into a box, light weight to 16.9kg, in the same industry leading. The graceful arc, smooth surface, no edges and corners, strong sense of design.

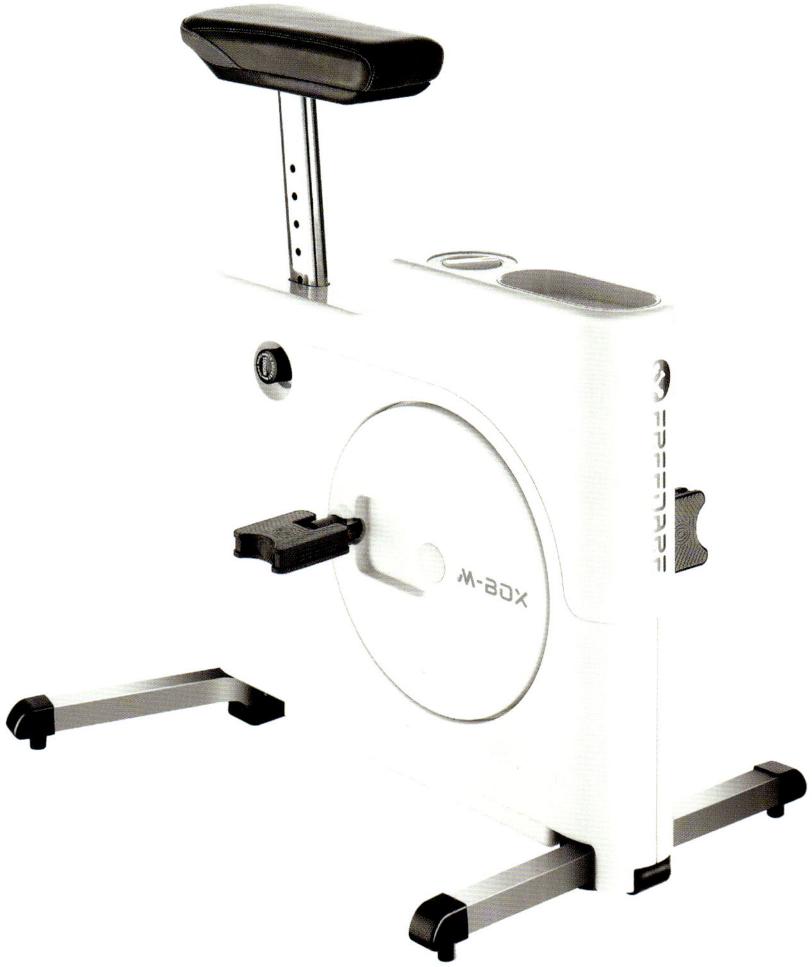

D300 锂电智能多功能工具
Thinkool D300

设计 / 溯洄（上海）设计咨询有限公司
生产 / 浙江恒友机电有限公司
Design / Sohui (Shanghai) Design and consult Co.,Ltd
Manufacture / Zhejiang Hengyou Machine&electron Co.,Ltd

这是全球首款触控式锂电智能多功能工具。拥有全新的智能控制系统，一块带有触摸功能的液晶显示屏，来实现所有的操作控制功能：智能电源管理、智能扭矩设定（螺丝批模式时）、剩余电量显示和电子式正反转转换等。主机仅拥有一套顶级直流马达、开关、智能电子控制芯片以及外壳，可通过不同功能头快速适配，实现冲击电钻、起子、锤击和多功能切割打磨等各种家用型工具应用。

Thinkool D300 is the world's first touch control Li-ion smart multi-function tool. It has all new intelligent control system, and a touch-controlled screen could realize all the control function: Intelligent power control, Intelligent torque setting(screw driver mode), battery bar and electric forward&reverse control. The masterboard has a top-class DC motor, switch, intelligent electric control chip and beautiful outshape, and it could realize the drill/driver, impact drill, cutting, sanding and scraping DIY applications by different function heads combinations.

RE 系列卷尺
RE Series Tapes

设计 / 朔洄（上海）设计咨询有限公司
生产 / 宁波欧博五金实业有限公司
Design / Sohui (Shanghai) Design and Consult Co.,Ltd
Manufacture / Ningbo Oubo Hardware Industrial Ltd

产品外观是颠覆传统的自主创新设计，线条的设计与人体工程原理结合，整体软胶包裹设计和合适的体积使握感更舒适。具有很多人性化的创新功能：领先的释放刹车按钮，可轻松自动锁定卷尺；上下双层挂钩尺带，方便多种情境下使用；尺带回缩减震装置，减弱尺带回缩时的反作用力使之不误伤人手。RE 系列卷尺年度销售量是 50 万个，市场主要集中在欧洲、日本。

The tape adds a lot of user-friendly innovations: the leading easy release brake button is adopted so that the tape can be easily and automatically lock. In position dual hook on case, it' s convenient to use in a different situations. The shock absorbing device at the blade retraction hole reduces the reaction force, thus it can' t hurt hands.

"器"——新型家庭绿植
Green Life

设计 / 夏旭
生产 / 上海艺凯设计有限公司
Design / Xia Xu
Manufacture / GK Design Shanghai Inc

该产品拥有能让水与空气并存的海绵体，它可以自动吸纳液态，同时始终保持气态与液态之间 3：7 的比例，让液态、气态、固态共存。具备植物健康生长、清洁、轻巧的特点，可以制成各种形状，可在横向垂直面或曲面上进行种植，让设计的自由度大大增加，具备"自由创意"的特点。人工土培 + 陶瓷（材料）+ 斗笠碗（造型元素），用东方元素体现自然的理念。

Here comes the artificial sponge soil. This makes water and air coexist in the corpus cavernosum, it can automatically absorb liquid, and maintain the ratio of 3:7 between air and liquid as well. Artificial soil also can be made into different shapes, thus we can plant in both vertical surface and curved surface, so that plant can be designed in any way. The artificial soil + ceramic (material) + Hat bowl (elements), Oriental elements symbolized the concept of nature.

普朗克过滤水壶
Planck

设计 / 李敏
生产 / 厦门建霖工业有限公司
Design / Mya Li
Manufacture / Runner-corp

普朗克水壶整体造型简约硬朗，把手与壶身采用无缝连接。把手全通透设计，赋予产品非凡的视觉穿透力。细长型注水口设计，在满足使用尺寸需求的前提下，使翻盖手感更轻盈。超薄壶身设计，使水壶能放置于冰箱侧门，方便直接饮用冰水。电显提示滤芯使用寿命，及时提醒用户更换滤芯，确保安全饮水。根据市场、水质的不同，可置换不同的过滤介质。

The overall shape of the Planck pot is simple and tough, the handle is connected to the body seamlessly. Extra slim design is applied in order to fit into the fridge for direct usage, reduce energy wastage & save time. To ensure the safety of the drinking water, the screen display reminds you to change filter in time.

GYENNO 睿餐勺
GYENNO Spoon

设计 / 深圳市佳简几何工业设计有限公司
生产 / 深圳市臻络科技有限公司
Design / Shenzhen XIVO Design Co.,Ltd
Manufacture / Shenzhen GYENNO Technologies Co.,Ltd

产品可有效抵消手部震颤进而稳定勺面，帮助帕金森或手部震颤患者自我进食，增加患者治疗信心。同时实时采集缓震震颤数据，建立可视化帕金森大数据库，用于医药企业或医疗机构的研究。360 度全方位的防抖效果，可有效抵消 85% 的手部抖动。自动识别并区分有意识运动和无意识抖动，通过数学模型将采集的震颤数据还原为 3D 图像，提供可视化的医学研究素材。

The GYENNO Spoon can effectively offset hand tremors and stable surface of the spoon to help those patients with Parkinson's or hands shaking feeding by themselves. Real-time acquisition shock vibration data at the same time, visualization Parkinson's large databases, to the study of medicine enterprises or medical institutions will become an important component of the Precision Medicine.

扫一扫查看产品 Pin3D 技术三维效果图
Scanning for the 3D image by Pin3D

Pixel Pro 智能墙面开关
Pixel Pro Smart Wall Switch

设计 / 北京东成新维设计咨询有限公司
生产 / 北京昊恒天科技有限公司
Design / FromD Innovation
Manufacture / HaoHengTian Technology Inc.

作为一款智能家居产品，可通过远程控制、无线开关联动等功能，实现更便捷的手机远程遥控定时开关、延迟关灯等。将诸多元器件整合在有限的空间内，是开关设计上的一大突破。基于人工智能技术，学习用户的日常使用习惯，可向用户推荐应用情景，推算用户将要进行的操作，并自行调整大按键的功能。基于云计算技术，可实现不同产品间的互联互通。

As a home automation product, Pixel Pro combines innovative Industrial Design and breakthrough technology, solves people's daily requirements and improves user's home life standard. With Artificial Intelligence, Pixel Pro could learn about user's daily habits. After the self-learning period, Pixel Pro may suggest some scenes to users, or adjust the Magic Button's function with prediction. With Cloud Computing, all smart products are connected with Product Cloud. Therefore, interconnections among different products are achieved.

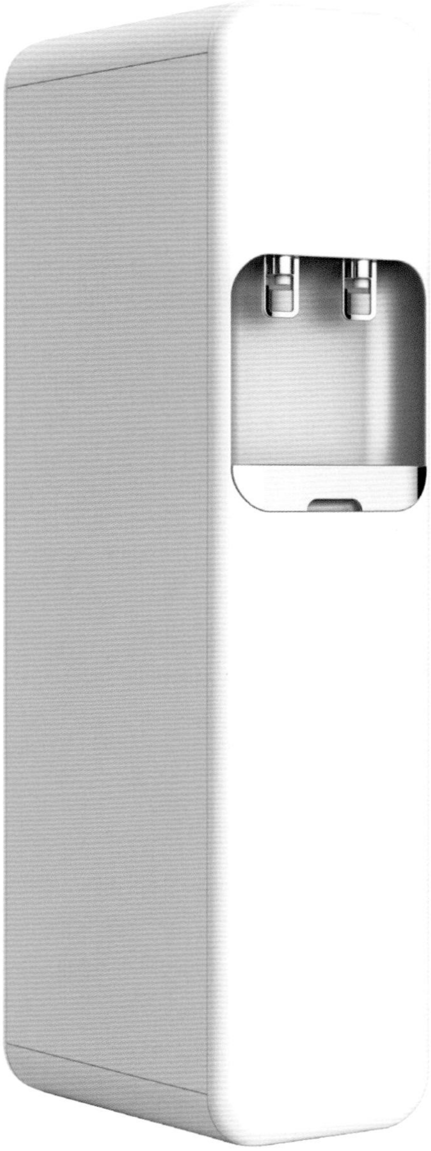

乐活净水机
Lohas

设计 / 徐智彬
生产 / 厦门建霖工业有限公司
Design / Xu Zhibin
Manufacture / Runner-corp

产品结合了 UV 消毒功效，加入了复合滤芯，确保用户在日常饮水中的健康安全性。同时一键触控式操作简化了操作，带来了便利性。造型拆件简单，上下左右面盖可共用模具，减少了公司的研发成本。成型工艺简单，良品率高。圆润整体的造型，简洁大方。整体简单的造型在包装运输上也可以减少材料浪费，降低成本。

Products combined with the UV disinfection, and composite filter, ensures that users in daily drinking water security, while a key touch action simplifies the operation and brought convenience. Multiple components can be shared by mold, cost savings. Simple overall styling package haulers can also reduce material waste and reduce costs.

茶花易洁系列扫把畚斗套装
Easy Clean Oustpan With Broom

设计 / 刘志斌、邱志荣
生产 / 茶花现代家居用品股份有限公司
Design / Liu Zhibin, Qiu Zhirong
Manufacture / Chahua Modern Housewares CO., LTD

畚斗上更长的梳齿能轻松地刮落扫把头上的毛发以及粘尘。一改传统固定的扫把头，引入活动扫把头设计，扫把的角度可调整，轻松适应各种身高的人群以及打扫房间内低矮的位置。整体化的设计美观且易于存放，形态特征明显，品牌识别性强。方便的可拆卸设计，轻松组装与配件替换，延长产品寿命与增强通用度。

The longer comb teeth on bucket can easily scrape hair and sticky dust of broom head. The broom angle can adjust which can easily suit people with various height and sweep low position in the room. Convenient detachable design, easily assemble and parts replaceable which can extend using life and enhance general use. The upside comb teeth on bucket can easily scrape hair and sticky dust of broom head into bucket.

延长水龙头
Lengthen Faucet

设计 / 郑金洪
生产 / 厦门建霖工业有限公司
Design / Zheng Jinhong
Manufacture / Xiamen Runner Industrial Corporation

本产品能够帮助宝宝够到水龙头，鼓励宝宝自己洗手，培养宝宝的自主能力。立体水槽与直流相比水流稍缓且顺畅，使水流更靠近，洗手更轻松。可折叠式的翻盖操作方式，新颖独特，造型、配色上也比较讨孩子喜欢，这更增加了洗手的趣味性。使用方法简单，方便实用。

This product can help baby reach the tap, encourage your baby to wash their hands, and cultivate the baby' s autonomy. Comparing with the direct flow, the stereo water tank enables the washing much easier. The foldable flip operation brings fun of washing hands of children.

婴儿体温计
Baby Thermometer

设计 / 东莞市浪尖产品设计有限公司
生产 / 康之元信息技术有限公司
Design / Dongguan Artop Product Design Co.,Ltd
Manufacture / Sybercare Technology Co.,Ltd

简洁又独特的气球外观造型，打破市场智能体温计单一的外观，适合幼儿佩戴。与手机软件结合使用，可长时间检测体温，满足半岁婴儿到 6 岁儿童的穿戴需求。医用级硅胶连体包裹设计，特别应用软胶增加了舒适度，体现对幼儿的关爱。气球外观造型线条流畅圆润，符合人机需求，2 毫米超薄表带环绕宝贝手臂，防脱落设计，测量更准确。

Simple and unique appearance of the balloon breaks the single appearance of the smart thermometer, suitable for children to wear. Connecting with the App, could detect the temperature of the infants and babies. The medical grade silicone piece package design conveys the care of children. Round shape of the balloon is ergonomics.

卡易刷
Swipeasy

设计 / 深圳市鼎典工业产品设计有限公司
生产 / 深圳市鼎典生活用品有限公司
Design / Shenzhen Designdo Industrial Design Co.,Ltd
Manufacture / Shenzhen Designdo Lifestyle Co.,Ltd

本产品用于安全刷卡，其中收纳模块为可翻转折叠的设计，减少整个安全刷卡包产品的体积，并在展开时，通过内部三块硬板互相支撑形成 180 度，来增加刷卡使用距离。整个安全刷卡包方便携带，操作简便，并可以提高使用的安全性，简单快捷的使用解决了生活中的问题。表面选择多种材质和色彩进行搭配，使产品精致美观。

This product is used for security card, in which storage module could be reversible folding, then reducing the volume of the whole security card. And when expanding, through internal three pieces of boards and support each other for form 180°, to increase the length of credit card use. The whole security card bag is convenient to carry, easy to operate, and can improve the safety of use.

竹纤维搅拌碗套件
Bamboo Fiber Mixing Bowl Kit

设计 / 宁波江北矩成创意产品设计有限公司
生产 / 宁波江东诚优进出口有限公司
Design / Ningbo Galachy Creative Product Design Co.,Ltd
Manufacture / BRIGHTMAN INTERNATIONAL TRADING Co., Ltd.

该系列餐具是用竹纤维混合材料加工而成，运用天然竹精加工成纤维颗粒，用高温压合而成，具有无毒害、天然材料、环境友好、质感丰富等特点。该材料拥有塑料产品的强度和韧度，不易碎不易破，不漏水不溶解等特点，可加快生物降解，进而减低环境压力。经过权威机构测试，耐高温 100℃可用于普通烹饪，并适用于洗碗机，大大提高了使用适应性。

The series cutlery is processed from bamboo fiber composite material, made of natural bamboo fiber finishing into granules, under high-temperature lamination. Replacing petroleum compounds with bamboo fiber accelerates biodegradation rate, which makes the products environmentally friendly. Since the material has the great features such as non-toxic, natural, environmentally friendly, rich texture and other characteristics, this material is widely applied for the household goods industry. After testing by authority, it can endure high temperature as high as 100℃ , and can be used for general cooking, and is suitable for dishwashers, greatly improving the adaptability.

便捷型 COB 工作灯
Portable COB Working Light

设计 / 宁波市法诺工业产品设计有限公司
生产 / 宁波市法诺工业产品设计有限公司
Design / Ningbo FANUO Industrial Product Design Co.,Ltd
Manufacture / Ningbo FANUO Industrial Product Design Co.,Ltd

该产品方便携带，在停电应急、维修、野营、车载等多种环境都可使用。采用市场最新流行的 COB 高功率集成光源技术，节省了电镀、贴片等工序，且高显色，发光均匀，无光斑，环保健康。产品背面有条形磁铁，可吸附在金属表面，结合COB光源技术，给人们带来创新的生活方式。手感舒适，体型小巧，能随时随地便捷迅速切换光源开关，使操作时倍感得心应手。

It is a portable COB light source working light, easy to carry and applied in a variety of occasions, such as power cut emergency, maintenance, camping, vehicle-mounted. Dust, corrosion and seismic design can resist all kinds of harsh environment. With the technology of COB light source, Bring people the innovative way of life.

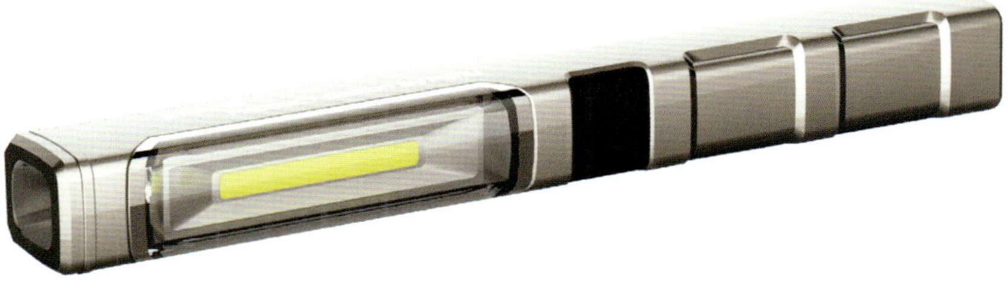

多功能安全排插
Multifunction Charging Station

设计 / 骆柏林
生产 / 深圳市绿联科技有限公司
Design / Luo Bolin
Manufacture / Ugreen Group Limited

这是一款集充电、防护、收纳、放置等功能于一体，专用于客厅中使用的多功能安全排插。带有儿童安全锁扣，把整个排插隐藏和锁住，避免了小孩接触到插孔中金属物而导致触电事故的发生。设有移动数码设备的放置槽及三个 USB 充电口，便于充电时放置及快速地为移动数码设备充电。设有八个新国标强电插孔，满足客厅家电设备的通电需求。

The childproof lock on top of the box locks all the sockets and leads inside the box, which effectively prevents your kids from inserting their fingers into the power socket and cause safety accidents. Long grooves on the top panel are for placing digital devices while charging. 3 universal USB charging ports are for charging more conveniently. 8 standard high-voltage power sockets are for safely charging various household appliances.

“旋霓”茶几
Water ripples tea table

设计 / 梁缘
生产 / 佰墨文化传媒（北京）有限公司
Design / Liang Yuan
Manufacture / BaiMo Culture Media (Beijing) Co.,Ltd

使用废旧报纸为产品主体材料，开发出一套新型环保家具。废旧报纸经过创新的塑形方法进行黏合、烘干、打磨，经过表面特殊处理，完全实现防水、防潮，解决了木质家具在南北方气候干湿差异产生的变形和开裂问题。结构采取榫卯和金属件结合的连接方式，材质硬度和结实度不低于一般的木质家具。原料成本低廉，大件家具成本在 220 元左右，小件成本在 160 元左右。

The designer is inspired by the large amounts of waste paper recycling, then designs a favorable value of people's lives. The main material is the waste paper through innovative shaping method for bonding, drying, grinding made. After special surface treatment, it can be fully realized waterproof, moisture-proof, to solve the problem of deformation and cracking wood furniture in the north and south Climatic difference. Take the connection tenon structure and metal combination, which can ensure durable structure.

一千零一夜
One Thousand and One Nights

设计 / 北京圣宝地工业设计有限公司
生产 / 河间市万里工艺玻璃制品厂
Design / CBD Group Corp.
Manufacture / HeJian WanLi Craft glass product factory

设计师将《一千零一夜》的故事投射到千家万户的家庭生活中。玻璃如山鲁佐德，白色陶瓷则是山鲁亚尔。打破传统的玻璃工艺，依托于生产工艺材质的特性，打造内旋形成自然倒流层，从根本上解决了消费者倾倒和清洁的苦恼。两种材质的搭配使用经过了长期测试与调整，在两种材料的公差范围内达到了最佳契合度。不仅可用来放置食物，还可用来装饰起居每个角落。

In this collection the glass and the ceramic part are like Sharāzād and Shāhriyār, so different but united that their matched is perfection. 1001 nights series products broke the traditional craft of glass, based on the characteristics of the material production technology, building internal rotation natural backflow layer formation, fundamentally solves the consumers to dump and clean. The collocation of two kinds of material is used after a long-term test and adjustment, in the two materials to best fit within the limits of tolerance.

至尊水槽
Proficency Sink

设计 / 殷刘春、卫凯 · 提鲁那嘎鲁
生产 / 珠海普乐美厨卫有限公司
Design / Yin Liuchun, Venkat Tirunagaru
Manufacture / Primy Corporation Limited

至尊水槽是可实现配件放置位置通用的多功能水槽，水槽壁顶部设有三对等长台阶，实现刀架组件、线篮、滤水篮之间的位置相互调换，使其摆放位置符合用户的使用习惯，提高用户的使用体验。刀架集成了皂液器，方便放置和更换，避免了人更换安装皂液器需要下蹲至橱柜里更换的繁复动作。

This is a multi-functional sink on which the accessories location could be exchanged. On the top there are three pairs of steps with same length so that the knife holder, wire basket and colander location can be exchanged. It is more user-friendly because customer can decide the location of accessories. The knife holder integrated with soap dispenser, hence it is more convenient to put and replace. Instead of going under the kitchen cabinet to replace the soap dispenser, the customer can do it just on the sink.

多功能切割机
Blade Runner 2X

设计 / 沃伦 · 布朗
生产 / 宝时得机械（中国）有限公司
Design / Warren Brown
Manufacture / Positec Machinery (China) Co.,Ltd

该产品创造了台式曲线锯的新品类，整机质量轻，台面有把手设计，方便携带。可实现多材料切割，使用者双手可以握住工件进行切割，提高可靠性与精度。拥有工件快速夹紧装置，调节方便。刀片容易更换，可满足不同材料的切割要求。台面附带斜切导尺和靠山，以提高切割精度。

This product creates a new category of desktop curve saw, a light-weighted tool, handle on mesa, convenient to carry. It realizes a cutting of multiple materials, enables the users to hold the workpiece to cut, greatly improving the reliability and accuracy. Fast clamping device is installed and easy to be adjusted. The blades are easy to change and fulfill the need of cutting different materials. Oblique guide rod and anchor are appended on the mesa in order to improve the precision.

扫一扫查看产品 Pin3D 技术三维效果图
Scanning for the 3D image by Pin3D

霾星人鼻用空气净化器
MaiXingRen Nasal Air Purifier

设计 / 北京万生人和科技有限公司
生产 / 北京万生人和科技有限公司
Design / Beijing Winsunny Harmony Science
Manufacture / Beijing Winsunny Harmony Science

该产品革命性解决了日常呼吸防护用品密封差、呼吸阻力大和过滤效率低三大难题。基于人脸 3D 扫描逆向设计密封单元，建立适用不同鼻周外形多规格密封件，100% 密封保证气体经过滤单元吸入体内。仿生鱼鳃水中取氧设计鳃瓣式过滤单元实现 4 倍过滤面积，过滤 99% 以上 PM2.5 颗粒。呼吸阻力小于 25 帕，低于传统口罩一倍使呼吸畅通。产品拥有多项实用新型专利、外观设计，且入选 14 年首都设计提升计划。

The nasal air purifier provides a revolutionary solution to the following three major issues in respect of protective devices for daily respiration: poorer sealing, bigger respiratory resistance and lower filtration efficiency. The purifier, based on 3D scanning on human face to make a reverse design sealing unit and setting up, is in accordance with the structure around nose, various sealing units closely joining on faces under slight pressure, ensures 100% sealing and air passing through the filtering unit. The design of bionic fish gill provides effective filtration, filtering PM2.5 of more than 99% with respiratory resistance < 25Pa, which is one time lower than that of the traditional masks, guaranteeing an unobstructed breathing.

汽车儿童安全座椅 太空城堡
R102A

设计 / 麦克英孚（宁波）婴童用品有限公司
生产 / 麦克英孚（宁波）婴童用品有限公司
Design / MAX-INF(Ningbo) Baby Product Co., Ltd
Manufacture / MAX-INF(Ningbo) Baby Product Co., Ltd

产品考虑到人体工程学，区别同类产品的常规调节方式，头枕采用向上调节为上拉方式，向下调节为下压方式的独特无级调节创新设计，肩带与头枕调节联动结构，使消费者使用更方便。产品适用于市面上的几乎所有车型，产品本身自带的角度调节功能，可满足儿童乘车时的睡姿、坐姿、躺姿。采用 ISOFIX+ 上拉带，避免常规的安全带安装座椅存在误装的可能。

Comparing with the traditional adjustment of the product, this baby chair adopts pull up and press down to make a innovation way of adjustment, the shoulder belt and head pillow are ganged to adjust then. The universal design could apply the baby chair to any vehicle in the market. The product could satisfy baby's sitting, sleeping it could be installed by ISOFIX + Top-tether and to avoid miss using caused by normal adult belt installation.

关怀手持花洒
Care

设计 / 厦门松霖科技有限公司
生产 / 厦门松霖科技有限公司
Design / Xiamen Solex High-Tech Industries Co.,Ltd
Manufacture / Xiamen Solex High-Tech Industries Co.,Ltd

常规花洒不方便手指不灵活或者手掌有残疾的残障人士使用，此款花洒设计增加了软胶把手，可以用臂膀或者脚掌套在软胶里实现操作，满足残障人士的沐浴需求，也可与家人共用一把花洒。设计匠心独具，白色与铬色巧妙搭配，优雅线条的，弧面与弧面自然过渡，巧妙隐藏分件线，形态轻盈。

Normal handshower doesn't take into account for the disabilities. This product specially adds soft rubber on it, so the disables could hold it with arm. The other family members could also use it. A perfect product shows its feature with the creative elegant design of white and chrome ingenious, elegant lines, natural transition between arcs and the cleverly hidden lines.

Douho 角阀
Douho

设计 / 九牧厨卫股份有限公司
生产 / 九牧厨卫股份有限公司
Design / JOMOO Kitchen & Bath Co., Ltd
Manufacture / JOMOO Kitchen & Bath Co., Ltd

产品超长的把手，间接联系着把手与阀体，使得产品更显整体。逗号的造型，新颖的方式，俏皮而又不失简约的姿态，诠释低调而富有深邃内涵的个性。黑与白，冷与暖，不同材质、颜色的相互交织，彰显别样的视觉体验。易操作，易识别。产品成本较低，采用 59 无铅黄铜，材料可回收利用，全新的出水网产品造型适合铸造工艺，易生产。

Douho faucet's long handle makes it integral in visual, and the fancy form is concise with its own character. This faucet is casted by 59 lead-free brass which could be recycled and the bubbler could save 20% water. It flows cold water out when open, so as to prevent sanitary and save energy. This faucet is concise and stylish with flowing lines and flexible handle.

开百合
I Opener

设计 / 梁振挥、蔡国伟
生产 / PSL Limited
Design / Fai Leung, Michael Choi
Manufacture / PSL Limited

百合开瓶器由金属和硅胶制成，透过巧妙外观线条设计，可适合打开多种樽瓶形状，包括易拉盖、樽装汽水盖、铁盒盖、圆形玻璃瓶盖等。同时运用硅胶物料吸吮特性，有助用户抓紧瓶盖，轻易打开瓶盖，方便女士、小朋友、老人及有需要人士解决生活中一个小麻烦。

I-opener is a multi functional kitchen tool enables to open cans , bottles and jar. The silicone materials offers extra grip. The main material is used silicone rubber, which is an eco-friendly material and durable.

卡莱氏滤水壶
HydroPure Filter Kettle

设计 / 上海木马工业产品设计有限公司
生产 / 上海卡莱氏净水科技有限公司
Design / Shanghai Moma Industrial Product Design Co.,Ltd
Manufacture / Shanghai HydroPure Water Purification Technology Co. Ltd

本产品采用法国 Micro-Filtration 高密度微孔过滤技术、Carbon Filtration 天然活性炭过滤技术及 Ion-Exchange 离子交换技术，可有效去除氯气、水垢、杂质，同时也可以去除如铅、铜等（来自家用管道的）金属物质，使水的味道更加天然美味。过滤水让茶和咖啡更香醇、更美味，并且有效防止水垢产生，延长家用电器的使用寿命。

The adoption of high density Micro-filtration technology, Carbon Filtration technology and Ion-Exchange ion exchange technology could effectively reduces chlorine and impurities as well as the scale and heavy metals (such as copper, lead, etc), while properly retain beneficial minerals such as calcium, potassium, magnesium and so on.

开水过滤器
Hot Water Filters

设计 / 马鞍山江东工业设计发展有限公司
生产 / 上海谷奇核孔膜材料科技有限公司
Design / Ma'an Shan Jiangdong Industrial Design Co.,Ltd
Manufacture / Shanghai GUCH Nuclear Poro Membrane Material Technology Co.,Ltd

此款开水过滤器利用高能加速器加速原子核所产生的强大穿透力，结合尖端化工技术，使 PET 薄膜形成致密、孔径均一的直通多孔薄膜材料，能在极低压力下过滤大量液体，极大提高了单位面积过滤液体的速度及抗染能力，使只能应用于高端科技领域的核孔膜为百姓服务。使人们健康、便捷饮水。物理过滤减少能源浪费。杯状漏斗形，圆润亲近。

Designers combined this sophisticated chemical techniques, making PET film a through-porous film material with dense and equal pores. Guqi hot water filter can effectively block harmful pollutants, by use of unique structure of cup and modification of the cell wall and membrane surface. On the basis of retaining all the advantages of conventional membrane, Guqi increases the speed and resistance to staining liquid filtration capacity per unit area of the membrane greatly. That makes it possible to filter large quantities of liquid at very low pressure.

幻雨魔法师 Select 淋浴管
Hansgrohe Rainmaker Select Showerpipe

设计 / 汉斯格雅卫浴产品（上海）有限公司 凤凰设计室
生产 / 汉斯格雅卫浴产品（上海）有限公司
Design / Hansgrohe Sanitary Products(Shanghai) Co.,Ltd Phoenix Design
Manufacture / Hansgrohe Sanitary Products(Shanghai) Co.,Ltd Phoenix Design

本产品设计简洁，线条清晰，用途多样，性能卓越。花洒控制组件和托盘部分合一，表面采用新型白色玻璃，可调节浴室环境氛围，使功能与设计结合。产品可与头顶花洒、手持花洒配合使用，不同出水方式带来独特感官体验。该产品采用智能节水技术，耗水量降低 60%，实现低能耗。出水喷孔采用高弹性硅胶材料，除水垢简单并可防止水垢生成。

This shower system delivers a compelling performance with its clear lines and unassuming design as well as diverse applications. The white glass and gleaming metal provide a visual link to the elements in the bathroom. The Showerpipe combines all advantages in a single system: ShowerTablet Select 700, Rainmaker Select overhead shower and a Raindance hand shower. The Hansgrohe Rainmaker Select Showerpipe uses EcoSmart, so that the water consumption reduces to around 60% compared with common products.

正姿护套
Corrective Sheath

设计 / 同济大学 & 晨光文具工业设计部
生产 / 上海晨光文具股份有限公司
Design / Tongji University & M&G ID Department
Manufacture / Shanghai M&G Stationery Inc.

该正姿护套使用强制型、引导型、正常型三步到位的原则，改善儿童的握姿问题。关注并矫正儿童的握笔姿势，可改善坐姿，预防近视，缓解肌肉疲劳和指部压力。产品使用无毒无害硅胶材料，运用双色模技术，工艺精细，凸显价值感。松鼠造型正姿护套，颜色亮丽，可爱不失功能性，使造型与功能巧妙结合。

The corrective sheath can improve children's grip posture problem through the three steps. The corrective sheath pays attention to children's posture of holding pen and corrects the wrong way, which can improve sitting posture, prevent myopia, relieve muscle fatigue and finger pressure.

全能营养料理机
Almighty Nutrition Food Machine

设计 / 青鸟工业设计有限公司

生产 / 广东顺德乐凡电器有限公司

Design / Bird Industrial Design

Manufacture / Guangdong Shunde Lefan Electrical Appliances Co.,Ltd

全能营养料理机是一款集料理、榨汁等功能于一体的厨房用具。拥有环绕立体加热破壁技术及强劲马力，能轻易击碎坚固的植物细胞壁，使营养全部释放，更易消化吸收。内设自动调速、关机、清洗等六种自动控制程序，设有酷炫液晶显示触屏，使用方便。产品采用高通透玻璃，晶莹剔透，防刮耐磨，无毒无味。防空转安全装置及过热自动关机保护，保证安全。

The almighty nutrition food machine is a strong power and high speed machine, can easily break down the plant cell wall, and releases all nutrients from the fruit, vegetables, flesh, seed plant biochemical, more easily to obtain the nutrition from the direct consumption of fruits and vegetables. The rubber base, bottom motor cooling and overheating protection are all for safely use.

榻榻米茶几凳
Tatami Teapoy Stool

设计 / 杭州博乐工业产品设计有限公司

生产 / 杭州橙舍文化创意有限公司

Design / Hangzhou Bole Industrial Design Co.,Ltd

Manufacture / Hangzhou Zen's Cultural and Creative Co., Ltd

榻榻米茶几凳是一款多功能的品质家居用品。采用拱桥形提手，符合人体工程学。独特设计，使产品既可用于室内喝茶聊天，又可用于户外闲情逸致，还可用于家中收纳整理。天然楠竹经高温强压成型，不易虫蛀、发霉和变形，经济耐用。取材天然，竹香清新，自然环保。茶几面采用弧线造型，圆润敦实，配麻料棉坐垫美观大方。

The combination design of tatami is innovative. The handle is in arch form, which considers about ergonomics and the convenience of carrying. The product is multifunctional. It could be both used indoor and outdoor as a teapoy or stool. The inner hollow space could be used as a storage space. The product is made from the natural bamboo which is molded through hot pressing process. It could prevent from the damage of worms and mold.

不锈钢真空保温焖烧罐
Stainless Steel Thermal Insulation Pot

设计 / 上海麦扑艺术设计咨询有限公司
生产 / 浙江武义山河工贸有限公司
Design / Map Art&Design
Manufacture / Zhejiang Wuyi Shanhe Industry

该焖烧罐杯身采用食品级不锈钢材质，具有良好的耐蚀性和耐热性。顶级工艺制造，应用超微波镀铜层，增强保温性能。顶部拎绳设计美观实用，可卡住折叠勺等小用具。外盖既是杯盖，也是盛放食物的小碗。内塞采用特殊结构，达到更好的焖烧效果，并加入空气阀设计，更易打开。底部硅胶垫延长使用寿命，且不划伤桌面。外观设计圆润，给人敦实感受。

The stainless steel thermal insulation pot adopts food grade stainless steel, which has good corrosion resistance, heat resistance. Special five layers top process manufacturing is adopted to enhance insulation performance. The tank cover is also a lid, by taking off which could turn to a small bowl. The air valve is designed to open it easily.

懒时光衣帽架
Lazy Time Coat Stand

设计 / 杭州博乐工业产品设计有限公司
生产 / 杭州橙舍文化创意有限公司
Design / Hangzhou Bole Industrial Design Co.,Ltd
Manufacture / Hangzhou Zen's Cultural and Creative Co., Ltd

懒时光衣帽架造型简约，用途多种，解决收纳问题。一物多用，可作为衣帽架也可作为家居装饰品。取材天然楠竹附加麻布、铝合金材料，自然竹香，低碳环保。竹制材质防虫防霉，可放置于多种环境。造型美观大气，边角圆润安全，银色铝制拼接画龙点睛，增添美感。接口拼接精细，连接浑然一体。产品轻便且易组合，经济实惠。

The shape of coat stand is simple and modern. The multi-functional hanging rod is design to fulfill the function of collection and organization. This product is made of bamboo, prevents damages from worms and mold. It could be placed at any place at home. The materials combine the bamboo with linen and aluminum, which is light weight and easily to assemble.

柜茗器
Gui Ming-Qi

设计 / 石大宇
生产 / 北京清庭文创文化发展有限公司
Design / Jeff Shi
Manufacture / Dragonfly Design Center

该茶柜由中国菜橱和英式茶柜获得灵感，用当代设计语言表达中华文化。产品改良了传统弯管竹家具易碎裂的缺点，将竹管剖开并包实心竹，保留原生美感，增加材料强度。竹条格栅设计简洁，比例拿捏准确，创造出通透的空间透视感。接合处为中式传统榫卯结构，无金属、塑料等材质。取材于竹，落形于竹，随着时间的增加更加古朴雅致。

The idea of "Gui Ming-Qi" symbolizes integration of food preservation cupboard from Southern China and British tea cabinet, which is a combination of the traditional Chinese food preservation method. Technical breakthrough in craftsmanship of "Gui Ming-Qi" was created where bamboo stalks were cut open to enclose another layer of solid bamboo to enhance its strength, an ingenious improvement that solved the issue of bamboo breakage among traditional arched bamboo furniture, at the same time preserved the natural aesthetic beauty of bamboo.

溪水间茶叶
Tea of XiShuiJian

设计 / 北京光彩无限管理咨询有限公司
生产 / 北京光彩无限管理咨询有限公司
Design / Shine Design Consulation Center
Manufacture / Shine Design Consulation Center

溪水间茶叶项目是农业溯源＋互联网创新的食品项目，注重后期服务与消费者体验。传统工艺制成茶叶，保留原始味道和营养。统一包装节省空间，使用标签易归类，提高管理效率，降低成本。具地域风情的中式水墨插画与金属包装盒结合，简洁雅致，使品茶人身临其境，并可收藏或回收。茶叶饮后晾干可用于除湿除味和枕边安眠，提高茶叶实用率。

This is an innovation design project combining agriculture and internet innovation which focuses on the latter service and consumer experience. From the tea produce, package design, tea products recycle usage and collection, the whole process is designed as a service chain which is a creative way of selling and promoting tea culture.

便携式烘鞋器
Portable Shoe Dryer

设计 / 杭州博乐工业产品设计有限公司
生产 / 台州市中联电器有限公司
Design / Hangzhou Bole Industrial Design Co.,Ltd
Manufacture / Taizhou Zhonglian Electrical Co., Ltd

便携式烘鞋器采用伸缩设计可适应不同尺码的鞋，使用范围广泛。开关采用多挡控制，内部采用双核发热结构，大大提高了烘干效率。散热孔分布均匀，烘干、杀菌、除臭效果明显。机身采用合金塑料，耐冲击不变形，耐热无异味，环保无毒。纯铜电源线设有防拉线卡，安全方便；加固加厚插头不易变形，防止短路。整体设计简洁大方，时尚感强。

The portable shoe dryer has several modes available to control. The inner structure uses the dual heating core to provide a better user experience. The even thermal porous surface could strengthen the drying effects and the dual core heating system could raise the efficiency of drying. The double strands of wire made by pure copper are much safer and more convenient than other wires.

实智 P1 智能插排
P1 Smart Platooninsert

设计 / 张长东、田春宇
生产 / 实智科技有限公司
Design / Zhang Changdong, Tink Tian
Manufacture / iSmart Science and Technology Co., Ltd

该插排采用智能控制技术，可在使用遥控器关闭电视后自动切断电源，减少待机消耗，延长电器寿命，安全节能。同时，可作为普通插排使用。产品采用锡磷青铜材料，高弹性、强导电、耐磨损。产品采用无断点连接和过载保护器，材质添加强力阻燃成分，提升安全性能。插排设计简洁，融合家居环境。前段设置显示界面，可直观方便看到插排工作状态。

This product can recognize TV status by using intelligent control technology. It will cut off the power of television and other related equipment automatically after 60 seconds when you turn off the TV. The quality of tin phosphor bronze material, high elasticity, conductive, abrasion resistance, to avoid the former brass material caused by virtual access, fever, fire safety risk. The 30 degrees interface window in front is in accordance with ergonomics which enables users to see the working state of the socket.

弹击式汽车安全伞
Shooting Safety Hambrella

设计 / 李若权
生产 / 深圳市喜途伞业有限公司
Design / Li Ruoquan
Manufacture / Shenzhen Xitu Umbrella Co.,Ltd

汽车安全伞将汽车破窗器、安全带切割器、反光警示条融入雨伞，实用易携带。破窗器与安全带切割器隐藏于伞柄盖内，操作简便。被困车内时，能迅速自救与逃生。伞边沿设置了反光警示条，起到警示作用。伞柄破窗器内置强化合金撞击针，硬度强，在水中也能轻松破窗。安全伞有红、黑、蓝色，男女皆宜，结实耐用又不失美观性。

Safety Hambrella is a multifunctional umbrella integrates emergency hammer, seat belt cutter and reflective stripe etc functions. The hammer and seat belt cutter hide in the umbrella handle, it takes only a few seconds to open it and assist to escape. The reflective stripe is placed at the side of the umbrella to remind passing cars. The strike needle is installed inside of the hammer, even trapping inside a car, it can helps to break the window.

果冻重力闹钟
JELLY Gravity Control Clock

设计 / 深圳市风格派家居用品有限公司
生产 / 深圳市风格派家居用品有限公司
Design / Shenzhen Stylepie Lifestyle Co., Ltd
Manufacture / Shenzhen Stylepie Lifestyle Co., Ltd

此款闹钟的设计灵感来自果冻，造型优雅圆润。创新地加入重力感应控制，闹铃响起后轻轻晃动可暂停 4 分钟；将闹钟倒扣即可关闭；闹钟翻回原状便进入待命状态。该闹钟节能省电，且无电磁辐射。采用橡胶油涂装，机身手感佳。闹钟呈圆锥体，满足机身自由滚动又不会太远的要求，造型和功能完美结合。

This gravity control clock is inspired from jelly, cute and smart. We develop gravity control alarm system for alarm-clock, it is a whole new experience. When clock rings, you just need to push or shake it, and the clock will snooze for 4 minutes. When you decide to get up, just turn it around and it will stop. The rubber oil finishing makes the clock feel nice.

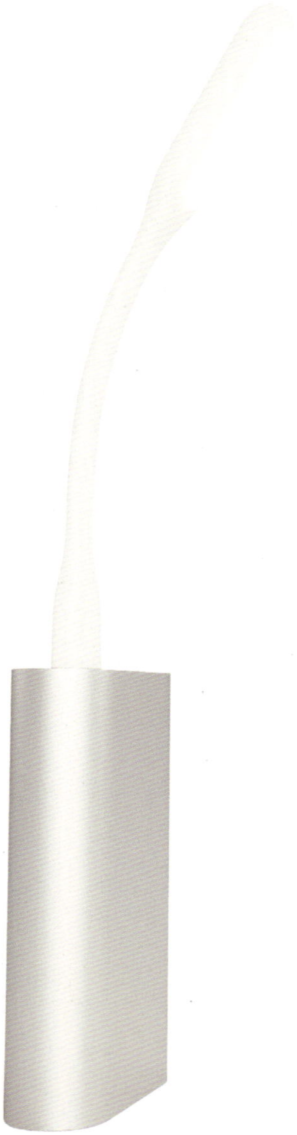

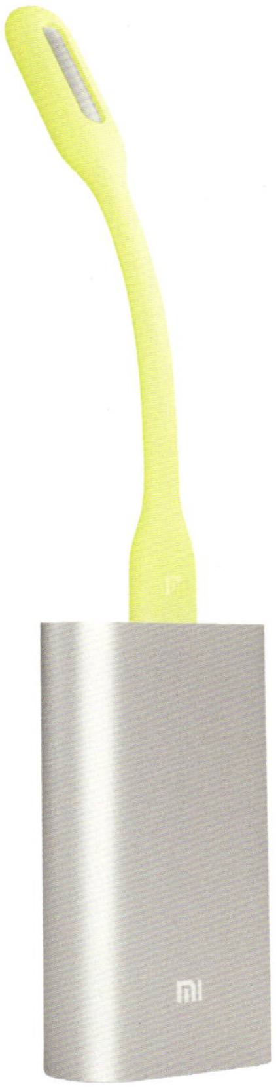

扫一扫查看产品 Pin3D 技术三维效果图
Scanning for the 3D image by Pin3D

小米 LED 随身灯 / 小米随身风扇
MI Portable Light/MI Portable Fan

设计 / 窦文博
生产 / 江苏紫米电子技术有限公司
Design / Dou Wenbo
Manufacture / Zimi Corporation

本产品是通过 USB 接口供电的便携 LED 随身灯和随身风扇，可连接于移动电源、笔记本电脑等设备使用。LED 随身灯可在光源不足的情况下使用；随身风扇可在炎热季节的户外或没有空调的场所有效地辅助个人通风降温。一体成型的生产工艺及柔软的 TPE 材质，使产品可随意调整角度，适合多种使用方式和环境，美观与功能结合统一。

MI Portable Light and Portable Fan is a product that can be powered by any kind of USB port from a power bank to a laptop / PC. The luminaire provides efficient lighting in various scenarios. Integrally molding and soft TPE material leaves great flexibility for direction and position adjustment. MI Portable Light is used under the circumstance of insufficient lighting. Portable Fan can efficiently help to do personal cooling under the circumstance of hot seasons outside and in places without air conditioner.

简 · 爱—4 平微厨
Simple Love-Mini Kitchen

设计 / 饶如泊、林建旋
生产 / 厦门金牌厨柜股份有限公司
Design / Rao Rubo, Lin Jianxuan
Manufacture / Xiamen Goldenhome Co.,Ltd

该厨房是针对小户型开发的空间利用率高的整体厨房，经济、实用、时尚。巧妙利用踢脚板空间，设计了储物、垫高、脚底按摩三功能合一的抽屉。垃圾桶与水槽设计成系统，方便倒垃圾。餐车融合梯凳，方便取放高处物品。产品采用秸秆作为门板和台面基材，环保经济。模块化设计 实现批量生产，并能快速无尘安装。配色为经典的黑白，造型简洁大方。

Mini- Smart kitchen is a space for the development of small high utilization of the overall kitchen. The clever use of the traditional kitchen cabinets without using the skirting board space, design the storage, high cushion, foot massage three functions of a drawer. The sink cabinet and trash bin are designed to form a system. Also, the dining car has integrated the stool for the convenience of fetching items from high. Standard modular design, realize large-scale production.

这里有我的一切（适老厨房）
One for All

设计 / 河南省大信整体厨房科贸有限公司
生产 / 河南省大信整体厨房科贸有限公司
Design / Henan Province Daxin Whole Cookroom Science
Manufacture / Henan Province Daxin Whole Cookroom Science

该厨房是根据老年人行动不便、视觉嗅觉衰退、适应能力减弱、安全感下降等特点设计的适合老年人使用的整体厨房。橱柜包括烟机、电磁炉、水槽、龙头、菜篮、垃圾分类篮、碗盘筷等，功能一应俱全。老人伸手可及用具，解决了腿脚不便的老年人做饭的问题。同时，具有可发短信遥控烟机和防干烧电磁炉设计，保障安全。台面边缘为圆弧，避免碰伤。

The design of age-friendly kitchen adopts the latest fixed point operational principle, such as remote hood which can send text messages and anti-dry induction cooker. Considering their infirm condition, the decline of vision and smell, the diminished adaptability, the descend of psychological sense and the appearing sense of loss and inferiority and other features, we design the holistic kitchen that is more convenient for the elderly to use and make sure that the elderly can do cooking chores and lead a confident and happy life.

拔火罐
Chinese Cupping

设计 / 杭州斯帕克造型艺术有限公司
生产 / 杭州斯帕克造型艺术有限公司
Design / Hangzhou Spark Industrial Design.,Ltd
Manufacture / Hangzhou Spark Industrial Design.,Ltd

该拔火罐改变了普通火罐罐印难看且需长时间消除的困扰，不仅能作为治疗仪器，其美感还可作为一种时尚。使用此款拔罐后，罐印为漂亮的图案，消除人们心里的抵触感，将有更多人使用拔罐器。拔罐器采用物理疗法，经济环保。产品使用 pc 塑料及注塑成型工艺，整体造型刚柔并济。运用简单线条勾勒外形，配色与中药色相呼应。

Ordinary cupping can is a traditional Chinese medicine therapy, applying which on the body will leave ugly imprint and takes long time to eliminate. This new product will turn the ugly imprint into a fashion. After the treatment, the cans imprint will leave a beautiful pattern of the cans. The product adopts PC plastic, using plastic injection molding process.

SILI—CUP 矿化杯
SILI-CUP

设计 / 黄辉荣
生产 / 广州韩能大健康产品有限公司
Design / Huang Ruirong
Manufacture / Guangzhou Han Energy & Health Products Co.,Ltd

该健康杯是国内首款应用水溶性硅元素的矿化水杯，让水具有超强水活性、益生矿物质、健康弱碱性、超微分子团等特点。杯身采用真空结构，具有保温功能。杯盖也可作杯子，一物多用。杯子由三个可拆解部分组成，更换灵活方便，环保经济。健康杯以沙漏为设计概念，感受时间，体验矿化过程。外观呈梭形，手感佳。外形采用圆弧切割而成，简洁时尚。

SILI-CUP is the first mineralization cup with water soluble silicon in China. The water soluble silicon can activate water, making it into mineral water. The mineral water is weak alkaline and contains healthy minerals. Besides, the silicon in water is easy to be absorbed by human body, which is good for your health. Hourglass as the design concept is in order to make users to feel the elapse of time.

“小心眼”护眼套装
Care Your Eyes Eye Protection Package

设计 / 深圳洛可可工业设计有限公司
生产 / 广东三块钱信息科技有限公司
Design / LKK Design Shenzhen Co.,Ltd
Manufacture / GuangZhou Three Yuan Information Technology Co.,Ltd

该产品为护眼套装，包括便携式洗眼液、一次性洗眼液和护眼胶囊，打破同类产品常规使用方式。便携式洗眼液开盖即用，流程简单便于对位；瓶身小巧易于手握，可带上飞机。一次性洗眼液将液体置于杯内，简化洗眼流程。护眼胶囊为一周药量，趣味外形与使用方式增加使用乐趣和包装的收藏性。产品线条简洁时尚，充满活力与亲和力，亮雾面对比提升品质感。

This product consist of portable eye washing liquid, one-off eye washing liquid and eye-safe capsule, which broken the using way of same type product. Portable eye washing liquid connected the eye washing liquid with container. Besides, it used spraying method to simplify operational process. The one-off eye washing liquid is putted into a cup directly and you can use it when you open it.

流金提梁壶
Golden Handle Teapot

设计 / 物舍设计团队
生产 / 三度品牌策划有限公司
Design / Mesh Design Team
Manufacture / Guangzhou Sandu Brand Strategy Planning Co.,Ltd

流金提梁壶保留传统提梁器形特点，以高硼硅玻璃为塑形材料，健康环保。提梁为黄铜材料，双喜标志采用烫金，营造流淌的金色之美。高硼硅玻璃与黄铜提梁的应用，使产品美观隔热。壶嘴为流线设计，出水流畅。配套茶杯采用双层玻璃，杯口以单层玻璃收口，隔热又能感知茶汤温度。玻璃可回收利用，无毒，耐高温，耐酸性。产品握持感佳，工艺精密。

The Golden Handle Teapot maintains the feature of the traditional teapot while using the high borosilicate glass as its material is a wise consideration. The streamline spout brings a good user experience and the cups are dual-layers borosilicate glass with single-layer edge makes users hold it with a comfortable temperature.

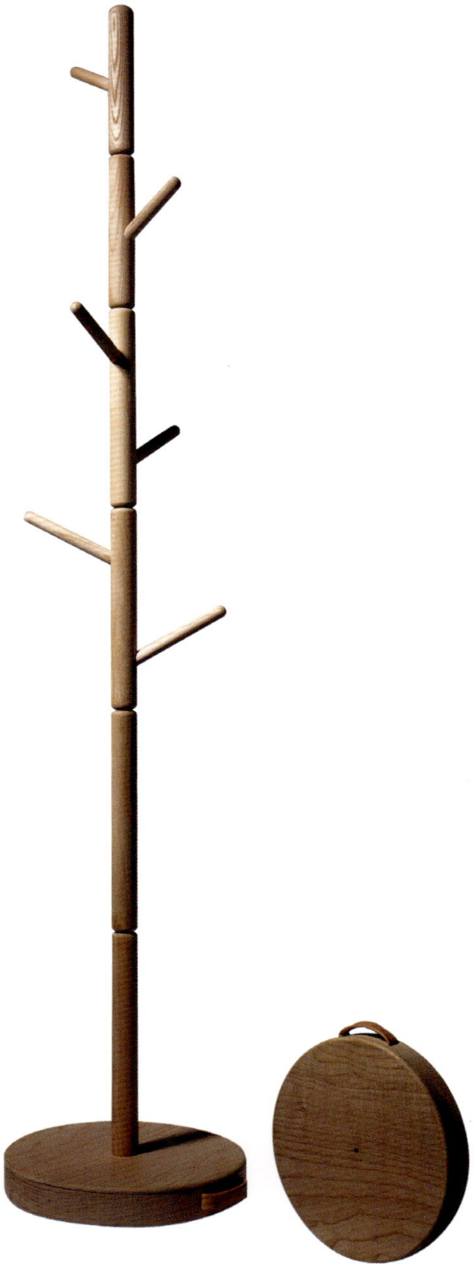

合
In One

设计 / 周安彬、雷南仕
生产 / 广州高尚生活文化传播有限公司
Design / Zhou Anbin, Lei NanShi
Manufacture / Guangzhou Han Energy & Health Products Co.,Ltd

“合”是一款具有易生产、易拆装、易运输、易使用等特点的衣帽架。衣帽架的支杆设计为倒圆角圆棍，长短不一，解决收纳问题，且有形式美感。部件经过精心设计与巧妙编排，可全部收纳于底盘，同时平衡衣帽架的使用高度与整体的比例美感。木头制成的底盘上设计有拉手，无需其他包装即可携带，适用于大众消费、礼品消费、线上线下消费等模式。

IN ONE is a coat stand with the concept of “no package needed”. The handle design on the pedestal can let consumers lift ALL WITH IN straight home to assemble without any unnecessary package. Good design and flat-panel packaging is suitable for mass consumption, gifts consumption, consumer online and offline consumer multiple models coexist.

叁
SAN

设计 / 周安彬、詹秋鸿
生产 / 广州高尚生活文化传播有限公司
Design / Zhou Anbin, Zhan Qiuhong
Manufacture / GaoShang Living (GuangZhou)Co.,Ltd

“叁”是一款合理利用包装、拆装运输简易、生产制造高效的衣帽架，适用于大众、礼品、线上、线下多种消费模式。三条木条通过两两相扣形成独特而稳固的三角形结构，三个特定角度斜孔连接衣帽架，三条凹槽使挂放简单方便。主杆连接口隐藏在三角结构中，简洁巧妙。每个部件的尺寸经过推敲，既保持衣帽架的实用与美感，又充分利用包装盒空间。

This coat stand is better use of packing space, easier to assemble & shipping and more efficient of manufacture. Three identical wooden sticks formed into a unique stable triangle by buckling each other. Three inclined holes of fixed angle is the key of installing the coat stand.Three simple indentations make hanging easy and convenient. Three main rods are installed by using double head screws twisting up and down, no installing tool needed, simple and clever.

中老年多功能健康座椅
Multi-functional Health Chair for Elderly

设计 / 清华大学美术学院健康医疗产业创新设计研究所
生产 / 博奥颐和健康科学技术（北京）有限公司
Design / Healthcare Design Research Lab, Tsinghua University
Manufacture / CapitalBio eHealth Science & Technology(Beijing)Co.,Ltd

中老年多功能座椅以解决起身不便为出发点，通过机械结构与程序控制设计，辅助行动不便人群独立站立和坐下，降低起坐难度和体力消耗。产品采用模块化设计，具有电动行走、辅助起身、按摩理疗、服药提醒等功能。材料符合环保标准，部分可回收利用。外观整合流线型元素，皮革与木质纹理支架相得益彰，既有科技感又不失时尚。

The unique design of sit-up structure fully takes the practical problem of inconvenient sit-up for user into consideration. It adopts mechanic and electronic technology to reduce the movement difficulty and physical exertion resulting from sit-up, and improve safety of sit-up. The entire machine uses modular functional design, wherein the functions such as electric walk, sit-up by support, massage and physiotherapy, medication warning etc. could be designed in one.

轻扇（屏风）
Light Fan（Screen）

设计 / 袁媛
生产 / 北京如翌家具有限公司
Design / Yuan Yuan
Manufacture / Beijing Rooy Furnishing Co.,Ltd

轻扇屏风的设计灵感来源于中国传统文化团扇。该设计作为空间隔断，利用团扇半透明的遮光特性，在若隐若现中传达东方含蓄之美，对室内空间既有隔断功能也有装饰效果。团扇和框架制作采用天然材料，体现人与自然和谐共处。产品结合了现代化工业制造工艺与中国传统团扇制作工艺，精巧的工艺细节和简洁的设计相辅相成，气质轻松优雅。

The artistically appealing the moon-shaped fans symbolizes union and happiness in ancient Chinese poetry and calligraphy. The design of Light Fan is precisely based on the traditional esthetics of moon-shaped fans. The spatial partitioning and the semi-transparency of the moon-shaped fans convey, in a faintly discernible way, the emphasis of Oriental cultures on implicit beauty. It combines the industrialization process and the traditional round fan production process, reflecting modern industrial manufacturing platform and Chinese traditional culture.

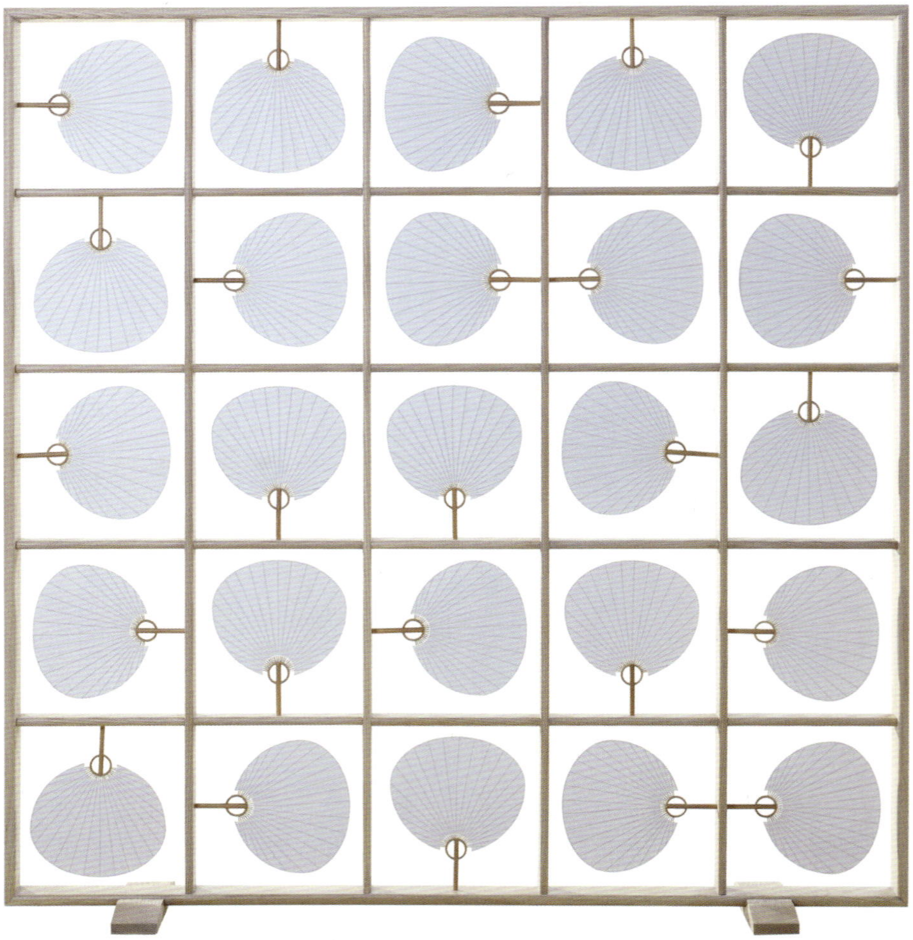

观石（沙发）
Stone Vision（sofa）

设计 / 袁媛
生产 / 北京如翌家具有限公司
Design / Yuan Yuan
Manufacture / Beijing Rooy Furnishing Co.,Ltd

观石沙发将中国独特的观石文化与人体工程学结合，外观设计为不对称的自然雕塑，饱满的造型与人体曲线贴合，兼顾舒适与自然之美，提供轻松愉悦又具有文化品位的生活方式。产品设计圆润亲切，采用天然材料，体现淡雅和谐的哲学内涵以及人与自然和谐共处。面套采用天然羊毛，通过巧妙的切割手法和特有工艺完成包覆，工艺水平精湛。

Combining this esthetics and ergonomics, the Stone Vision sofa matches its plump design with the curvature of the human body and thus pays equal attention to comfort and natural beauty. The Stone Vision sofa was to create a lifestyle that's relaxed, pleasant and tasteful. Design mellow kind, reflects the elegant harmony of philosophical connotation, materials are made of natural materials.

通气面罩
Nasal Mask

设计 / 毅达（北京）医疗科技有限公司
生产 / 东莞市毅达电子有限公司
Design / EDA (Beijing) Medical technology Co.,ltd
Manufacture / Dongguan EDA Electronics Co.,ltd

通气面罩应用于对睡眠呼吸暂停综合症患者进行无创通气治疗。产品追求简约、轻薄的理念，去掉其他繁复设计，用简单结构实现了理想效果，提高舒适度。产品采用医用硅橡胶和 PC 材料制成，无毒无害。采用液体硅橡胶注射技术，保证产品立体成型。产品采用简洁的设计风格，突出细节之美，整体高透明度，制造工艺精良。

Sleep apnea syndrome patients need to use a nasal mask with the respirator noninvasive ventilation in the treatment while sleeping. In the guarantee of the effect of treatment, the product is lightweight and comfortable, remove unnecessary complicated design, with the simplest structure, it realizes the most ideal product comprehensive effect.

婴儿浴盆
Bathtub

设计 / 深圳市问鼎工业设计有限公司
生产 / 深圳市懒妈妈生活用品有限公司
Design /Shenzhen Wing-id Co.,Ltd
Manufacture / Shenzhen Lazymum Daily Supplies Co.,Ltd

婴儿浴盆采用活水理念设计，分储水区和洗澡区，流动水源使清洗更健康方便。躺板为柔软的抗菌材质，呵护宝宝幼嫩肌肤，安全舒适。拖轮设计，方便移动。盆底设计排水塞，方便倒水。背部挂钩设计，美观且节省空间。水温贴监控水温，科学安全。产品取下躺板可使用到 8 岁，持久耐用，环保经济。产品造型简洁大气，外翻卷边弱化底部，提升档次感。

This bathtub is divided into two areas – Storage Area and Bathing Area. Clean water in Storage Area will naturally flow into Bathing Area. A board is specially designed according to ergonomics to protect bab's neck and back. Your baby can lie on the board whose surface is covered by soft anti-microbial EVA materials, in which way, your baby will feel safe and comfortable. As a whole, this product is concise and simple in its shape, and it will always be a pleasing view.

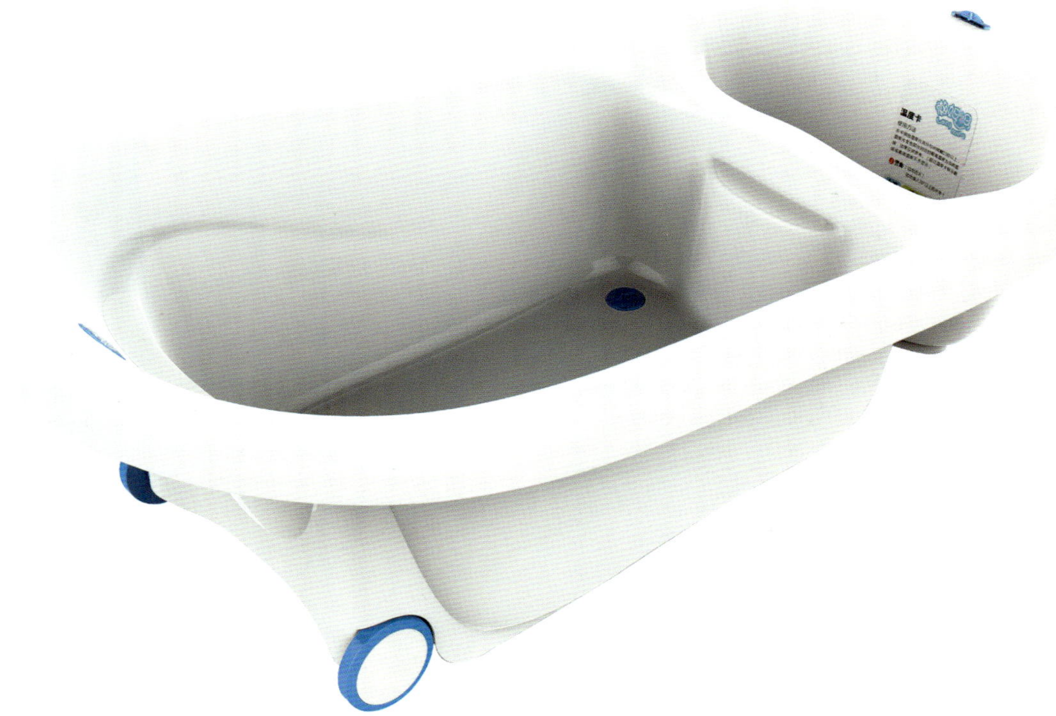

五环茶——和之缘
Five Rings Tea

设计 / 焦哲
生产 / 北京老舍茶馆
Design / Kurt Jiao
Manufacture / Beijing Laoshe Tea House

该产品是老舍茶馆为弘扬中国传统文化特别设计的茶礼。外包装设计为抽屉式，有效控制体积，选用红色、棕色和金色搭配，有中国味道。茶叶罐设计为圆形，选用奥林匹克五环颜色，包装全部打开时形成五环形状，茶精神与奥林匹克精神完美结合。该产品既是汇聚中国六大名茶的珍贵茶礼，也是颇具象征意义和收藏价值的奥运会纪念品。

The Five Rings Tea is a tea set gift based on Lao She Teahouse, which carries the traditional Chinese culture. The package uses a drawer design for arranging space; red, brown and golden colors are adopted for a sense of China. Tea jars are round in shape, choosing the colors of the Olympic Rings. When opening the package, the five rings shape implies a perfect combination of the tea spirit and Olympic spirit.

两忘角壶
Liangwang Teapots Set

设计 / 石大宇
生产 / 北京清庭文创文化发展有限公司
Design / Jeff Dayu Shi
Manufacture / Dragonfly Design Center

扫一扫查看产品 Pin3D 技术三维效果图
Scanning for the 3D image by Pin3D

两忘角壶是新形态当代茶具。首次使用 3D 打印技术制模以准确掌握角度规格。无壶钮外形跳脱传统规范，取材于老岩泥，成色古朴，可软化水质、保持香气，使茶汤更甜美甘醇。壶嘴与壶把成利于倒茶的角度，单柄握把符合人体工学，可单手使用不烫手。壶盖四边因吸力紧附于壶身，倒茶时不掉落不溢水。茶漉呈半球型突出状，增加过滤面积。

The Liangwang Teapots Set is designed specifically for fine Chinese tea drinking with the aim to revive tea culture. For the first time, 3D printing technique was used for teapots moulding to enable intricate details of teapots can be achieved. “Laoyan clay”, containing mineral components, is used in making this product, which improves the flavor of tea and adds extra natural sweetness. Between the spout and the handle, a defined angle is best suited for tea pouring. While the tea is steeping, 4 sides of the lid attach to the teapot body so tightly as to prevent the lid from falling off and the tea from spilling over.

优尚自动吸墨钢笔
OASO Ink Self-sucking Fountain Pen

设计 / 上海优尚文具有限公司
生产 / 上海优尚文具有限公司
Design / Shanghai OASO Stationery Co.,Ltd
Manufacture / Shanghai OASO Stationery Co.,Ltd

该自动吸墨钢笔根据气压平衡原理，特制上墨器与配套墨水瓶一并使用，简化过程，无需擦拭墨水残留，节约墨水和纸张。产品采用进口优质 ABS、AS、PP 材料，使用德国精密注塑机制造。墨水瓶造型稳重，笔帽采用借景手法，透过外圈缺口看到里面色彩。配件采用黄铜电镀，减轻重量，长时间书写不疲劳。握手采用三切面结构，贴合手指，书写舒适。

The OASO Ink Self-sucking Fountain Pen is an automatic ink absorbing pen. Based on the pressure balance principle, an ink extracting bottle is specifically made to be used with an inkwell, where the ink is extracted into the pen without any residual ink and wiping. It is made of imported high quality ABS, AS and PP material and manufactured by the German injection molding machine, which is light weight, comfortable for holding and can support long writing time.

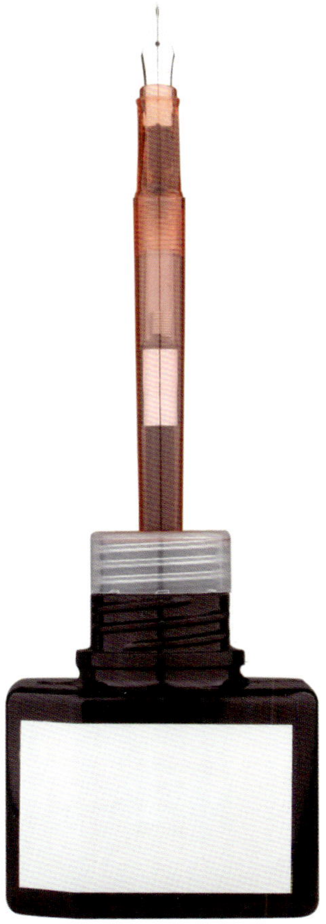

折角一圆珠笔
Flod-Ballpen

设计 / 欧赛笔业
生产 / 杭州欧赛笔业有限公司
Design / OWNSEAS
Manufacture / Hangzhou OWNSEAS Pen Co.,Ltd

该产品是一款造型设计为折纸的中性笔。笔夹犹如翻折的纸角，充满想象力，同时可做名片夹使用，更添巧思。超大面积笔夹设计，满足广告印刷需求。双色笔身，巧妙显示出手握区域，两种颜色叠加充满活力。充满童趣和实用性的独特造型，使人过目不忘，增加企业辨识度。笔芯采用德国进口油墨，使用寿命长，减少笔芯替换率，环保经济。

The FLOD-BALLPEN is a gel pen with a paper folding style. The pen clip looks like a folding paper angle, which can also be used as a name card holder. The large scale of clip area can be used as advertisement printing. The ink cartridge is imported from Germany which can last for a long time thus reduces the frequency of replacement.

飞亚达立体读时手表 GA8606.BBB
FIYTA 3D Time Watch GA8606.BBB

设计 / 孙磊、高仍东
生产 / 飞亚达（集团）股份有限公司
Design / Sun Lei, Gao Rengdong
Manufacture / FIYTA Holdings Co.,Ltd

该手表在读取时间的方式上进行了功能性创新，突破常规平面化读时方式，将时针盘设计为立体有倾斜角度的形态，可从正面侧面等多角度读时，开创了手表立体读时的先河。手表整体线条简洁硬朗，颜色对比鲜明，富有科技感和未来气息，拥有功能性的同时，是一件工业设计艺术品。手表采用自动机械机心，靠手臂摇摆产生动力，自然环保。

The FIYTA 3D TIME WATCH GA8606.BBB has an innovated design for time reading from the side, which breaks through the traditional way of reading time only from the top. It is an industrial design artwork combining the function of technology and the sense of future. The watch design is simple yet powerful and the color contrast is distinct, in order to highlight the function of the stereoscopic reading. The whole watch design is a partial modern design style, in line with the current aesthetic trend.

望乡——城市主题纪念创意花盆设计
Looking Hometown

设计 / 盐城工学院
生产 / 盐城卡洛泽科技有限公司
Design / Yancheng Institute of Technology
Manufacture / Carousel Technology Co.,Ltd

该创意花盆设计选取城市轮廓图作为砖模，配合当地地图轮廓，植入当地土壤，种植当地特色植物。产品使用中国传统建筑材料青砖，质密且具有多孔结构，可以缓慢吸水并有较高含水性。花盆分为上下两层，上层是青砖花盆，下层是亚克力盛水容器，具有一次加注长时间保湿功效。材料易于找到，加工成本低。造型简洁，青砖和透明亚克力结合十分美观。

The design as local cultural product is full of strong Chinese traditional humanistic spirit, choose a profile view of the city as a brick mold. Pots divided into two layers, the upper is flowerpot brick material, and the lower is the water container acrylic material. Pots can draw water from matching acrylic container with a raise for a long time moisturizing effect. Material is very inexpensive, easy to find and low processing costs.

口袋城市——模块化风情背包
City on Backpackers

设计 / 盐城工学院
生产 / 盐城卡洛泽科技有限公司
Design / Yancheng Institute of Technology
Manufacture / Carousel Technology Co., Ltd

该产品是采用模块化设计的时尚毛毡包，内胆包外形设计为城市代表性建筑剪影，同时将市花作为装饰穿插在包扣上，是特色鲜明的地域文化产品。毛毡包的模块化内胆包可根据需要更换，满足日常放置雨伞、手机、收纳袋等需求。毛毡材料采用天然羊毛制成，可再生。产品时尚美观且经济实用，适合年轻人使用和作为城市旅游纪念品销售。

This is a modular design fashion felt bag, the city's landmark as a design element, the use of color in the inner bag and liner bag designed for these different utility and functionality. In addition, the floral emblem of the city as a decorative element will be interspersed in the bag buckle, and the liner bag echoed the distinctive geographical and cultural products. Sleeve contour silhouette is typical buildings of the city. Modular expansion sleeve meet daily travel needs, such as: place an umbrella, pen, mobile phone bags, hubs pouch, glasses bag. It is a popular souvenir for the tourists.

飞图 UV 单双面同步喷绘机 SDM3300i
SKYJET UV Double Side Printer SDM3300i

设计 / 沈阳国度真爱设计咨询有限公司
生产 / 沈阳飞行船数码喷印设备有限公司
Design / Shenyang Sky Air-Ship Digital Printing Equipment Co., Ltd
Manufacture / Shenyang Sky Air-Ship Digital Printing Equipment Co.,Ltd

该喷绘机应用 UV 喷绘与同步双面喷绘相结合的新技术，解决了灯箱打光后色彩衰减的难题。产品集双机同步双面打印、双机单面各自打印和双机协力倍速打印三种功能于一身，具有无人职守、辅助上布、墨桶监控、打印统计等功能。使用环保墨水，无毒无味，更换方便。可在布、车身贴、皮革、纸张等介质上喷绘，应用广泛。造型以简洁折边为主，体现科技感。

The multifunctional new UV inkjet technology combining the UV inkjet technology and synchronous double-sided inkjet has been applied to SDM, the worldwide original product patent for invention, in order that the worldwide problem about color attenuation after the lighting of light box pictures has been completely solved. The environment-friendly ink, free of harmful substances and undesirable odor, featuring the energy saving and environmental protectionThe equipment appearance and molding is overall dominated by concise edgefolds.

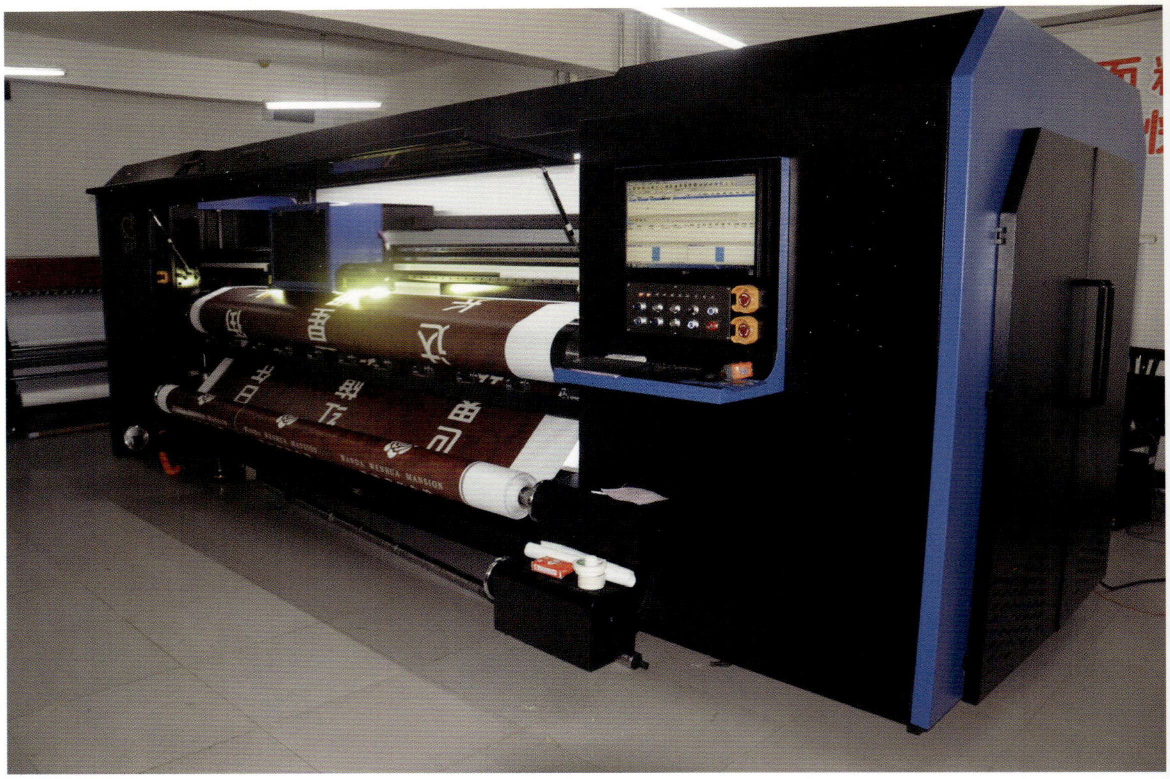

混凝土振动棒驱动电机
Universal Motor for Concrete Vibrator

设计 / 张炯辉
生产 / 上海摩图机电科技有限公司
Design / Zhang Jionghui
Manufacture / Shanghai MOTOR Electromechanical Technology Co., Ltd.

本产品通过工业设计优化功能，提升用户体验，美观时尚。产品对电机冷却进风过滤结构进行改进，在过滤棉下方增加排水槽。产品将更换或清理耗材整合于后盖中，外观简洁平顺，耐脏易清理。尾部增加手柄，双手柄操作便利可靠。产品使用寿命提高至 12 到 24 个月。零部件为金属和塑料，可再生。主体注塑成型，外壳采用耐冲击材料，强化结构设计。

The product get a stylish appearance. We improve the air floating system, which cool down the motor and take out the wearing carbon powder in working, then improve the lifetime of motor.Convenient for maintenance, an integrated rear cover is applied to protect the filter and carbon brush holder, it is easy for assembling & disassembling.

电动车控制器
DMC2950

设计 / 刘永进、秦龙
生产 / 阳光电源股份有限公司
Design / Liu Yongjin, Ben Qin
Manufacture / Sungrow Power Supply Co.,Ltd

电动车控制器旨在让电动汽车更高效。产品的高效率和可靠性使能源充分利用，电机参数辨识使控制方便准确，丰富的控制功能使驾驶更自由。控制器通过控制电动机电流，完成电动机驱动转矩和旋转方向的控制。产品通过对部件巧妙的整合，给人全新的视觉感受。微弧度面可增加结构强度，更利于散发积水积油。形态仿生，让科技充满人文趣味。

DMC2950 is an electrical vehicle controller to make electrical vehicle running more efficiently. The high efficiency and high reliability of the product make the energy use fully; the identification of motor parameters makes the control of the EV more accurately. The EV motor controller controls the rotation direction and the driving torque of the motor via controlling the electric current of the motor. Although it is technically a complete new product design, its functional components are of industrial-standard rather than customization.

远程智能药箱
Remote Intelligent Medicine Cabinet

设计 / 深圳市柏斯工业设计有限公司
生产 / 陕西世强实业集团有限公司
Design / Shenzhen Perth Industrial Design Co.,Ltd
Manufacture / Shaanxi Shiqiang Industry Co.,Ltd

远程智能药箱将互联网与传统医疗结合，病人在家中即可接受诊疗，解决看病难问题。药箱可将测量数据、用药情况实时发送到监护者手机应用程序，方便监测患者身体状况，及时安排就医。系统可显示药品名称、所剩计量及售卖位置。设计采用塑胶外壳和金属骨架结合，外观以“牛”为设计元素，传达敦厚特质，结构注重实用性和操作性，外观整洁。

Remote intelligent box by remote Internet system, complete the connection between medical institutions and users.Solved the problem of the individual, the family, the doctor NanZhiBing difficult, to fill the market vacancy, product testing by the basic data for hospital as a direct reference and analysis of data, do not need to line up to the hospital to check, make reasonable use of resources of hospital effectively, reduce hospital operating costs.

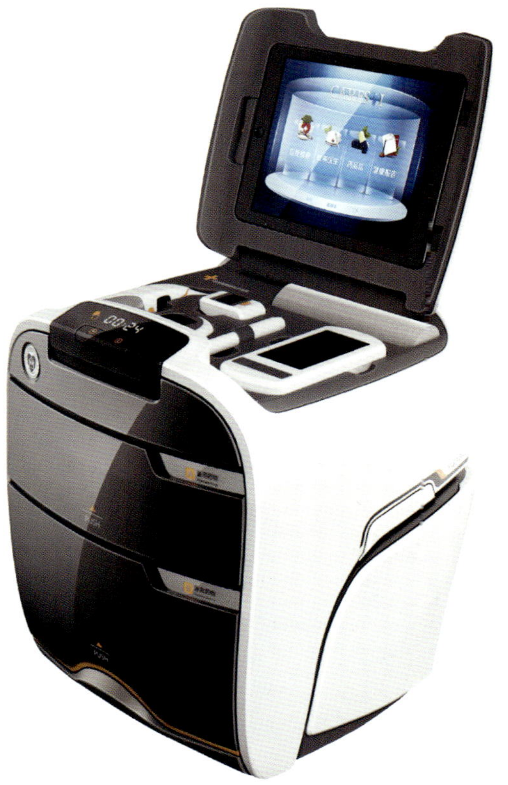

车床结构及内外防护设计
The Design of Internal and External Protection

设计 / 大连后青春工业设计有限公司
生产 / 大连吉润企业集团
Design / Dalian Post-Spring Industrial Design Co.,Ltd
Manufacture / Dalian Jirun Enterprise Group

该设计采用低能耗高效主轴高压电机及环保油脂润滑线轨，减少气体油料消耗和排放。人体工程学设计提升操作宜人性和安全性。遵循整合性，设计为内部走线。分板可互换，减少加工次数和装配出错率。通过造型设计树立全新产品形象，在细节上使用黄金分割比，色彩搭配和谐优美，形成整齐划一的系列化风格。产品节约材料和空间，减轻重量。

We use the low consumption but high efficient mainshaft high voltage power and grease lubrication rail line to decrease the gas oil consumption and emission. Hydraulic station, electrical boxes, ladders and other highly are integrated into the protection. We persist in interchangeability, and our purpose is to reduce the number of processing times and the possibility of errors while assembling.

QLYC3015 激光切割机
QLYC3015 Laser Cutting Machine

设计 / 武汉华夏星光工业产品设计有限公司
生产 / 武汉华夏星光工业产品设计有限公司
Design / Wuhan Huaxia Star Industrial Products Design Co., Ltd
Manufacture / Wuhan Huaxia Star Industrial Products Design Co., Ltd

该激光切割机采用光纤传输和柔性加工，适用于切割铜、铝等高反材料，实现了任一点上的等质量切割。严谨的排屑区域设计将对加工产生的废料有更合理的处理方式。产品表面处理采用喷塑形式，达到零污染。产品采用钣金折弯焊接工艺，使用进口切割机及折弯机，保证所有部件的精细度。产品整体造型设计时尚灵动。

This laser cutting machine adopts fiber transmission and flexible processing, applied to cutting copper and aluminum, realizing equivalent cutting to different materials. Sheet metal bending welding process, before each parts production drawings are subject to reasonable review optimization, behind to ensure that the production line every link will not appear any mistakes.

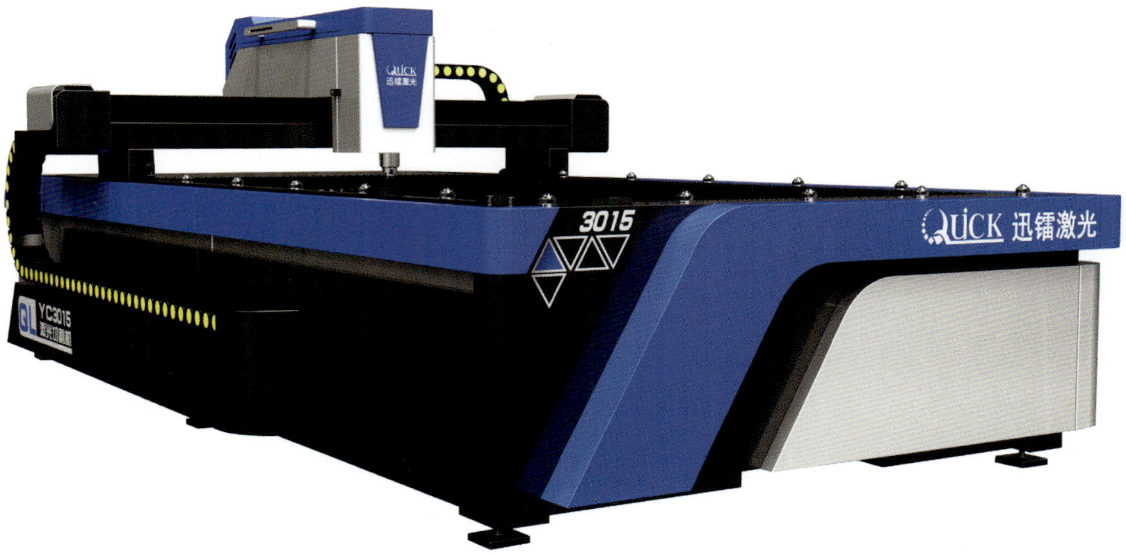

XG-3015E 全罩激光切割机
XG-3015E Cover All Laser Cutting Machine

设计 / 武汉华夏星光工业产品设计有限公司
生产 / 武汉华夏星光工业产品设计有限公司
Design / Wuhan Huaxia Star Industrial Products Design Co., Ltd
Manufacture / Wuhan Huaxia Star Industrial Products Design Co., Ltd

该全罩激光切割机具有光电转换率高和能耗低的优点，节省运行成本和维护成本。使用光纤传输，节省外光路镜片，结构稳定，减少机床故障率。排屑区设计严谨，合理的处理加工废料。表面处理采用喷塑，零污染。产品使用钣金折弯焊接工艺使线条硬朗、部件精细。正面与侧面采用线条包边、局部使用不锈钢板以及使用灯带作为修饰，都是产品设计亮点。

This optical fiber laser cutting machine is good of the high photoelectricity transformation rate and low consumption rate. Adopting fiber transmission saves light path outside the lens, and has a stable structure, effectively reduce the failure rate.

智能深槽匀翻机
Intelligent Deep Groove Turner

设计 / 北京中科博联环境工程有限公司
生产 / 北京中科博联环境工程有限公司
Design / Beijing GreenTech Environmental Engineering Ltd
Manufacture / Beijing GreenTech Environmental Engineering Ltd

智能深槽匀翻机是城市污泥、生活垃圾、畜禽粪便等废弃物好氧生物发酵处理的关键设备，具有处理能力强、效率高、翻抛均匀、智能化控制等特点。电动机和减速机于旋转滚筒内，动力传输效率高。应用自动定位等技术，实现远程智能化控制。采用不锈钢加抗氧化喷漆工艺，耐腐蚀、抗脱落、寿命长。局部亮色及声光电有提醒功能，黑白相间体现未来感。

Intelligent deep groove turner is the key technological equipment in aerobic fermentation (compost) engineering, dealing with municipal sludge, municipal solid waste, poultry manure and other organic solid wastes. This product is characterized by large processing capacity, high efficiency, uniform turning and intelligent control. With a unique structure design which sets motor and speed reducer in the rotating drum, the power transmission efficiency is raised to 95%. Moreover, with the automatic positioning method, the remote monitoring and other modern scientific and technological achievements, intelligently remote control is achieved, preventing operators from direct contact with poisonous gas.

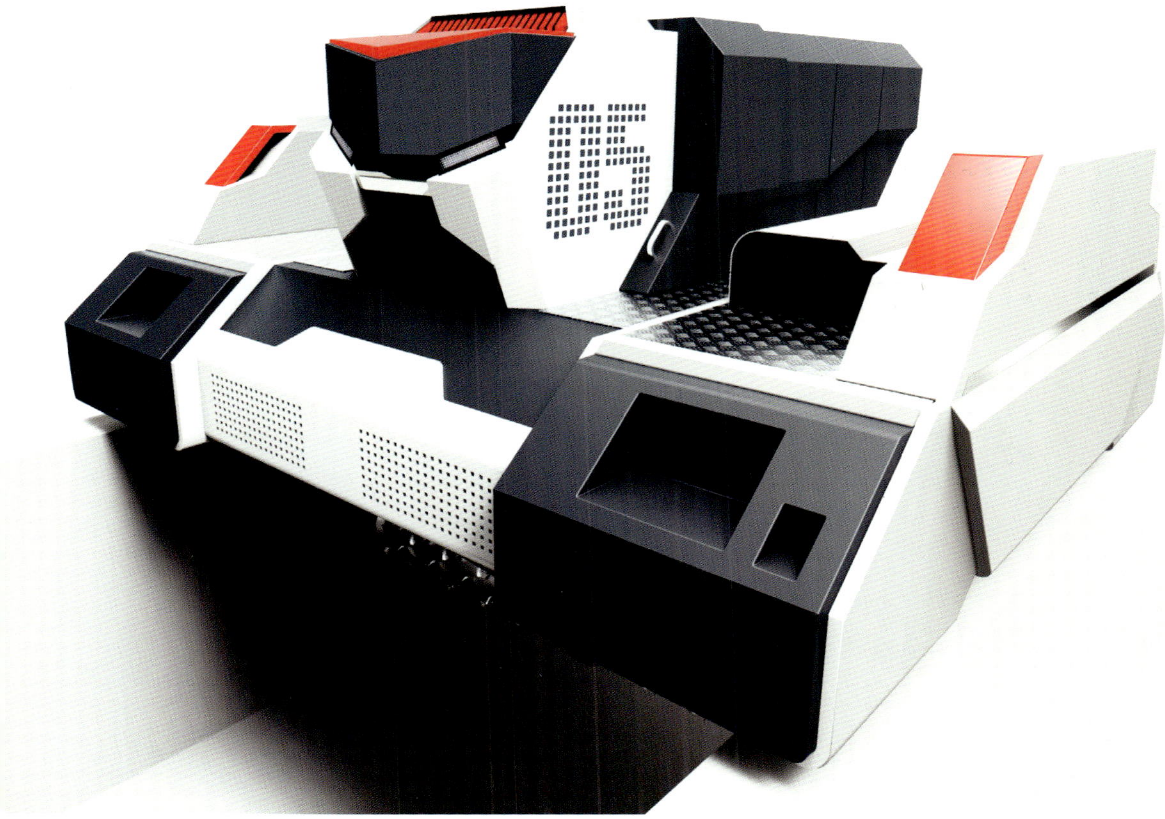

扫一扫查看产品 Pin3D 技术三维效果图
Scanning for the 3D image by Pin3D

XM1003S 铣刨机
XM1003S Milling Machine

设计 / 江苏徐州工程机械研究院工业设计中心
生产 / 徐州工程机械集团有限公司
Design / ID Center of Jiangsu Xuzhou Construction Machinery Research
Manufacture / Xuzhou Construction Machinery Group Inc.

该产品为国际先进中型铣刨机，使用自动找平系统、自动功率控制、全液压四驱驱动，铣刨深度实现精确控制与自动控制。大容积油箱和水箱，一次工作持续更久。采用机械折叠输料装置，便于整机运转。铣削旧料实现二次利用，降低生产成本，工作效率高。外观设计将“龙”元素融入其中，色彩分割合理，造型细节丰富，品牌识别感强。

XM1003S is an international standards medium-sized milling machine, which is a pioneer of using the automatic leveling system, automatic power control and fully hydraulic four-wheel drive technology in China. The large volume of fuel tank and water tank enables a longer duration of operation. The mechanical folding conveying device is a clever installation to operate the machine easier. The "dragon" modeling language is integrated into the new design of XM1003S.Tank hoardings and tank's both sides of hem are absorbed the shape of dragon head and dragon horn.

单光子发射计算机断层成像系统
Single Photon Emission Computed Tomography, SPECT

设计 / 北京智加问道科技有限公司
生产 / 北京天地智慧科技有限公司
Design / ZCO Design Co.,Ltd
Manufacture / Beijing TianDi Zhihui Technology Co.,Ltd

本产品是国内首款具有自主知识产权的单光子发射计算机断层成像系统，可同时产出 SPECT 图像、CT 图像或两者融合图像，实现高对比度和细腻图像效果，方便诊断数据图像的采集，综合性能领先国际。产品采用可回收医用级塑料和金属，外观采用精密模具注塑成型。设计灵感来自海豚，融入简约流畅的生命曲线，富有生命感，消除患者的恐惧感。

This product is the China's first independent intellectual property rights of the single photon emission computed tomography(SPECT), which can optimize SPECT and CT and produce fusion SPECT image or both fusion images, and achieve higher contrast, more subtle image effect, the overall performance of leading international similar manufacturers in the low dose level of radiation. The product uses the recyclable medical grade plastics and metal and the finishing of color injection molding.

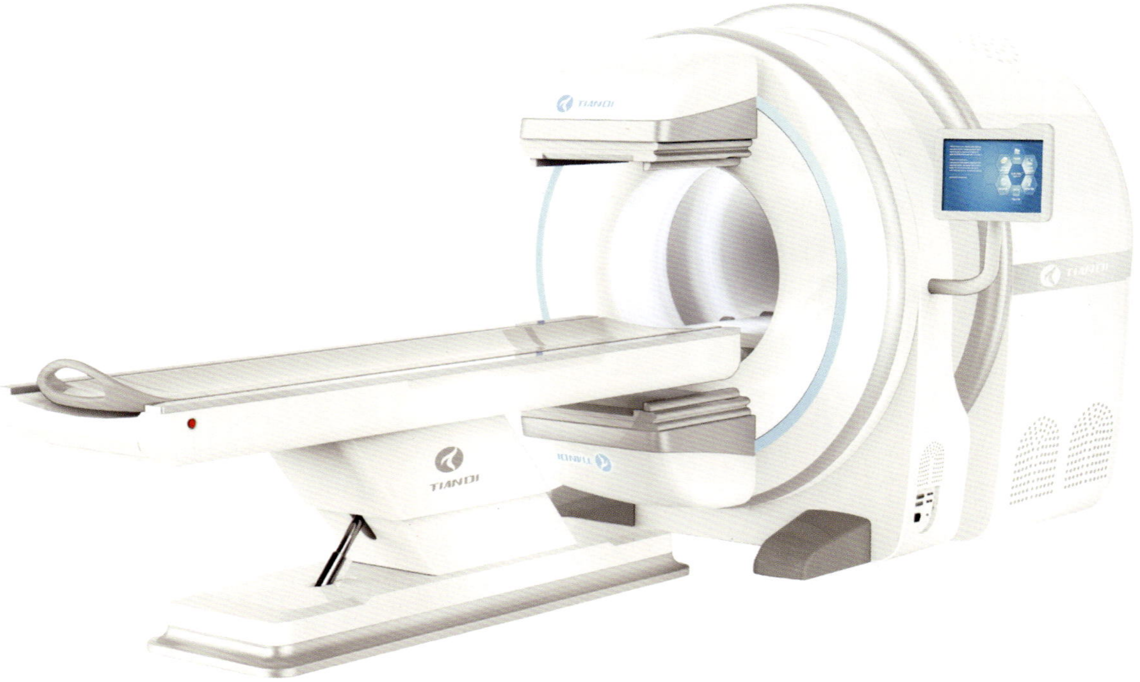

3C 行业大幅面专用镭雕机
3C Industry Large Special Laser Engraving Machine

设计 / 武汉华夏星光工业产品设计有限公司
生产 / 武汉华夏星光工业产品设计有限公司
Design / Wuhan Huaxia Star Industrial Products Design Co., Ltd
Manufacture / Wuhan Huaxia Star Industrial Products Design Co., Ltd

该镭雕机采用单模输出，光斑精细，峰值功率高。工作幅面大小可定制，伺服驱动，精度高。操作区把散乱按钮组合一起，操作舒适。产品适合恶劣环境，界面友好。产品采用局部包围设计，减少装配难度及外围钣金数量，节约成本。产品运用黑色贯穿大面积白色中，运用红色点亮，更加生动。产品采用圆角穿插造型，硬朗的线条突出大型机械设备美感。

This laser etching machine adopts single mode output which is spot fine and high power during the peak period. Integration of the separate buttons makes a better user experience. Highlighted by red, the all black and white body looks more vivid. The sharp lines indicate a beauty of heavy equipments.

C400K 斜轨式数控铣床
C400K Inclined Rail Type CNC Milling Machine

设计 / 武汉华夏星光工业产品设计有限公司
生产 / 武汉华夏星光工业产品设计有限公司
Design / Wuhan Huaxia Star Industrial Products Design Co.,Ltd
Manufacture / Wuhan Huaxia Star Industrial Products Design Co.,Ltd

该数控铣床采用伺服主轴无极调速，液压卡盘，卧式八工位刀架和封闭式防护。伺服电机通过弹性联轴节与精密滚珠丝杠直连，精度高，丝杠两端固定，提高支撑度。采取减少主轴热变形的措施，提高稳定性。本产品设计为不规则形态，如船帆耸立，运用灯带设计寓意清晨阳光，采用红黑白经典配色。产品造型简单大方，装配简单，功能强大。

This CNC milling machine adopts servo spindle infinitely adjustable-speed, hydraulic chuck, the eight horizontal location tool post and the enclosed protection. The spindle box has taken measures to reduce the spindle thermal deformation to keep the relative stability of the main axis, making the main shaft to work as long as possible. The irregular shape implies the sails, light belt is designed the sunshine of the dawn.

全自动装卸车
Automatic Loading and Unloading Car

设计 / 武汉华夏星光工业产品设计有限公司
生产 / 武汉华夏星光工业产品设计有限公司
Design / Wuhan Huaxia Star Industrial Products Design Co.,Ltd
Manufacture / Wuhan Huaxia Star Industrial Products Design Co.,Ltd

该全自动装卸车采用外置式智能充电器，可靠方便。大功率泵站电机缩短起升时间，提高工作效率。低重心设计，彰显更好的稳定性。采用全电动动力，经济环保。装卸车大体采用钢架结构，在电机和操作区域采用注塑工艺，刚柔并济的材质对比彰显叉车体量感。产品配色为黄与黑。叉车前部设计棱角分明，充满力量感。

This auto-loader is a reliable and convenient product comparing with the others. The super power pump motor could shorten the time of lifting and greatly raise the efficiency. The low gravity design makes it stable. Powered with electricity, the loader adopts an external smart charger, is more eco-friendly. The steel frame structure and the lines bring a powerful feeling.

蓝宝石切割机
DGNXQ300 Sapphire Cutter Machine

设计 / 沈阳梵天工业设计有限公司
生产 / 重庆机床（集团）有限责任公司
Design / Shenyang Fantian Industrial Design Co.,Ltd
Manufacture / Chongqing Machine Tool (Group) Co., Ltd

该设备是为切割手机、手表等蓝宝石屏幕而设计的专用设备，全球领先，广泛应用于高端精密产品制造。采用最新专利切割技术，提升成品率，降低成本。优化结构，防护更严密，提升安全性，同时减少占地面积和材料使用。产品外观色调以蓝白黑为主，将专用的三色带识别系统至于侧面，正面采用全亚克力，彰显产品科技感和稳重感。

The DGNXQG300 is a new leader of sapphire cutter in sapphire screen cutting equipment. The product utilizes the newest patented cutting technology, raising finishing rates above 30% and drastically reducing sapphire cutting costs. After structural adjustments, we have not only decreased its area but also correspondingly reduced material usage, thus optimizing the product's overall price ratio. The special-use three-ribbon identification system is located on the machine's side. Its front is made exclusively from acrylic, highlighting the product's high-tech, stable feel.

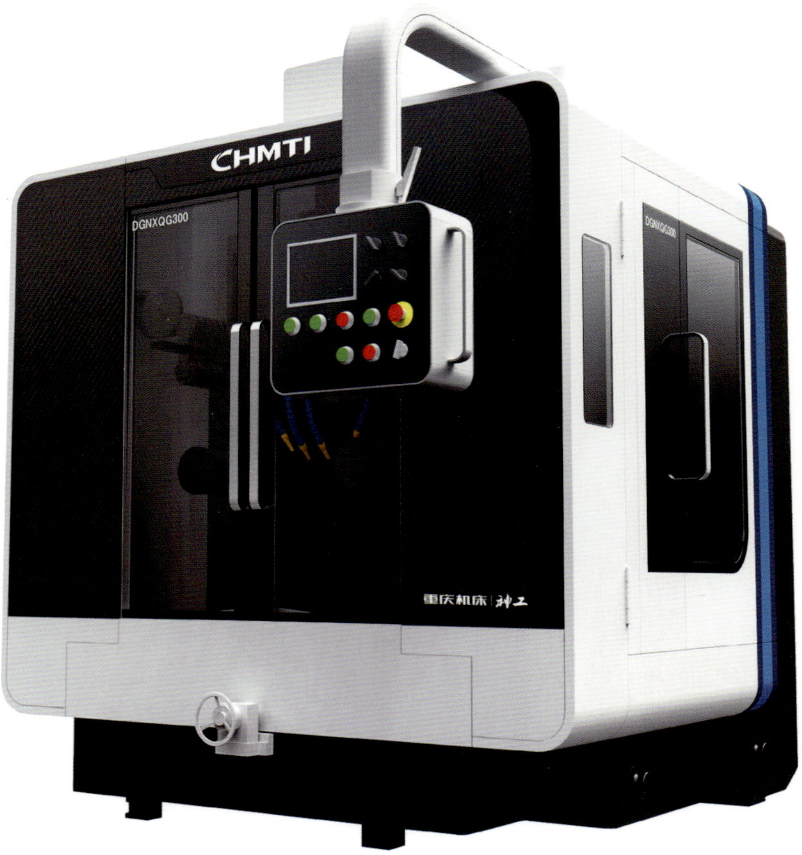

SGTH160 滚车复合机床
SGTH160 Compound Machine Tool

设计 / 沈阳梵天工业设计有限公司
生产 / 重庆机床（集团）有限责任公司
Design / Shenyang Fantian Industrial Design Co.,Ltd
Manufacture / Chongqing Machine Tool (Group) Co., Ltd

SGTH160 滚车复合机床，采用了创新的模块化设计和制造，以简约的设计理念去除不必要的结构部分，大大降低了采购费用和维护成本，且在排油排污方面引入了最先进的环保技术，具有绝对的市场竞争优势。其左右两侧防护板和主要部件的防护立面都采用了圆弧造型，这一设计提升了品牌识别力，使其成为真正意义上的高端机床典范。

The SGTH160 Compound Machine Tool utilizes an innovative modular design and manufacture, creating machines or machine production lines. According to users’ manufacture needs, we offer users different modules, allowing our product to offer single functions such as gear hobbing, turning, chamfering for burr removal, milling of metals, drilling, measuring as well as automatic workpiece transport. Unlike the partial edge arc modeling of past machine products, the SGTH160's side fender panels and fender walls of primary components utilize arc construction.

五星 V 型刹把
The Five-star V Brake Handle

设计 / 杭州汉度工业设计有限公司
生产 / 五星车业有限公司
Design / Hangzhou HUMTA Industrial Design co., Ltd
Manufacture / The Five-star Vehicle Industry Co., Ltd

五星 V 型刹把，其 V 型平行转动结构为刹把提供了均匀平行的间距，减少了转动刹把时需要的用力，对女性和手较小的使用者来说更容易掌控。精简了刹把的零部件，使产品整体强度增强的同时节省了模具生产成本。在设计方面，新型结构使刹车线靠近自行车手把，便于刹车线的固定。产品采用可回收型 PC 材料，减少对环境的污染。

V-shaped structure design provides a uniform parallel spacing, it's easy for women and hand smaller users to control. Adopted in the design of a new type of V type structure, such product's internal structure can be streamlined, greatly reduce the production cost. V-shaped structure design makes the brake line does not need to have very big outer arc to ensure brake line pull flow. The adoption of recycled PC material could minimize pollution to the environment.

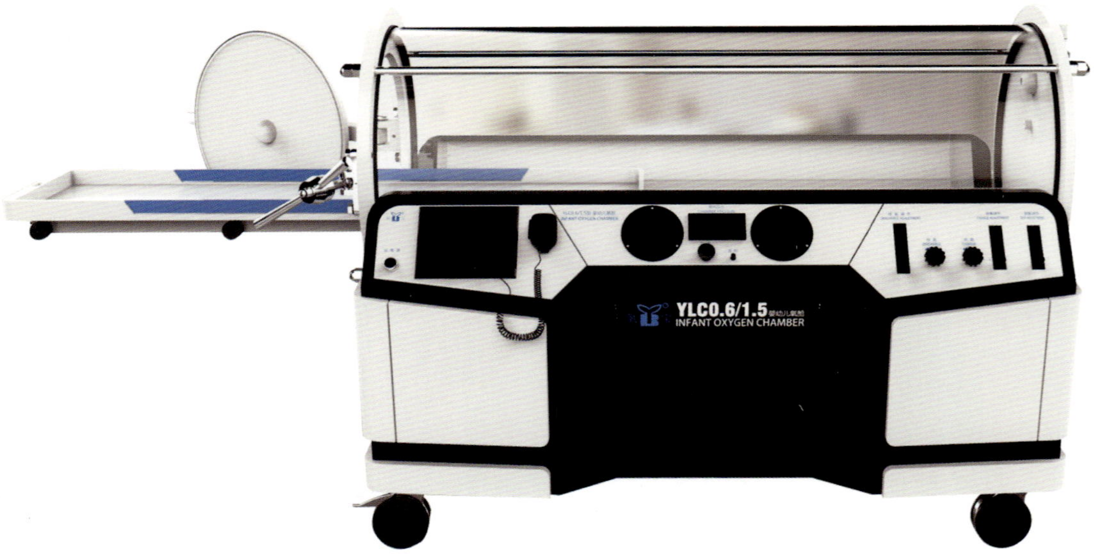

婴幼儿氧舱
Infant Oxygen

设计 / 武汉华夏星光工业产品设计有限公司
生产 / 武汉华夏星光工业产品设计有限公司
Design / Wuhan Huaxia Star Industrial Products Design Co.,Ltd
Manufacture / Wuhan Huaxia Star Industrial Products Design Co.,Ltd

婴幼儿氧舱，融入了先进的科技与概念，有效地保障了婴儿在呼吸供养不足时的生命安全。产品以大面积白色为主，圆润的造型充满着整个产品，局部凌厉的线条圆中带方，显得稳重又充满亲和力。功率小，省电节能。加工简单，易于装配量产。作为国内首批婴幼儿氧舱，基本上垄断了 90% 的市场占有率。

The infant oxygen cabin could save the infants' live while they are lack of breathing. Large area of white, the round but partially square shape is the main impression of the product. The lower power consumption makes it an energy saving product. As the first domestic product of the congeneric products, it is a 99% monopoly one in the market.

数控等离子回转割炬
CNC plasma rotary cutting torch

设计 / 武汉华夏星光工业产品设计有限公司
生产 / 武汉华夏星光工业产品设计有限公司
Design / Wuhan Huaxia Star Industrial Products Design Co.,Ltd
Manufacture / Wuhan Huaxia Star Industrial Products Design Co.,Ltd

数控等离子回转割炬，运用了模块化设计，机床龙门架采用重负载结构，割炬回转结构采用轻负载结构，机床整体结构动态特性精度高，割炬摆动结构采用新型材料，运用专利设计，轻巧耐用，角度调节速度快。数控多轴运动控制，可完成复合坡口切割。割炬初始定位采用接触电阻式方法，防碰撞装置采用了滑动结构，稳定性高。

The modular design of the gantry machine frame adopts the structure with heavy load, rotary cutting torch structure with light load structure, the overall structure of the machine dynamic characteristics and high precision, stable and smooth cutting. Through the composite motion of cutting torch, NC multi axis motion control can complete complex groove cutting. The initial positioning adopts resistance cutting, the sliding structure is utilized for the anti-collision device, enables high reliability and stability

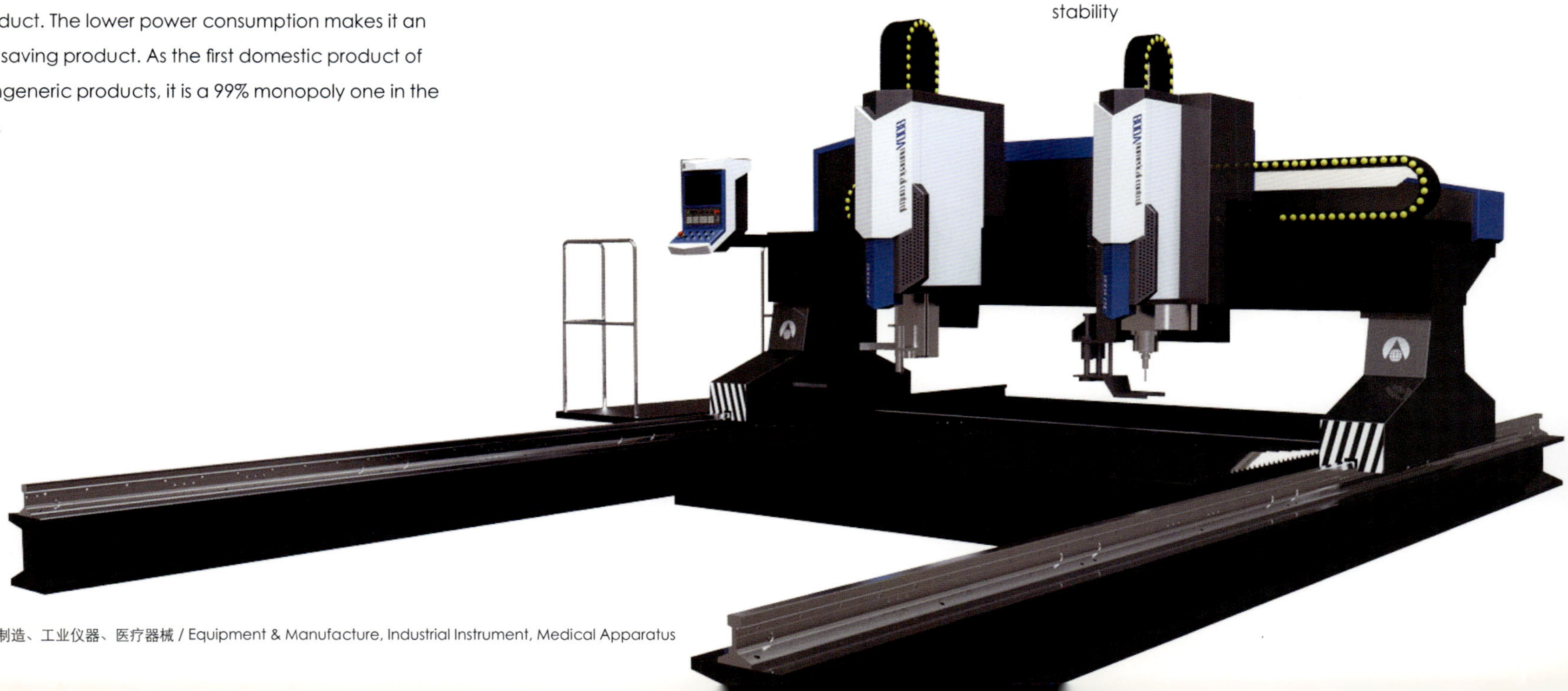

STAR3015 全罩激光切割机
Star3015 Cover All Laser Cutting Machine

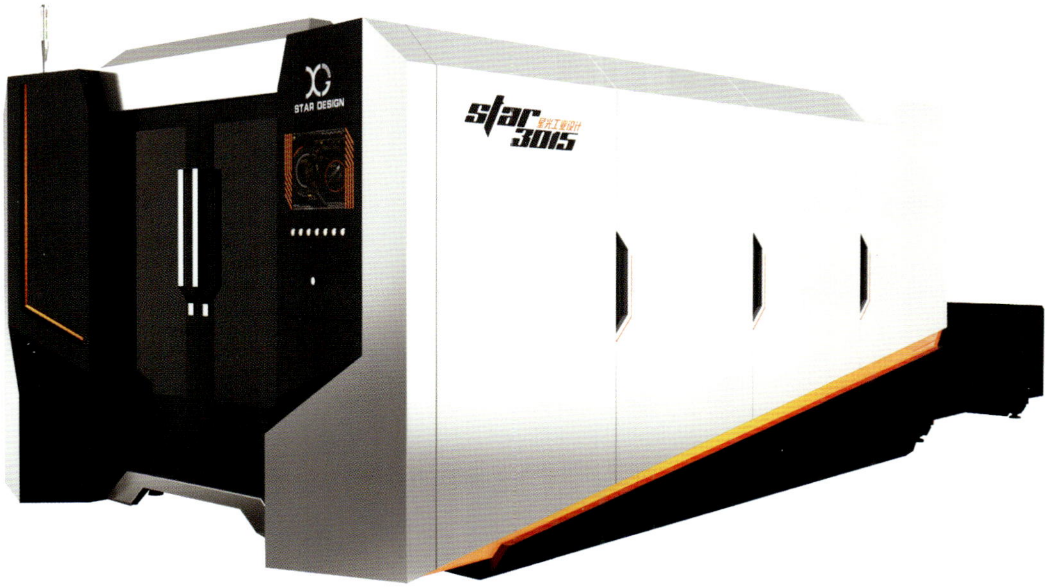

设计 / 武汉华夏星光工业产品设计有限公司
生产 / 武汉华夏星光工业产品设计有限公司
Design / Wuhan Huaxia Star Industrial Products Design Co.,Ltd
Manufacture / Wuhan Huaxia Star Industrial Products Design Co.,Ltd

STAR3015 全罩激光切割机，该产品设计风格简洁，通体采用黑白搭配，以橘红色为点缀。外光路免维护，减少机床故障率；光纤激光切割机在薄板切割方面有明显优势；高光电转换效率，节省运行成本；使用光纤传输，严谨的排屑区域设计，对于加工时产生的废料，有了更加合理的处理方式。表面处理均采用喷塑的形式，真正地达到了零污染。

The STAR3015 laser cutting machine has obvious advantages in sheet cutting, it is concise and compact, black and white adopted on the main body, highlighted with red. The use of the optical fiber transmission saves the light path outside the lens, the outside light path is free of maintenance. The high rate of fiber transmission saves running cost.

XS395 单钢轮振动压路机
XS395 Single Drum Vibratory Roller

扫一扫查看产品 Pin3D 技术三维效果图
Scanning for the 3D image by Pin3D

设计 / 江苏徐州工程机械研究院工业设计中心
生产 / 徐州工程机械集团有限公司
Design / ID Center of Jiangsu XuZhou Construction Machinery Research
Manufacture / XuZhou Construction Machinery Group Inc.

XS395 单钢轮振动压路机，借助了中国传统龙文化的设计元素。采用徐工自主知识产权的定向振动轮，能够输出强大的有效对地作用力；基于人机工程的操纵系统设计，确保操作者的安全舒适性；采用模块化设计，整机工作质量 36 吨。结构设计的优化和新材料的使用，降低产品模具的费用。采用满足欧 Ⅲ 排放标准的进口发动机，满足排放要求。

In the process of design, the dragon element was melted into the product, realizing the of product design. Using the directional vibration wheel with XCMG's own independent intellectual property right, it can output powerful effective ground forces with high impact depth and high compaction efficiency. The design of control system is based on ergonomics, ensuring the safety and comfort to the operator. Adopting modularity design, the machine's working weight is 36 tons, maximum 39 tons. Roller, as one of the earth-moving machinery, was mainly used for road compaction work.

GR215K 平地机
GR215K Motor Grader

设计 / 江苏徐州工程机械研究院工业设计中心
生产 / 徐州工程机械集团有限公司
Design / ID Center of Jiangsu XuZhou Construction Machinery Research
Manufacture / Xuzhou Construction Machinery Group Inc.

GR215K 平地机，采用变功率控制技术、独立散热技术、负荷传感等多项国际先进技术，降低了整机油耗；采用加强型作业装置，提升了作业性能，减小了操纵力，并创新引入全新双控手柄操作模式，降低了操纵者的劳动强度；采用了多种减震降噪技术，降低了驾驶室内噪声；采用满足欧 Ⅲ 排放标准的进口发动机，满足排放要求。

Adopting a brand-new design platform and appearance, the new GR215K Motor Grader uses many international advanced technologies, including the variable power control technology, the independent cooling technology and the load sensing technology, etc. Moreover, the application of enhanced operation device improves the operating performance and decreases the operating force, greatly reducing the labor intensity of the driver. It is innovatively equipped with two handles for operation, instead of ten handles of the old version, giving a better experience to the driver.

扫一扫查看产品 Pin3D 技术三维效果图
Scanning for the 3D image by Pin3D

电动座驾式叉车
Electric Forklift

设计 / 杭州领跑者工业设计有限公司
生产 / 杭州昱透实业有限公司
Design / Hangzhou LPZ Industrial Design Co. Ltd
Manufacture / Hangzhou Yu Tou Industrial Co., Ltd

电动座驾式叉车，进行了结构的重新布局，将警示灯置于车架顶端，加高护顶架，打造出一款国内最小的电动平衡式叉车。底盘动力后置的三轮驱动形式，使产品转弯时更易控制速度，增加稳定性。产品采用经久耐用的玻璃钢材质配合钢制门架来完成支撑需求。而表面的喷涂工艺带来了产品的主要色调表现，以及产品表面质感的视觉传达。

The design aims to create a compact, more flexible and adapt to different environments refined type car truck. The warning lamp is placed to the top frame, causing the driver to avoid visual interference. The postpositional 3-wheel driven form of the chassis makes the product easier turning around.

电动托盘搬运车
Electric Pallet Truck

设计 / 杭州领跑者工业设计有限公司
生产 / 杭州昱透实业有限公司
Design / Hangzhou LPZ Industrial Design Co. Ltd
Manufacture / Hangzhou Yu Tou Industrial Co., Ltd

电动托盘搬运车，将护臂做成翻转的形式，让产品适应不同复杂的使用场景。置物台的首创引入是为了解决工人随手工具放置的问题。产品保证核心部件尽量与产品重心保持一致，提高了驾驶时的安全系数。前端叉具的校准帮助驾驶员直观地测量叉取货物的安全范围。细节的喷涂工艺和人机分析，使得产品成为工业和美学完美结合的典范。

Electric Pallet Truck flips up the armband parts to adapt the product to different scenario of using, innovatively solve the problem of placing tools. The core components are in accordance with the product gravity center to improve the security. Front fork's calibration could help the operator to measure the safe scale of lifting the cargo.

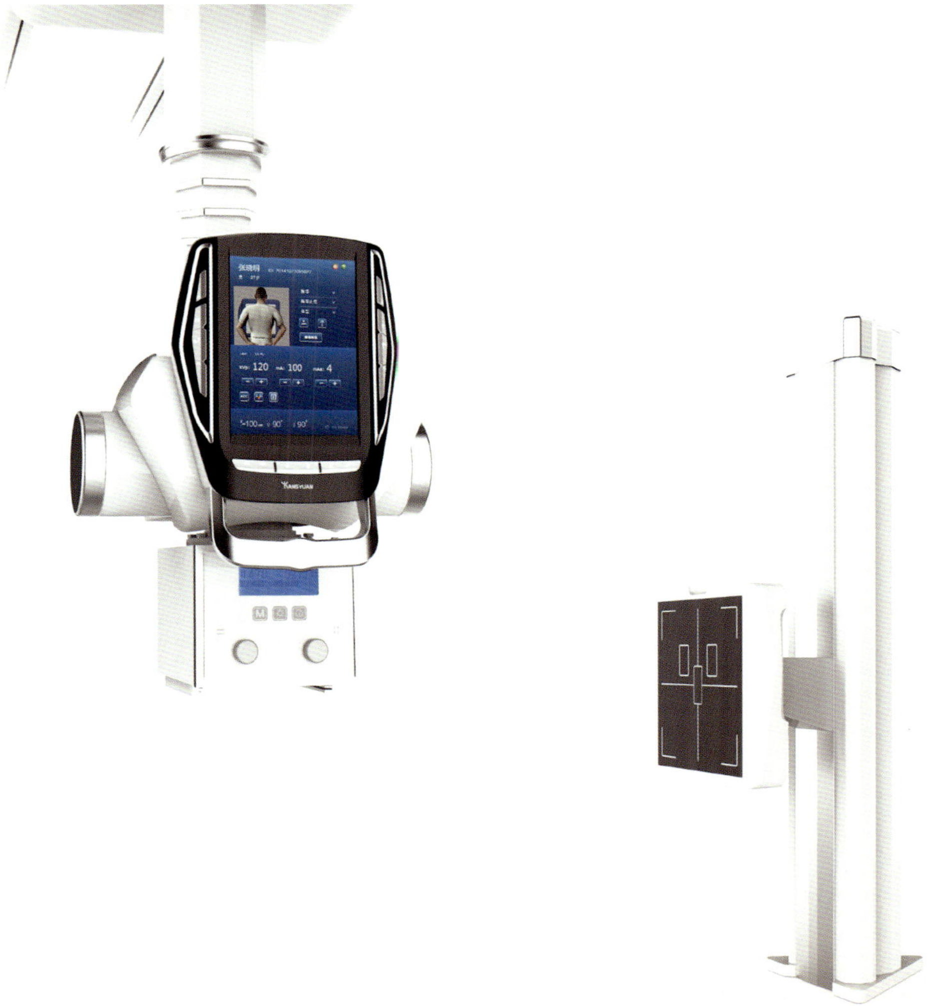

数字 X 射线摄影系统
X-Ray Digital Radiographic System

设计 / 杭州领跑者工业设计有限公司
生产 / 浙江康源医疗器械有限公司
Design / Hangzhou LPZ Industrial Design Co. Ltd
Manufacture / Zhe Jiang Kangyuan Medical Devices Co., Ltd

X 射线摄影系统，是运用 X 射线进行病变诊断的医疗产品。产品将按键设计在主要视觉特征的主屏幕周围，既符合操作人员的医疗作业习惯，也帮助操作人员更高效地进行操作。在工艺上，结合并引入了吸塑、注塑、电镀工艺，提高了产品的高端品质感。突出的色彩对比可帮助提高操作行为的流畅度，彰显了工业设计之美。

X-ray imaging system, is the use of X-rays the lesion diagnostic medical products. Home screen button design around main visual features is consistent with the medical work habits of the operator, to distinguish between different shades of color and texture contrast different visual senses, but also help the operator to operate more efficiently, while avoiding the misuse. In the process, we combine the introduction of plastic, injection molding, plating process, is to improve the high quality feel of the product.

摩天轮防雾霾口罩
Motlun

设计 / 杭州领跑者工业设计有限公司
生产 / 北京雷果科技有限公司
Design / Hangzhou LPZ Industrial Design Co.,Ltd
Manufacture / Beijing Leiguo Technology Co.,Ltd

摩天轮防雾霾口罩，是具有特种滤棉能真正过滤 PM2.5 的口罩。面罩主体部分采用食品级硅胶，耳带采用防水材料，呼气阀主体加工工艺为原色塑料注塑，干净环保。硅胶内壁通过人机工学设计紧贴面部，进气口采用独创的旋涡式，舒适的佩戴形式从硅胶到耳带全部按照人体头部的曲线设计，将工业美学与产品功能性紧密结合。

PM2.5 filter is realized by leading special filter cotton, silica gel inner wall through the man-machine engineering design close to the face, to ensure absolute seal, the original vortex type air inlet, in giving the appearance of a more dynamic and to solve the traditional masks for sealed, lead to high pressure influence respiratory comfort degree.

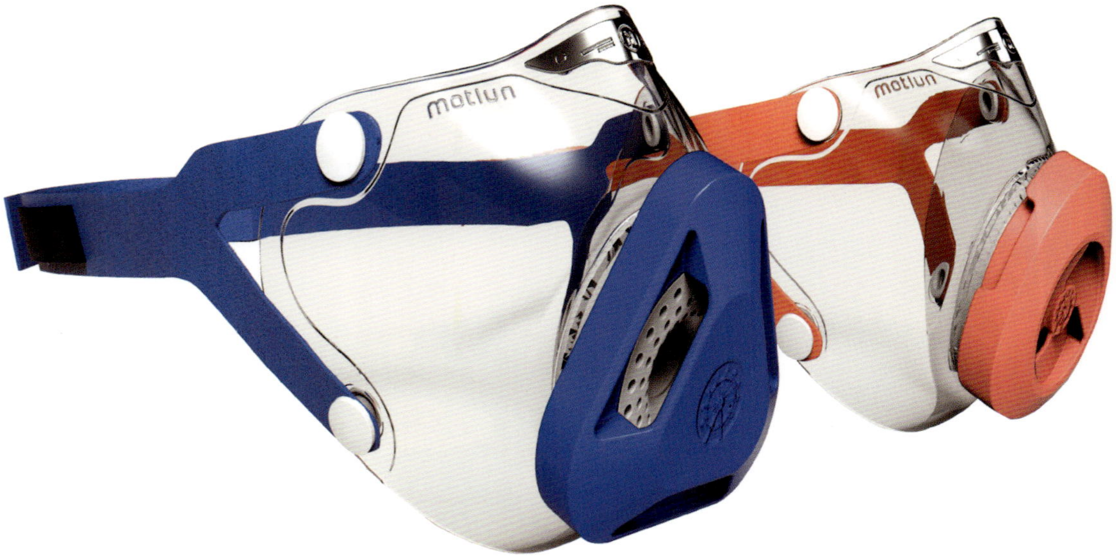

静脉注射辅助器
Intravenous Auxiliary Device

设计 / 杭州汉度工业设计有限公司
生产 / 杭州普勒佳生物科技有限公司
Design / Hangzhou HUMTA industrial design Co.,Ltd
Manufacture / Hangzhou PLJ Biomedical Instrument Co.,Ltd

这是一款为完善婴儿及儿童的静脉注射辅助系统开发的辅助器械。通过蘑菇头的设计解决了婴儿手腕固定难、自然弯曲难的问题。造型简洁圆润，将辅助注射区、储存区和胶带区整合起来，产品整体性强。产品采用塑料件，局部使用硅胶材质，增加使用舒适感。该产品能为新护士带来注射便利，减轻婴儿及儿童在静脉注射时带来的疼痛。

The auxiliary equipment is designed for intravenous injection for infants and babies. The mushroom head design solves the issue of the infants' wrist fixing and bending. Overall shape is round and concise, effectively integrates the infection area, storage area and tape area. Silicon is adopted partially to make patients more comfortable.

SY485H 液压挖掘机
SY485H Hydraulic Excavator

设计 / 三一重机有限公司
生产 / 三一重机有限公司
Design / Sany Heavy Machinery Ltd
Manufacture / Sany Heavy Machinery Ltd

SY485H 液压挖掘机，采用电控正流量、AOCT 自寻优控制系统、增功率控制等多项技术，优化主阀内部结构及再生通道，并通过自主研发控制系统实时调整流量。其主要结构件采用加强型设计，使得整机作业性能更稳定。整机造型大气、简洁、轮廓硬朗，使用切割手法处理，色彩分明，注重立体表现，彰显出矿石机刚毅、稳重的个性形象。

SY485H Hydraulic Excavator features electrical control, positive flow, AOCT optimisation control system and power boosting control technologies. The overall machine design is noble, strong and with sense of simplicity. The way lines are designed and the way colors are segmented make the machine look powerful, dynamic and easy to stand out.

大小便护理机
Urine Nursing Machine

设计 / 杭州汉度工业设计有限公司
生产 / 浙江新丰医疗器械有限公司
Design / Hangzhou HUMTA Industrial Design Co., Ltd
Manufacture / Zhejiang Xinfeng Medical Instrument Co., Ltd

全自动排泄处理系统的感应器可以自动感应，自动冲洗粪便，用温水和暖风清洁病人的排便部位。产品通过收集粪便，负离子净化以及触媒除臭，能够消除室内异味，减少由于空气污染而引起的感染。吸座采用分离设计，硅胶护罩易于替换，能有效避免病人的交叉感染。产品主体采用白色，造型简洁亲和，符合医疗行业的特有属性。

Automatic excretion processing system could automatically detect and clean the faeces, wash and dry the defecation. The product could eliminate the smell by collecting the faeces, also decrease the infection by polluted air. The separation design especially for suction chassis could avoid the second infection.

冷媒检漏仪
Refrigerant Leak Detector

设计 / 陈浩
生产 / 江苏省精创电气股份有限公司
Design / Chen Hao
Manufacture / Jiangsu Jingchuang Electronics Co.,Ltd

冷媒检漏仪，创新采用半导体纳米技术传感器，对所有卤化（包括氯和氟）制冷剂起作用，能快速检测到更小的制冷剂泄漏量。采用工程塑料(POM)热塑性材料，经模具注塑成型，前壳体采用本体不透明 POM 加透明 PC 双色成型工艺，防护等级显著提高。产品外观酷似鲨鱼，以曲线贯穿整体，符合人机需要。体积小巧，操作简便，携带方便。

Innovative sensor, the semiconductor nano technology create a new leak detector industry benchmarking. Compared with the traditional leak detector, product service life extension of the 3-5 times. Can work in more bad environment, rapid detection to the smaller amount of refrigerant leakage, save the user's system maintenance and the cost.Product materials meet the ROHS standards, through the CE certification, in line with the eu testing standard, materials can be recycled.

桌面智能 3D 打印机
Table Smart 3D Printer

设计 / 詹德勇
生产 / 青岛奥德莱三维打印有限公司
Design / Zhan Deyong
Manufacture / Qingdao Oda, 3D Printing Co.,Ltd

桌面智能 3D 打印机，运用了智能化操作系统、基于云端存储技术及可实现打印自动送料与退料。标准料盘结构，安装简单，可反复利用，避免浪费。产品采用冷轧板与工程塑料相结合，在外观造型与成本之间找到平衡点，采用“大斜倒角”的元素，来体现产品的独特风格，具有很高的识别性，既有工业感，又不失时尚感。

This smart 3D printer is specifically designed for designers and artists, the precision is ±0.1mm. This product uses intelligentized operating system, basing on the cloud storage technology and automatically feeding and returning materials.It has intelligentized operating system, 6 cun touch screen, getting rid of the traditional 3D printer complicated operation method. The printer feeds and returns materials automatically, reduces the situation of cutting and blocking materials, improves the material utilization.

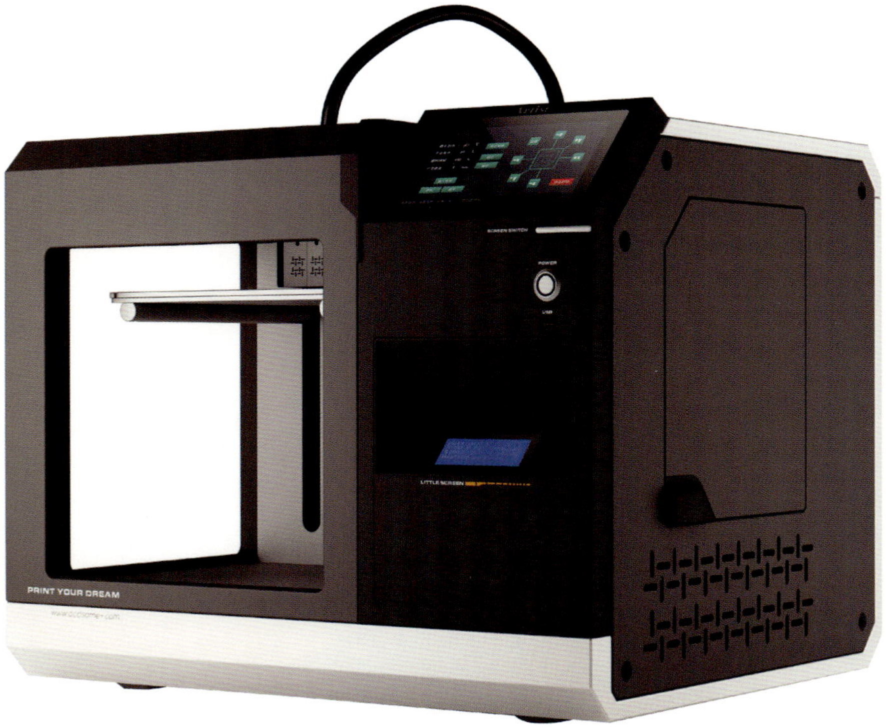

阿波罗
Apollo

设计 / 陈良格、彭博锋
生产 / 厦门唯科健康科技有限公司
Design / Chen Liangge, Peng Bofeng
Manufacture / Xiamen Voke Health Technology Co.,Ltd

本背包设计采用特殊防水材料与快接自封阀门相结合，净水过滤系统，淋浴器及增压泵可以快速地接入或拔除，从而实现一包多用。产品非常适合户外休闲、登山、露营、国内和国际旅行以及应急准备。背包涉水表面所用材料 TPU 为食品级无毒材料。外观设计上体现其简约而不简单的卓越品质，滤芯模块体积小巧精致，容易携带且使用方便。

The portable backpack is designed with waterproof fabric materials and the combination of self-sealing valve connector. It is a multi-functional outdoor backpack There are several filter cartridges available according to the actual water quality and personal needs. It is flexible and economic to get the clean water outdoor. Ideal for outdoor recreation, hiking, camping, domestic and international travel and emergency preparedness. The backpack is designed to equip a quick connect self-styled valve in the bottom side, so that products can be converted between the backpack and water storage backpack easily.

夹力持
Jawhorse

设计 / 沃伦 · 布朗
生产 / 宝时得机械（中国）有限公司
Design / Warren Brown
Manufacture / Positec Machinery (China) Co.,Ltd

夹力持是一款可折叠移动、夹紧及释放操作方便的虎钳。产品适用多种工况，可夹持门、柜子、自行车及常用工件。支撑脚可踩踏，提高稳定性，可折叠，存储方便。机身自带轮子设计， 携带方便， 无需搬运。产品采用弹性复位系统，有效保证了虎钳自动复位、连续进给等要求。整机深色金属搭配黄色操作部件，体现高品质感。

For a variety of conditions, but holding the door, cabinet, bicycle and the commonly used artifacts;Clamping and releasing of easy to operate;Supporting feet trample, improve stability; Support foot foldable,convenient storage. The fuselage with wheel design, easy to carry, without handling.It has achieved sales of 4.5 million,sales 33 million.The fully automatic robot welding technology, improving the production efficiency, guarantee the weld appearance and quality.

智能交流充电桩
AC Charging Pile

设计 / 郑州市浪尖产品设计有限公司
生产 / 凯迈（洛阳）电子有限公司
Design / Zhengzhou ARTOP Design Co.,Ltd
Manufacture / CAMA Electronics Co.,Ltd

智能交流充电桩的外观造型简约，整屏的操作界面让产品充满科技感，使界面设计也更加人性化易操作。钣金机身，具备输出侧的漏电保护功能，输出侧过流和短路保护功能、可通过手动或远方通信的方式紧急停止充电。机身使用钣金件加工，避免较大部件用塑胶件开模，以减少制作成本。产品减少了对石油资源的依赖，保护环境和空气。

In the context of the global energy crisis and environmental crisis is serious, the charging pile application can effectively reduce dependence on oil resources, to promote the development of electric vehicle industry and is conducive to environmental protection. Simple appearance, the entire screen of the operating interface to make product technology and future sense.Sheet metal body, with the output side of the leakage protection function,can be through manual or remote communication mode of emergency stop charging.

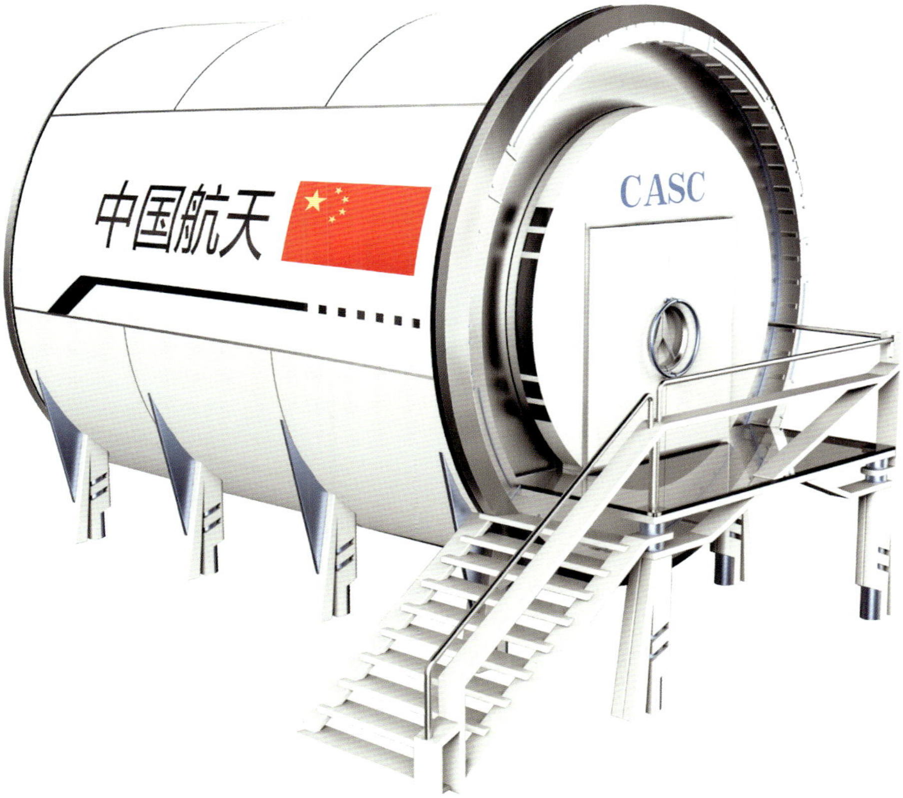

中国空间站太空试验舱
China Space Station Space Capsule

设计 / 北京智加问道科技有限公司
生产 / 北京轩宇空间技术有限公司
Design / ZCO Design Co.,Ltd
Manufacture / Sunwise Space technology Co.,Ltd

中国空间站太空试验舱是中国空间站计划中，用于地面培训宇航员体验训练的空间站模拟实验舱。设备在准确还原功能的基础上，着重强调了人性化设计。内部设计灵感来源于时空隧道，外壳和内饰承重部分多采用太空铝材质。产品采用了太空铝折弯、切割、无缝焊接等工艺，可进行模块化拆装，打造了中国新一代太空设备的高端形象。

This product which is in China Space Station Project is called space station simulation. When astronauts get into the chamber, as to simulate space station scene, they can communicate with personnel outside by operating relevant interface. On base of improved functions, the equipment focuses on humanized design, for instance, soft materials are innovatively integrated into the interior design, which makes the chamber more secure and comfortable.It highly increase speed and quantity of training and reduce training cost.

单举升机器人
Single Lifting Robot

设计 / 广东顺德潜龙工业设计有限公司
生产 / 广东嘉腾机器人自动化有限公司
Design / Chinno Industrial Design Co.,Ltd
Manufacture / Guangdong Jaten Robot

单举升机器人具有全新智能化导航系统，能够更精准地到达生产线指定位置。多重人性化设计，减少装配工人工作伤害。产品外板采用简单实用的钣金结构，激光切割焊接，内体采用框架式结构，便于批量生产、后期产品升级维护。产品运用三色 LED 灯条，具有统一鲜明的 PI 特征，操作面板集中，科技智能化外观，符合汽车生产线产品形象。

Use natural gas as fuel, reducing the environmental pollution;Efficiently recycles abandoned heat to preheat ceramic processing; reducing carbon emissions and greatly improving the energy use efficiency;New product brand image design enhances the brand and product class Ergonomic design reflects the care to the users. Synchronous with brand concept - green & energy saving, let more happiness.Uses the streamline form elements, levels varied, full of rhythm, toan otherwise boring appliances adda affinity.

UV 万能平板打印机
UV Flatbed Printer

设计 / 广东顺德潜龙工业设计有限公司
生产 / 北京上富卓勤科技有限公司
Design / Chinno Industrial Design Co.,Ltd
Manufacture / Beijing Singfull Joint Technology Co.,Ltd

UV 万能平板打印机是一台更易维修、更小巧、更易操作的万能平板打印机，不仅统一了杂乱的内部结构，更加统一了机器的外观识别系统，具有独创的唯一性。产品会对打印过程中产生的墨蒸汽进行回收处理，避免散播到空气中去。产品采用全新全透明操作视窗，让操作过程变得更加直观；操作面板升级，操作视角更人机。

Based on the research of users inter face, we creatively changed the original structure and the operation of this uv flatbed printer, finally which bring the differentiation and core competitiveness to our product.This uv flatbed printer has a smaller appearance, easy operating and easy repairing.New transparent window design, makes us easily to watch the printing process.The transparent window makes it look much smaller; Rounded design is recognizable and difficult to counterfeit; The upgraded control board offers a good operating experience.

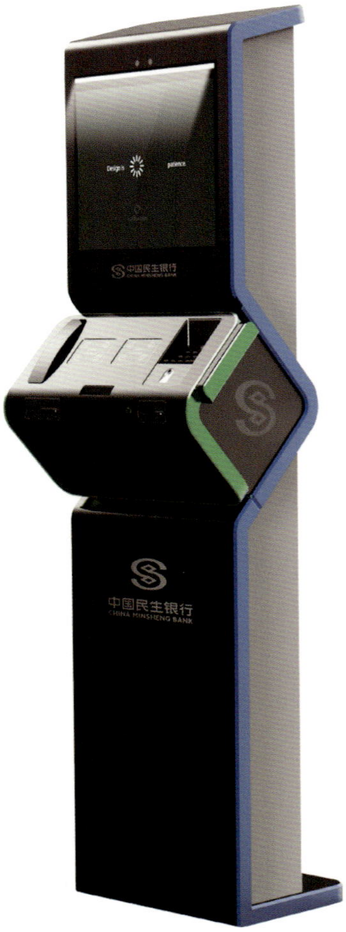

民生银行智能终端
Minsheng Banking Self-service Terminal

设计 / 成都浪尖工业设计有限公司
生产 / 深圳凯欣达信息技术股份有限公司
Design / Chengdu Artop Industrial Design Co.,Ltd
Manufacture / ShenZhen Kingstarit Information Technology Co.,Ltd

民生银行智能终端实现了智能，高效率的一体化设计，立式和壁挂式方案的模块化组合，灵活多变。产品既可分解银行办卡业务，减轻民生银行业务人员工作量，又可扩展民生银行物业市场。钣金和玻璃经久耐用、功能布局合理、环保细致。一体操作台，形态简洁、流畅，具有创造力动感，色彩搭配以品牌色为主，时尚且富有生机。

The design features a "S" shaped form extracted from the brand' s logo which symbolizes growth, with a diamond shape that vaguely represents ancient Chinese coin blended into its flowy surface profile, achieving smart and high efficiency. Modular design provides flexibility over both floor-standing and wall-mounting.Minimum decorative parts help reduce production cost.Premium materials combined with precise manufacturing process conveys an impression of quality and high-tech.

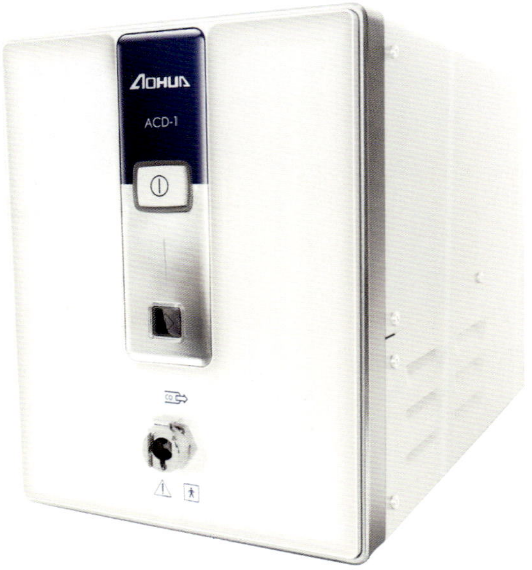

二氧化碳送气泵
Carbon Dioxide Gas Pump

设计 / 王秋波
生产 / 上海澳华光电内窥镜有限公司
Design / Wang Qiubo
Manufacture / Shanghai Aohua Photoelectricity Endoscope Co.,Ltd

二氧化碳送气泵结合使用塑料和金属，塑料具有可塑造性，金属钣金具有优良的抗压性，保护内部装置，同时对于电子屏蔽具有很好的效果。在肠胃手术过程中需要将外部的二氧化碳气体导入人体，这款产品可以减轻病人的疼痛，也更方便医生操作手术。该产品采用简洁的设计，便捷的操作方式，颜色采用大面积的白色，更具有亲和力。

In the detection of gastrointestinal diseases, endoscope is needed to penetrate into the body.Intestinal surgery, without the use of carbon dioxide gas, the patient will be very painful，the carbon dioxide pump is very practical. It follows the medical industry standards, can be put into use, at the same time,it has through clinical validation, product processing and must follow the environmental protection.

LNG 加气机
LNG Gas Dispenser

设计 / 刘晓婷
生产 / 北京联创锦程科技有限公司
Design / Liu xiaoting
Manufacture / Beijing Jincheng LIAN Technology Co.,Ltd

LNG 加气机是一款用于重型卡车、大型公交车等交通工具加液化天然气的设备。不锈钢双线金属配件，提高气密封口保护和阻止振动疲劳；高清液晶屏显示，提高了夜间的显示能力；电力调节性能，消除在供电不稳的情况下造成损坏。表面采用深灰与白色的颜色搭配，突出了设备的专业性，镂空设计又减轻了设备的沉闷感。

Independent integration, no more external control required; high-performance gas pipelines and long-lasting anti-corrosion; single Control board, and simple and high-performance design, can be operated separately and fully automatic.The product is designed as double-sided operation and symmetric display, it can be installed in different places, no customized Accessories required;

PLUS4020 全罩激光切割机
Laser Cutting Machine PLUS4020

设计 / 武汉玛吉工业设计有限公司
生产 / 武汉卡特激光工程有限责任公司
Design / Wuhan Magi Industrial Design Co.,Ltd
Manufacture / Wuhan Carter Laser Engineerir g Co.,Ltd

PLUS4020 全罩激光切割机采用电脑编程、激光切割、焊接、喷涂整套国际化流水线工艺。在结构设计上，解决了外钣金件与床身结构件在装配时间与配合上的前后配合冲突问题。产品运用柔和的手法去概括外观，使其更富灵活性。产品运用汽车碳纤维膜去强调表面质感，运用 led 炫光灯带去强调其现代科技感，促使设备类产品更现代化。

This product in the design of the first and second change devices on the semantic mechanical cold feeling, emphasize its soft, feedback from the vision to experience is a kind of friendly feeling, rather than a dull, old sink a pile of "iron".

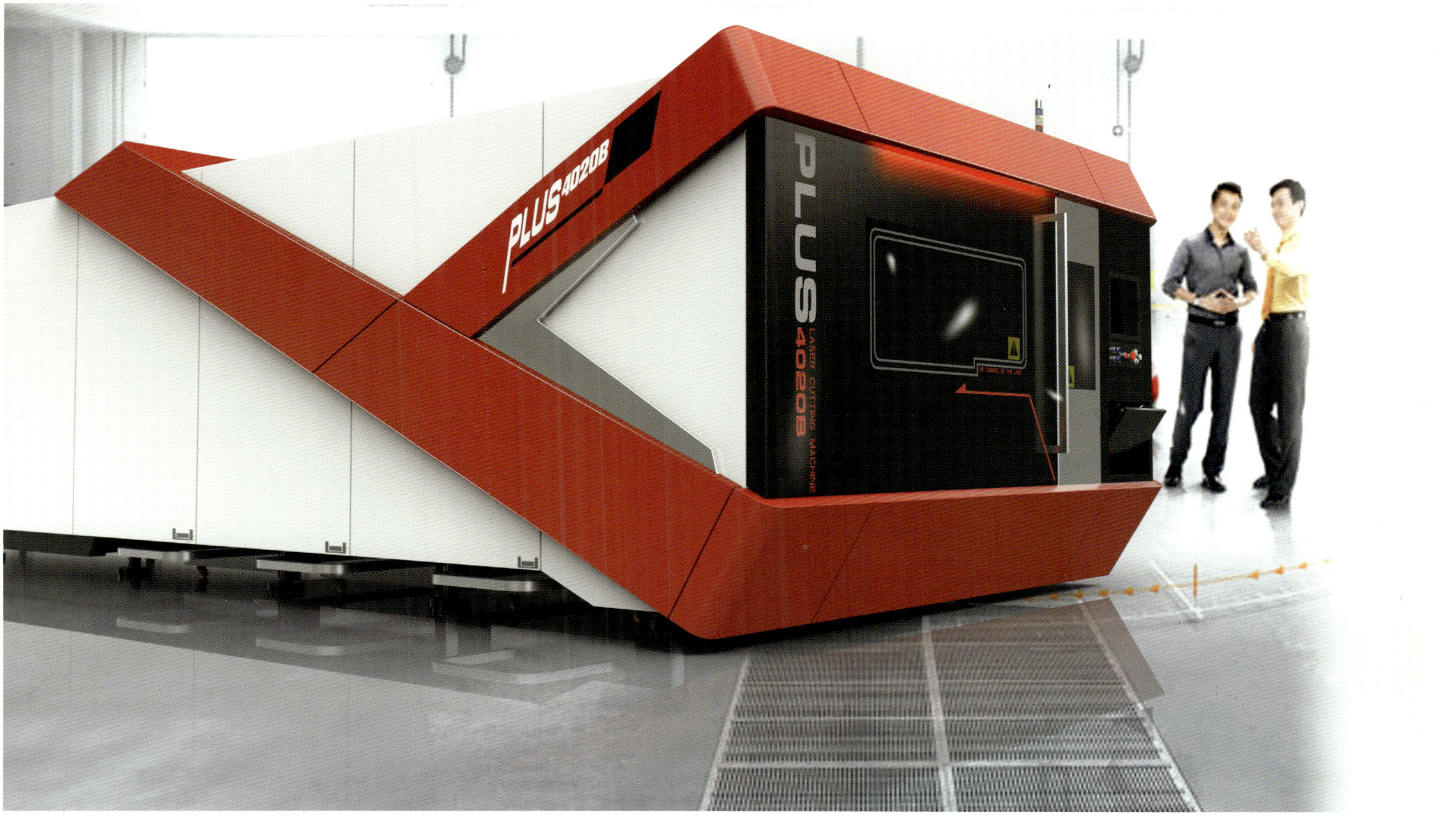

高压清洗机
Pressure Washer

设计 / 苏州本丞工业设计有限公司
生产 / 苏州洁宝机械有限公司
Design / BENCH DESIGN
Manufacture / JIEBAO

高压清洗机的主体像是一只凶猛的动物，硬朗的线条给人干净明了的感觉。左边镂空部分方便安装各种接口，右边镂空部分可以观测机油容量和收纳喷枪，机壳与产品框架巧妙连接，防止震动产生的摩擦声响。机器操作和收纳简单便捷，机体结构强度高。把手部分采用吹塑工艺，主壳体采用吸塑，泵头采用铜材质，防止生锈，最大限度延长使用寿命。

The body looks like a ferocious animal, machine head is two eyes, the left part of the hollow design, easy installation of various interfaces and other inlet and outlet, the right hollow portion can be observed and the storage capacity of oil gun pierced around each use. Enclosures and product framework ingenious connections, prevent friction sound due to vibration.The pump head is made of copper material, to prevent rust and maximum service life.

便携式个人新风系统
Respirator

设计 / 深圳市匠意科技开发有限公司
生产 / 深圳市新乐正环保科技有限公司
Design / Shenzhen Jiangyi Science
Manufacture / Shenzhen Xinlezheng Environmental Technology Co.,Ltd

该产品是世界上首款主动送风口罩，体积小，风量却是人呼吸空气量的 6 倍，适合雾霾天气下使用。口罩接触皮肤部分采用硅胶材料，可清洗消毒循环使用。用户可以自行更换滤网，耗材廉价。整个产品从模内直接注塑出来，没有经过喷涂处理，材料安全环保。设计上采用“U”和“微笑”的设计语言，整体设计成有机曲面，使产品更加舒适。

The products with the smallest volume, which guarantees the comfort in the use.It is suitable for the outdoor people in hazy weather. Besides, it is easy to carry, which ensures the breathing of fresh air at any time.In the hazy environment, the product solves the problems of low purification efficiency and disturbance in respiration of anti-dust respirator. The whole part adopts the direct injection molding with no spraying. The medical material is friendly to skin with safety and environment protection.

航母控制台
Aircraft Carrier

设计 / 上品设计机构
生产 / 中船重工
Design / Top Design
Manufacture / CSIC

此款控制台的操作面板采用了模块化设计，不仅对功能区域做了重新划分，且根据不同的操作需求对造型及结构都进行了升级，使其易拆装易操作，同时符合人机工程学，提高了单兵的工作效率。超大显示屏搭配体感摄像仪，使设备功能更加完善，操作更加方便精准。产品选择环保材料，提高了产品的使用寿命，从而节约了资源，避免浪费。

The operation panel of the console uses a modular design, not only to do a re division of the functional area,the shape and structure have been upgraded. it is easy to assemble and easy to operate.By changing the internal structure, large sculpted blocks, and functional areas of the re division, to enable the products to more in line with the ergonomics, thereby making the console operation more convenient and simple, accurate.

美容仪
Beauty Instrument

设计 / 深圳市东方艺辰工业设计有限公司
生产 / 深圳市纬安共创生物科技有限公司
Design / Shenzhen Oriental Yichen Industrial Design Co.,Ltd
Manufacture / Shenzhen Weft Ann Create Biological Technology co.,Ltd

该美容仪造型来源于鸡蛋的自然形态，柔美舒适，亲和力强，操作区域独立出来，使用方便舒适。携带方便，设计小巧，金属和塑料的完美结合，手感舒适自然。产品预置数百种自动护理程序，实现护理过程的智能化，完善运行检测功能，实现安全可靠的自检和自保护功能。产品具有较强市场竞争力，主要面向欧洲市场。

Product ideas from eggs, is inextricably linked, like a shadow like one. To achieve safe and reliable self-test and self-protection, the beauty instrument display module output advanced graphical menu interface, quick operation via color LCD information, providing beautiful and make products with strong market competitiveness, mainly for the European market.

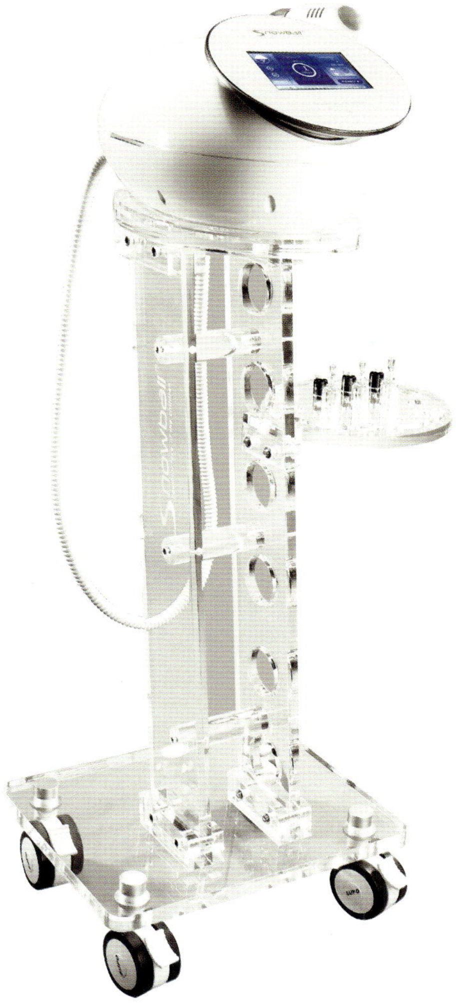

Kast 3D 打印机
Kast 3D Printer

设计 / 深圳市嘉兰图设计股份有限公司
生产 / Photon Fluid Inc.
Design / Shenzhen Newplan Design Co.,Ltd
Manufacture / Photon Fluid Inc.

Kast 3D 打印机是一种采用立体光刻（SL）技术的 3D 打印机，使用紫外线逐层照射并硬化液态光敏树脂以构建 3D 对象。它具有 96 微米的打印分辨率，能打印出表面十分光滑的 3D 对象，甚至能够打印出透镜的效果。Kast3D 打印机全身采用铝合金机身，且打印材料为光敏树脂，打印耗材损耗率非常低。设计上采用极简的风格，旋转开门的方式更节省了空间。

Kast 3D printer adopts the stereoscopic (SL) technology. It is to construct the 3D object by ultraviolet (UV) irradiation layer by layer and hardened liquid photosensitive resin. It has the 96μm printing definition (Dots Per Inch) to print the smooth 3D object without postprocessing and even with lenticular effects. Its body is made of aluminum alloy, which are recyclable materials.

医用胶片打印机
Medical Film Printer

设计 / 深圳市浪尖设计有限公司
生产 / 重庆联佰博超医疗器械有限公司
Design / Shenzhen Artop Design Co.,Ltd
Manufacture / Lianbai Medicine Co.,Ltd.

这是一款能打印出检查化验单据及胶片的医疗自助终端，具有独特又合理的模块化整合方案。采用胶片盒报告区域独立分区的形式，使外观轻盈。结构合理，符合人机工程学，操作可在一种无意识中连贯的完成。产品采用原色注塑，加工简易，便于批量生产。透明件的运用增加该产品的通透，造型与灯光的结合更具展现产品的科技感。

Using the form of separated partition in the film box reporting area, visually the machine becomes lighter, changing the original heavy square form. The report collection area is in the height above the knee on the right hand side, to ensure the coherent operation, adopting the principle of ergonomics.It allows to self print the examination documents and films with easy and simple use, and the functional zone is separated by the lights to guide the proper use.

光纤切割刀
Cutter for Fiber-Optic Cables

设计 / 深圳市浪尖设计有限公司
生产 / 中国电子科技集团公司第四十一研究所
Design / Shenzhen Artop Design Co.,Ltd
Manufacture / The 41st Research Institute of China Electronics Technology Group Corporation

这款切割机体积小、重量轻、携带方便，切割断面整齐，并采用超高硬度刀片，使用寿命长，适合单模或多模石英光纤的切割。它具有光纤一步式切割、自动回位以及切断的碎光纤自动收集功能。碎光纤收集装置中的碎光纤收集盒可方便的取出，在手操作位置有明显标识，手拿部位手感舒适，材料上使用 ABS 塑胶原色注塑，避免二次处理，免喷涂。

It has small size and light weight, portable and easy to use. It is for single-mode or multi-mode quartz fiber cut, and if replace the fiber clamp, even can cut 12-core ribbon optical cable.The cutter has one-step cutting function, automatic reset and collection of broken fibers.It applies recyclable metal and plastic injection molding process, to avoid secondary treatment and paint.

眼科 OCT
OCT Machine

设计 / 深圳市浪尖设计有限公司
生产 / 深圳市斯尔顿科技有限公司
Design / Shenzhen ARTOP Design Co.,Ltd
Manufacture / Shenzhen Certainn Technology Co.,Ltd

此款光学相干断层扫描仪提供了一个直接的、实时的视网膜各层组织剖面图，并对视网膜神经纤维层做出精确分析，提供准确的诊断数据。造型提取天鹅优美曲线，而且使用灰白蓝色彩使得产品更大方优雅。伸缩硅胶防护探头受损，内部合理的传动装置确保摇杆操作的顺滑性和平稳性。产品均采用医学专用材料，确保产品的健康环保性。

Bionic white swan, extract its dynamic delicate form of swimming. Streamlined body is full of affinity, helps eliminate the tension and pressure of patients, so that having both users and patients have a good user experience.This OCT provides a direct and real-time retina tissue profile of each layer with accurate diagnostic data. The flexible silicone protects the probe from damages and the internal gearing ensures smoothness and steady of the rocker.

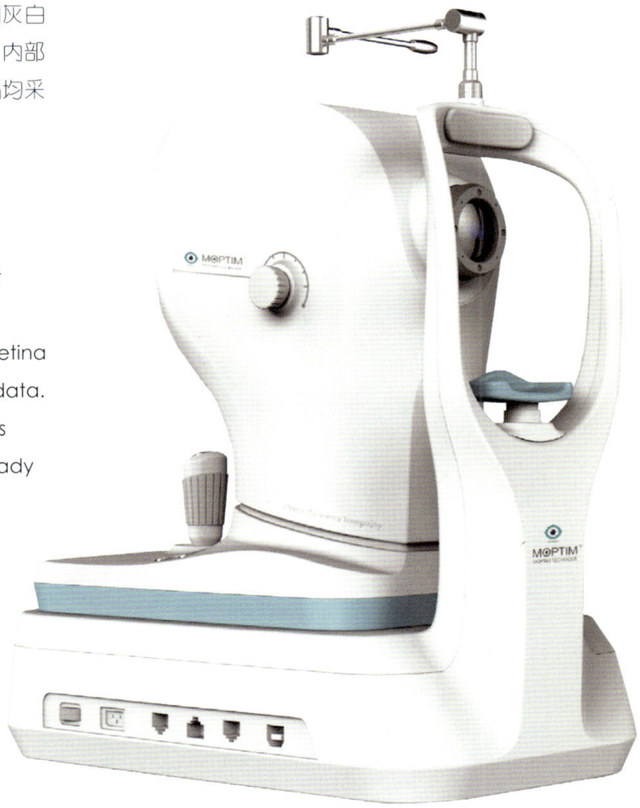

FR 云机器人
FR Cloud Robot

设计 / 武汉龙兴工业产品设计有限公司
生产 / 武汉奋进电力技术有限公司
Design / Wuhan Rising Industrial
Manufacture / Wuhan Feng Jin Power Technology Co.,Ltd

这款全新概念机器人具备远程监测、远程诊断、远程操控、远程示教等功能，还能担负起工业现场物理信息系统的信息枢纽职责，为制造执行系统的部署、机器人集群的协同工作提供了基础。产品外形采用有机的形态，柔和的边缘、缓斜的角度减少了操作过程中磕碰对操作人员以及机器本身的伤害，同时增加了视觉的柔和感。

This work relies on strong network function, the robot tasks, track, parameters and production schedule information real-time sharing to industial cloud, but also as an information hub will around the machine, cloud sensor, cloud execution and personnel information collection fusion sharing to industrial cloud.This work is more convenient and efficient mode of operation and core part are domestic parts and effectively reduce cost of the product itself.

樱花核磁共振成像
Sakura MRI

设计 / 胡海权、赵妍
生产 / 东软集团股份有限公司
Design / Hu haiquan, Zhao yan
Manufacture / Neusoft Corporation

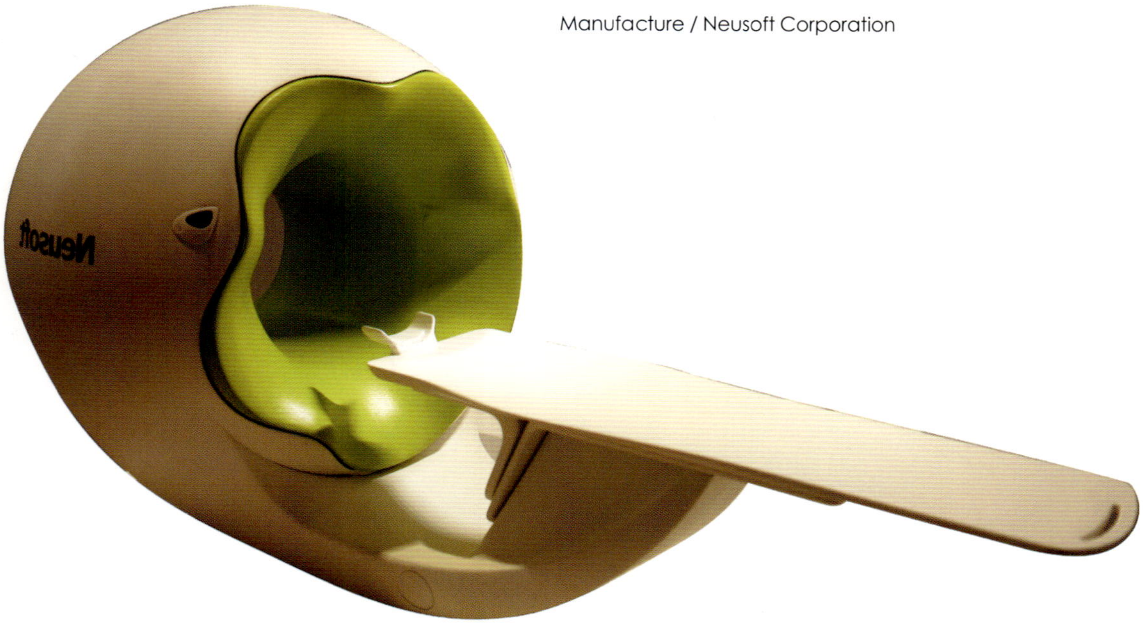

Sakura 核磁共振医疗设备摆脱了现在医疗设备冰冷的触感，整体机身呈现蛋形，内部结构以樱花为原型，犹如花瓣张开，塑造了一个充满生气活力的形态。整体外表呈现是中性的米白色，给人舒适、稳定的安全感。床体上半部分凸起，边缘便于手握和把扶，对上床和下床都有助力的作用。材料上选择绿色环保的材料，可回收再利用。

Sakura MRI equipment chooses Sakura as the prototype, shaping a form full of vitality, the overall appearance uses the white color, give people a comfortable and stable sense. It gives full consideration to the relationship between the machine and the patients. When design the MRI equipment, the upper part of the bed can be raised, and the edge is easy to hold.

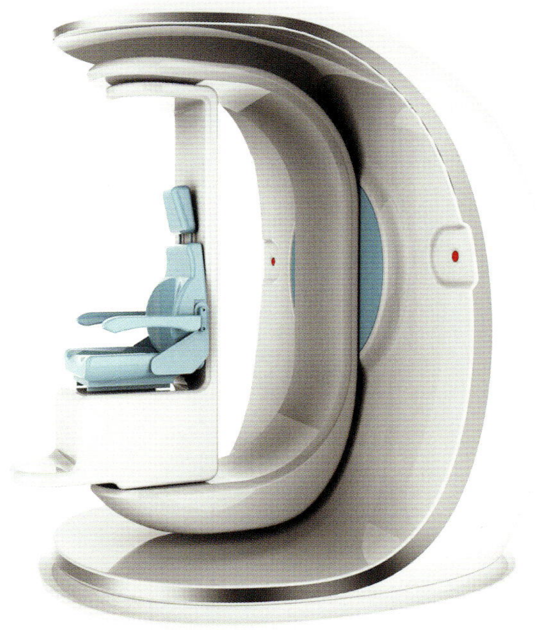

四维平衡诊断系统
Four-dimensional Balanced Diagnosis System

设计 / 温凯翔、刘程
生产 / 上元医疗
Design / Wen Kaixiang, Liu Cheng
Manufacture / Shangyuan Medical Co.,Ltd

这套四维平衡校治系统是针对有眩晕病患者的治疗诊断系统，经过从内到外的全新设计，让诊断时间更短、诊断结果更精确、治疗的效果更好，节省患者的治疗费用。我们采用新的玻璃钢加工工艺来生产整套设备，让模具达到了较高的结构强度和平整度。在设计上运用了“蛋壳”造型元素，寓意呵护，康复，传递出亲和，舒适的视觉感受。

The four-dimensional balanced school system is a diagnostic system for patients with vertigo, which has only two medical companies in China. First in the appearance of breakthrough innovation, get rid of the rigid traditional equipment and huge, heavy visual experience.This set of equipment in the design of the new process, first of all in a piecemeal approach, we do the try less demolition quantity, is reduced in the process of waste, and in late in the painting process, we adopt is environmentally friendly paint, ensure the equipment at the same time the effect, to meet the requirements of environmental protection.

手持静电纺丝仪
Hand-held Electrospinning Device

设计 / 青岛桥域产品设计有限公司
生产 / 青岛博纳生物科技有限公司
Design / Qingdao Nearbridge Product Design Co.,Ltd
Manufacture / Qingdao Bona Bio-Technique Co. Ltd

该产品是目前世界最小的电纺仪器，具有体积小、质量轻、实用性强的特点，黑白色经典搭配，简约流畅的线条，让本身小巧的体积更加轻盈、浑然一体。产品无需外接电源，单人单手手持操作，并且与手型完美结合；移动携带灵活，操作方便；能够灵活的实现多种聚合物纳米纤维材料的原位、定向沉积，实现了静电纺丝设备的跨越式的发展。

This product is the smallest electro-spinning equipment in the world, characterized by small volume, light quality and strong practicability. Having no external power supply, it is operated by single hand by one person and carried portably and flexibly, which enable various polymer nanometer fiber to complete the procedure of oriented deposition. At present, this product is the only type of portable electro-spinning equipment at the domestic and foreign market,it is concerned by researchers in the field of nanometer technology and medicine.

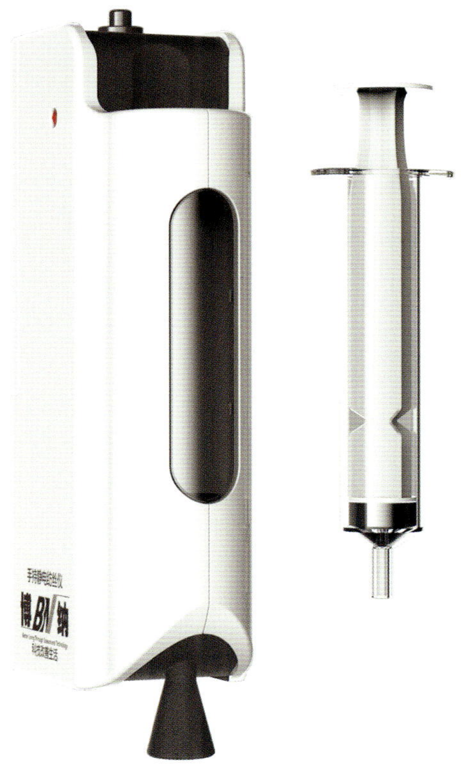

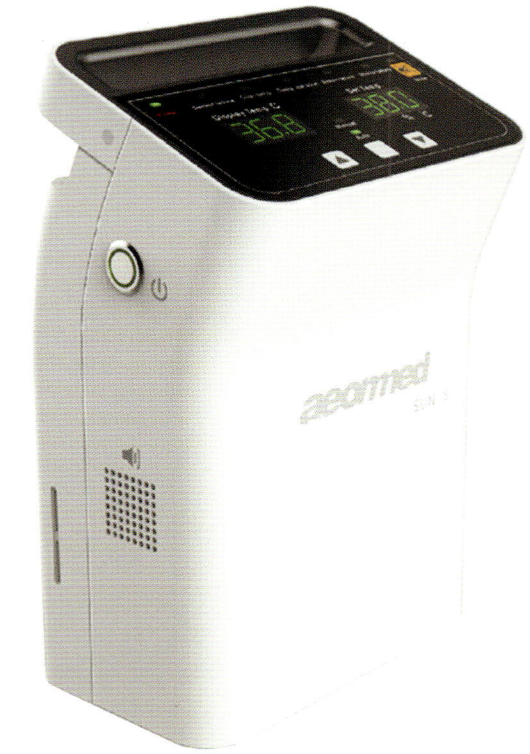

SUN 5 医用升温毯控制器
SUN 5 Medical Heating Blanket Controller

设计 / 北京谊安工业设计团队
生产 / 北京谊安医疗系统股份有限公司
Design / Beijing Aeonmed Industrial Design Team
Manufacture / Beijing Aeonmed Co.,Ltd

这是一款全国首创用电加热方式帮助手术中的患者保持体温恒定，避免低温症的出现的温控设备，拥有体积小，精度高，控制性强，加热均匀快捷等优势。整体采用钣金作为支架，医用塑壳包覆的结构方式，保证强度又减少模具投入，同时医用塑料具备抗腐蚀、抗氧化的能力，方便消毒清洗。产品外观以白色的简洁风格为主，整体简约大方。

Compact design - Equipment can be put on support arm and vertical pole by using the handle and derrick installation pieces.This is the first temperature control equipment in domestic country which applied electric heating technology to maintain patient' s body temperature and avoid hypothermia. This machine is more compact and accurate with ultra silence and stable heating function.

绅宝 CC
Senova CC

设计 / 北汽股份汽车研究院
生产 / 北京汽车股份有限公司
Design / Baic Motor
Manufacture / Baic Motor

绅宝 CC 安全性及操控性卓越，配置丰富，还有超大的后备箱储物空间。车的设计开发过程中高度重视车体轻量化设计，底盘铸铝件、碳纤维格栅及尾翼的应用，有效提高整体刚度，降低车身重量，提升安全性与加速性。简约设计的环绕式驾驶座舱，基于战机引擎矢量喷口设计的单眼双色航空科技仪表盘，尽显绅宝优异的工程设计。

Innovation design of the Senova CC uses the "BEST concept" (Big T performance, Excellent technology, "Safety" comprehensive protection, "Trend" innovative fashion design) and applies new technology and materials at the same time. Senova CC is the first model of sports car in BAIC. It has not only very excellent performance of safety and handling but also wealth configuration, such as SVA, keyless entry/startup system, stop-start system, automatic AQS dual zone air conditioning system.

绅宝 X65
Senova X65

设计 / 北京汽车股份有限公司
生产 / 北汽（广州）汽车有限公司
Design / Baic Motor
Manufacture / Baic Guangzhou Automotiue Co.,Ltd

绅宝 X65 创新继承了萨博的涡轮增压、轻量化底盘等技术因素，配备个性的 Night Panel 模式，充分实现了动力性、操控性和安全性的完美融合，搭载了车载移动互联技术等高智能化电子配置，为驾乘者带来科技感的驾驶体验。车内 3D 仪表盘设计，营造出更加立体的效果，冰蓝色背光更显科技时尚。肩线贯穿到车头，尾部线条飘逸，整体流畅又不失坚毅。

Saab X65 is equipped with Night Panel model, the full realization of the perfect dynamic performance, handling and safety of fusion, equipped with mobile Internet technology and intelligent electronic configuration. With rich configuration, equipped with a 360 degree panorama parking assist system, Telematics system, seat memory system, keyless entry,can achieve the highest level of security.

新型 100 %低地板有轨电车
The New 100% Low Floor Tram

设计 / 南车青岛四方机车车辆股份有限公司
生产 / 南车青岛四方机车车辆股份有限公司
Design / CSR QINGDAO SIFANG CO.,Ltd
Manufacture / CSR QINGDAO SIFANG CO.,Ltd

新型 100 %低地板有轨电车包括传统受电弓模式有轨电车、储能式混合动力有轨电车及氢能源有轨电车，采用永磁同步电机驱动，体积小，效率高，粘着利用好，是目前世界上最先进的驱动技术。该车造型流线、富有张力。在外观与内装色彩搭配上选用橙红色与黑色，时尚现代。客室空间宽敞通透，木质座椅富有家居性，乘坐体验舒适。

The hydrogen powered tram uses hydrogen fuel cell as the power source, operating with no catenary along the line. The hydrogen fuel cell has outstanding advantages of high efficiency and high energy density. Its rolling off the operation line fills up the blank of application of hydrogen power in tram globally.Good controllability operates relatively independently with no dependence on any external power.

电动独轮车
Powered Unicycle

设计 / 北京梦想者工业设计有限公司
生产 / 北京梦想者工业设计有限公司
Design / Beijing Dreamer Industrial Design Co.,Ltd
Manufacture / Beijing Dreamer Industrial Design Co.,Ltd

此款电动独轮车采用独特的超级跑车流线型设计风格，充分地体现了设计与科技的完美结合。它采用可以折叠的踏板设计，给使用者带来超便捷的体验。并且以电源为动力源，对环境成功实现“零污染”。本产品还采用注塑模具的加工工艺，此工艺的成本低，批量化一致性很高，加工误差小。

This electric unicycle adopt unique supercar streamline design style, fully embodies the perfect combination of design and technology. The security, intelligent, low carbon, trendy brand image in the service of every detail of life.This product can be folded pedal design, to consumers in use process, with super convenient experience, consumers in both cycling and storage, without any auxiliary tools, can be at ease.Injection mold processing technology on the product processing technology, the process than the machining process of low cost, mass consistency is very high.

悦翔 V7
Alsvin V7

设计 / 重庆长安汽车股份有限公司
生产 / 重庆长安汽车股份有限公司
Design / Changan Automobile Co.Ltd
Manufacture / Changan Automobile Co.Ltd

悦翔 V7 犀利的腰线贯穿车身，配合波浪式的进气格栅与漩涡状的轮辋，把动感的气质发挥得淋漓尽致。V7 配备了无钥匙进入一键启动系统、ESP 车身电子稳定系统、HHC 坡道辅助、STT 怠速启停、侧气帘和雾灯转向辅助照明等潮流配置，科技感强。在动力方面，长安悦翔 V7 搭载了在竞品车型中排量最大的 1.6L Bluecore 高效发动机，更省油、提速更快。

The abundant technology configuration is a highlight of Changan Realfly, and with trend-setting configuration, such as keyless entry and push-button starting system, electronic stability program (ESP), hill hold control system (HHC), STT idle stop-go system, side curtain air bags and fog lamp turning auxiliary lighting.The sportive and sharp appearance is one powerful tool to attract the attention of target buyers. The design inspiration of Realfly is derived from the structure aesthetics of modern architectural design and the new flow aesthetic concept.

BJ40

设计 / 北京汽车研究总院有限公司
生产 / 北京汽车股份有限公司
Design / Beijing Automotive Technology Center
Manufacture / Baic Motor Corporation Limited

BJ40 设计风格秉承“坚固、简练、征服” 的纯正越野车特质，线条刚毅，简单纯粹。产品多处可拆卸，满足用户个性化体验，拥有功能全面的越野生存讯息系统，经典的分时四驱系统，坚固的非承载式车身，无与伦比的高通过性，能最大限度提升人们日常户外越野的安全性和趣味性。车内零部件的材料、工艺更是严格控制，提升车内空间舒适性。

The products of BJ40 which with removable doors、removable roof, overturn the front windshield, quickly removed the rear seats, can give you more personalized distinctive experience.BJ40 applies not only in the urban environment, namely in roads and highway driving, while more can and rocky area in a variety of bad road, country road, trackless areas.GMT materials is used in the front and rear bumpers and side bumpers of BJ40 innovatively, it has the Characteristic of lightweight and high strength.

200km/h 客运机车外形及驾驶室设计
200km/h Passenger Locomotive Exterior and Cab Interior Design

设计 / 西南交通大学人机环境系统设计研究所
生产 / 中国中车股份大同电力机车有限责任公司
Design / Institute of Human Environment and System Design, Southwest Jiaotong University
Manufacture / CRRC Datong Electric Locomotive Co.,Ltd

机车网络控制系统采用基于以太网的分布式列车网络控制系统，并可扩展实现与 ATP 系统及客车的接口功能。转向架为 B0 转向架。传动方式为主动齿轮空心轴 + 弹性膜片联轴器传动，牵引力传递采用中心销加 Z 字形牵引杆结构。机车整体是全钢的焊接结构，采用圆与方的设计元素，使其硬朗与圆润的造型感相互融合，使机车更具力量感和亲和力。

Bogie to bogie B0. Transmission to active gear hollow shaft + elastic diaphragm coupling drive, traction transfer with central drawbar pin + Z-shaped structure.Traction circuit using IGBT modules of four-quadrant rectifier and inverter, an independent axis control technology, the main and auxiliary converter integrated design, share a water cooling system, only one set of each locomotive converter cabinet.Motorcycle Body with the overall carrying steel welded structure, the main choice of car body steel structure high strength low alloy steel S355J2G4, Q345GNHL.

成都低地板有轨电车
Chengdu Low-floor Tram

设计 / 西南交通大学人机环境系统设计研究所
生产 / 成都市新筑路桥机械股份有限公司
Design / IInstitute of Human Environment and System Design, Southwest Jiaotong University
Manufacture / Chengdu Xinzhu Road

该电车车头造型整体线条根据企业文化logo造型进行设计，提取“Z”型为设计元素。车头造型整体线条流畅而简洁，在前方划分车窗、车钩、防爬器的结构和层级关系，使车头呈现出柔和的一面，再通过局部面的转折变化来呈现与柔和互补的刚硬一面。车的主色调为黑白灰，彰显其科技感。车身涂装简洁大方，体现出成都天府之国的文化内涵。

The overall shape of the front lines of the corporate culture based on modeling logo design, extract "Z" type of design elements. Mainly reflected in the window of the transition surface. The overall shape of the front line is smooth and simple, divide the front windows, couplers, anti-climbers structure and hierarchy.Vehicle charm index increased to attract passengers and increase economic benefits.

马来西亚 ETS 米轨动车
Malaysia ETS Meter-Gauge EMU

设计 / 李鹏飞、高楠
生产 / 中国中车株洲电力机车有限公司
Design / Li Pengfei, Gao Nan
Manufacture / CRRC Zhuzhou Electric Locomotive Co., Ltd

ETS 米轨动车是我国第一次出口最高速度的米轨动车组，拥有五星的驾驶系统和环境及全维度可调安全座椅。高强度全焊接铝合金车体，满足 EN15227 的碰撞安全要求。客室内空调系统完全满足人体最佳体感舒适性要求。外观造型运用仿生设计，采用马来西亚当地常见的长梭鱼风格，内饰设计中也特别融入马来西亚文化元素。

The first design of top speed meter-gauge EMU, which is also the first time of export the top speed meter-gauge EMU of our country;Rely on the technology of disc brake meter-gauge bogie, we realized parking in 1 kilometers within 1minutes and a half.Five-star driving system and environment as well as fully adjustable safety seat, considering the driving habits.The vehicle has streamlined carbody design with the help of simulation analysis and optimization design of aerodynamics flow field.

八轴交流传动快速客运电力机车
Eight Axle AC Drive High Speed Passenger Electric Locomotive

设计 / 易琼、高楠

生产 / 中国中车株洲电力机车有限公司

Design / Yi Qiong, Gao Nan

Manufacture / CRRC Zhuzhou Electric Locomotive Co., Ltd

该机车功率大、牵引力强、加速性能好。头型采用曲面流线型，两节车之间采用双包折棚气密风挡式贯通道，降低运行时的空气阻力和噪声，优化空气动力学性能，极大节约能源。能适应 −40℃ ～ +40℃环境温度，可在 2500 米海拔的西北地区运用。机车采用机械、电磁混合制动，确保行车安全。当司机刹车或减速时，可采用再生制动，实现能量高效循环利用。

Major innovations in the appearance of Chinese locomotives. The world's first eight-axle passenger locomotive. The highest speed electric locomotive in China (Vmax: 230km/h). Power, traction, acceleration performance is good. It Meets the needs of China's railway network plan. It has streamlined surfaces, double fold between two car canopy-air windshield through the road, reduce air resistance and noise when running.

乐行 V3 电动独轮车
Inmotion SCV V3

设计 / 邱宇鹏、蔡优飞
生产 / 深圳乐行天下科技有限公司
Design / Qiu Yupeng, Cai Youfei
Manufacture / Inmotion Technologies Co.,Ltd

乐行 V3 采用“井轮”设计，稳定性强，易学易用。其独有内嵌式伸缩拉杆，与“水滴型”车身外观完美融合，结合乐行独创的“助力模式”，在不骑行的情况下，可以轻松推动。V3 独创前后智能车灯，前行和后退行驶都有灯光。它配置集娱乐和社交功能为一体的手机软件，不仅能够实现车体自检，故障诊断，还能够发现附近车友，发挥社交娱乐功能。

V3 adopts the "dual wheel" design with super stability and easy hand-on learning experience; It has a unique integrated hand-bar which blends in with the water-drop shaped vehicle body without any sense of abruptness; V3 is equipped with unique front and rear lights. The vehicle uses lithium battery as power source, which achieves zero carbon emission.It is by far the most comfortable product in the market. V3 adopts highly responsive rubber footboard with protective design that makes users more comfortable when driving.

Solo Wheel 天蝎
Solo Wheel Scorpio

设计 / 北京尚果创想科技有限公司
生产 / 英凡蒂（北京）科贸有限公司
Design / Beijing SUNGO Industrial Design Co.,Ltd
Manufacture / Invanti Co.,Ltd

SOLOWHEEL 电动独轮车是世界上最小、最环保、最便捷的自平衡电动独轮思维车。驾驶者可通过身体的前倾后仰改变重心控制车子的运动方向。混合纳米塑料使车体更坚固，航空铝制踏板减轻车体重量，增大负重强度。铝型材弯折把手贴合车身，功能与造型贴合，同时兼容提手、拉杆、停靠三种功能。造型上线条流畅，黑银配色高贵且炫酷。

SOLOWHEEL is a self-balancing electric unicycle which is the smallest, the most environmentally and the most convenient in the world. The maximum speed of SOLOWHEEL is 16km/h and the charging time need 45 minutes at a time.Meanwhile SOLOWHEEL can take you to anywhere without any road restrictions. Driver changes barycentre by leaning forward and back body to control the direction of movement of the unicycle.The viation-aluminum pedals reduce unicycle's weight and make the maximum load strength.

防雨头盔
Rain Helmet

设计 / 杭州斯帕克造型艺术有限公司
生产 / 杭州斯帕克造型艺术有限公司
Design / Hangzhou Spark Industrial Design.,Ltd
Manufacture / Hangzhou Spark Industrial Design.,Ltd

该产品将头盔和雨衣完美地结合在一起，解决了人们在雨天出行不戴安全头盔的现象。本产品运用先进的产品加工工艺，在材料上使用环保性强，耐磨度高的材料。设计上运用空气动力学原理，将盔体设计成流线状。面罩采用内外两层的设计，内部设计防高亮度光源和紫外线，外面罩防大风和雨雪。整个产品设计时尚，具有现代感。

The products are mainly for the rain to ride for people to travel without wearing a safety helmet design issues, the helmets and raincoats two products into a single product design, the combination of increased helmet use environment, reducing the probability of accidents. Helmet use is high-grade ABS plastic biodegradable, rugged and durable, wear-resistant lenses using wellhead PC material, resistance to ultraviolet radiation.

扫一扫查看产品 Pin3D 技术三维效果图
Scanning for the 3D image by Pin3D

传祺 GA6
Trumpchi GA6

设计 / 广州汽车集团股份有限公司汽车工程研究院
生产 / 广州汽车集团股份有限公司
Design / Guangzhou Automobile Group Co., Ltd Automotive Engineering Institute
Manufacture / Guangzhou Automobile Group Motor Co., Ltd

GA6 是广汽全自主研发的 B 级家轿，外观设计融入了中国文化元素。它采用了 1.8T 发动机、7 速手自一体双离合变速箱的黄金动控系统，油耗低。GA6 采用以驾驶员为中心的“包裹式”非对称设计，为驾驶者体验驾驭轿跑的乐趣提供设计上的可能。其内饰选材秉承“同级中选优”的策略，内饰做工、品质可媲美甚至超过同级合资车。

"Pride and Progressiveness" design philosophy: Trumpchi GA6 is a B-segment family sedan independently developed by GAC. It is also applied on to all of our Trumpchi models. Creative combination with Chinese culture: GA6 creatively brings Chinese culture into its design. Best at environmental legislation and Environmentally friendly for the user.All the details are evolutionarily applied to GA6 for better perceived quality.

普罗娜智慧照明路灯系列
PRONA Intelligent Lighting Streetlight Series

设计 / 上海木马工业产品设计有限公司
生产 / 创导（上海）智能技术有限公司
Design / Shanghai Moma Industrial Product Design Co.,Ltd
Manufacture / ChuangDao Alliance (Shanghai) Co.,Ltd

PRONA 不仅是路灯，它集光伏发电、LED 照明、微基站、城市视频探头、多媒体广告、信息发布、智能交互、便民服务、充电桩为一体，实现硬件可植人，软件可叠加，应用可拓展。普罗娜路灯在造型方面拥有极简风格、未来主义风格、简欧风、中国风四种创意造型，可满足任意场馆需求，设计别具匠心。

Prona is more than a streetlight because of its ingénue design. Prona is fitted with high power LED. On the top there are a solar panel, a micro mobile communication station and a CCTV camera. In the middle part, the multi-media system can release commercials, city public information according to the time and their locations. At the bottom, an interaction screen is fitted to serve people with real-time information.It takes full consideration of energy saving and environmental protection.

“鱼骨”桥梁设计
"Fishbone" Bridge Design

设计 / 西南交通大学人机环境系统设计研究所
生产 / 西南交通大学建筑勘察设计研究院
Design / Ilnstitute of Human Environment and System Design, Southwest Jiaotong University
Manufacture / Survey and Design Institute of Architectural Southwest Jiaotong University

桥以“鱼骨”为设计元素，将鱼抽象化，赋予桥新的形象——仿佛一条鱼游于江河之上，鱼骨式的桥梁结构增加了桥的层次感和稳定性。主桥采用了承载式有推力拱桥结构和轻钢材料，鱼骨的镂空设计更是大大减少了建造成本。桥梁使用醒目的红色为主色调，与周边环境相对比，更加突出桥梁流动性线条的独特。

With "bones" for design element, overpass oridge statuses and middle part of the facade to maintain consistent, the formation of multiple hollow out design, the whole of the bridge is very transparent, distinct. Ingenious use of natural relationship between fish and water, the bionic implication among them, thus achieved the highly harmonious relationship with surrounding environment. Take the necessary engineering control measures, and establish environmental monitoring and protection system, minimize adverse effects.

CHINA RED STAR DESIGN AWARD

Most Popular Product Prize

最受大众欢迎奖

智能后视镜行车记录仪
Smart Rearview Mirror Car Driving Recorder

设计 / 深圳捷渡科技有限公司
生产 / 深圳捷渡科技有限公司
Design / Jado Technology Co.,Ltd
Manufacture / Jado Technology Co.,Ltd

Nubia Z9

设计 / 努比亚技术有限公司
生产 / 努比亚技术有限公司
Design / Nubia Technology Co,.Ltd
Manufacture / Nubia Technology Co.,Ltd

CXW-220-TJ20 吸油烟机
CXW-220-TJ20

设计 / 帅康集团
生产 / 帅康集团
Design / Sacon
Manufacture / Sacon

乐行 V3 电动独轮车
Inmotion SCV V3

设计 / 邱宇鹏、蔡优飞
生产 / 深圳乐行天下科技有限公司
Design / Qiu Yupeng, Cai Youfei
Manufacture / Inmotin Technologies Co.,Ltd

弹击式汽车安全伞

Shooting Safety Hambrella

设计 / 李若权

生产 / 深圳市喜途伞业有限公司

Design / Li Ruoquan

Manufacture / Shenzhen Xitu Umbrella Co.,Ltd

Amazing Box Lite 智能家居控制中心

Amazing Box Lite

设计 / 张嘉泳

生产 / 大连华信计算机技术股份有限公司

Design / Mark Cheung

Manufacture / Dalian Hi-Think Computer Technology, Corp

折角 - 圆珠笔

Flod-Ballpen

设计 / 欧赛笔业

生产 / 杭州欧赛笔业有限公司

Design / Ownseas

Manufacture / Hanzhou Ownseas Pen Co.,Ltd

智能湿水牛皮纸包装机

Water Soluble Kraft Paper Packer

设计 / 宁波市法诺工业产品设计有限公司

生产 / 宁波赛美达环保科技有限公司

Design / Ningbo FANUO Industrial Product Design Co..Ltd

Manufacture / Ningbo Media Environmental Technology Co.,Ltd

公交自动售水机

Bus Automatic Water Dispenser

设计 / 北京乐品乐道科技有限公司

生产 / 北京君汇港沣科技发展有限公司

Design / Beijing LEAD Technology Co.,Ltd

Manufacture / Beijing Junhui Hong Kong being technology development Co.,ltd

魅厨套系

N+ Series

设计 / 北京圣宝地工业设计有限公司

生产 / 华帝股份有限公司

Design / CBD Group Corp.

Manufacture / Vatti Corporation Limited

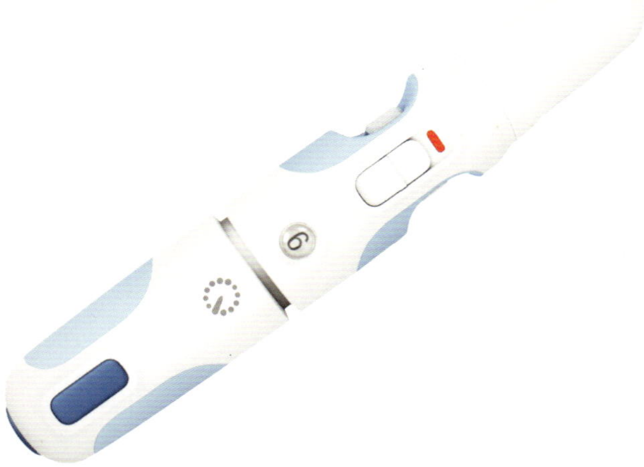

QS-M2 无针注射器

IQS-M2 Needle-free Injector

设计 / 陈苏宁

生产 / 北京快舒尔医疗技术有限公司

Design / Chen Suning

Manufacture / Beijing QS Medical Technology Co.,Ltd

电动车控制器

DMC2950

设计 / 刘永进、秦龙

生产 / 阳光电源股份有限公司

Design / Liu yongjin, Qin Long

Manufacture / Sungrow Power Supply Co.,Ltd

智能深槽匀翻机
Intelligent Deep Groove Turner

设计 / 北京中科博联环境工程有限公司
生产 / 北京中科博联环境工程有限公司
Design / Beijing GreenTech Environmental Engineering Ltd
Manufacture /Beijing GreenTech Environmental Engineering Ltd

这里有我的一切（适老厨房）
One for All

设计 / 河南省大信整体厨房科贸有限公司
生产 / 河南省大信整体厨房科贸有限公司
Design / Henan Province Daxin Whole Cookroom Science
Manufacture / Henan Province Daxin whole cookroom Science

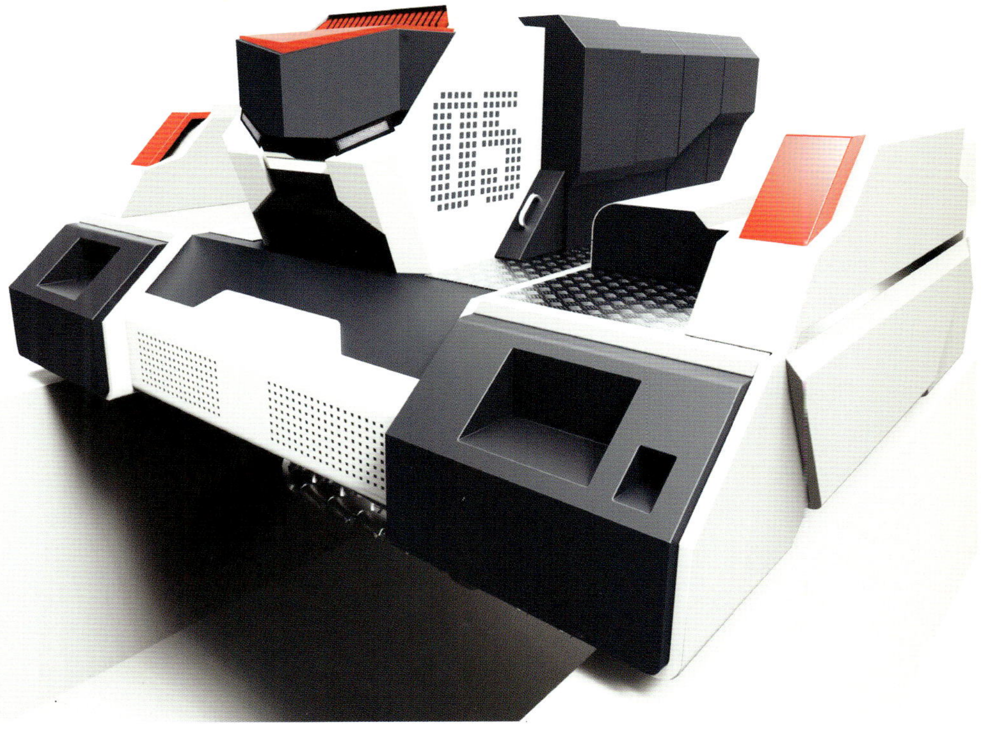

CHINA RED STAR DESIGN AWARD

Most Popular Team Prize

最具人气团队奖

捷渡中国
JADO Re-DESIGN

捷渡中国是一支富有经验且具备国际视角的设计团队。核心成员由多年从事一线品牌汽车设计的设计师及经验丰富的产品 CMF 设计师、结构工程师组成。基于对汽车和周边产品多年的设计经验以及对未来“人与车生活”的研究，团队将每一次捷渡中国产品的设计过程作为一次对未来美好的“人与车生活”的创新实践，而每一次设计成果旨在为消费者带来更加安全与富有乐趣的驾乘体验。作为专业从事汽车智能后视镜设计和研发的团队，捷渡中国将在行驶记录、安全预警、GPS 定位、互联网 +、智能语音操控等方面不断完善，致力于创造一个更加安全、便捷且富有乐趣的未来“人与车生活”。

JADO Re-DESIGN is a design team with rich experience and international perspective. The core team is composed with experienced car designer, CMF product designer and structure engineer. Based on the research of vehicle and its accessories as well as the research of future "People & Car life", JADO regards its design as an innovation practice of "People & Car life", which brings a safer and more joyful experience for the consumers. As a professional design and research team, JADO Re-DESIGN will improve the products on driving recording, safety alarm, GPS positioning, Internet+, smart devotes to create a more safety, convenient and joyful future for "People & Car life".

祈福的芽——燃香阻燃器
Praying Bud — Incense Burning Flame Retardant Device

设计 / 张剑
Design / Zhang Jian

此款燃香阻燃器由金属制成，形态为两瓣“小芽”，“芽”的底部设有与香粗细一致的圆形孔，并有小磁铁相互吸牢。燃香时选择需要燃烧的长度，将两瓣芽靠磁铁吸附在香柱上，当香燃烧到金属芽底部圆孔位置时，燃香遇金属阻隔自然熄灭，达到控制香燃烧长度的目的。香熄灭后与阻燃器形成一个破土而出的“芽”造型，寓意着“祈福”萌发出希望的“嫩芽”。如需要继续点燃，将阻燃器摘下，点燃香即可。该设计既满足了使用需求，又创造了一种奇妙的心理感受，同时暗合了东方文化气质与神韵。

This type of incense burning flame retardant device is made of metal. The appearance consists of two "little buds"; the "bud" bottom is designed with a circle hole of the same diameter with the incense, and they are interactively firmed by small magnets. When burning the incense, it requires to select the length of incense to be burned; get the two parts of buds attach to the incense column by the magnet effect. When the incense is burning to the circle hole at the bottom of metal buds, then the incense will be naturally extinguished due to metal isolation, which realizes the objective of controlling the incense combustion length. After the incense is extinguished, it shapes a "bud" model of protruding from the soil, which means "praying" for the "fresh bud" sprouting the hope. If it needs to continue to burn the incense, take off the flame retardant device, and ignite the incense easily.

可清洗的塑料袋
Washing Plastic Bag

设计 / 匡珈莹
Design / Kuang Jiaying

设计师能够敏锐观察到现实生活中户外果蔬清洗的需求，在不具备专有清洗器具时，利用装运果蔬的一次性塑料袋，巧妙地在袋子的下方制作几个出水的小孔，不增加更多设计与制造成本，改变装运功能为清洗工具。该设计为一次性产品增添了更多的使用功能，为环境保护和减少白色污染做出实际的设计贡献，成为可持续设计在现实生活中的经典案例。

It is keen for the designer to observe the need of washing fruits outdoors. It is clever to take the plastic bags to wash the fruits, only a few holes on the plastic bag could solve the problem without adding cost. This design enables more function of the disposable product, for the good of environment, by reducing white pollution, could be a classical case study of the sustainable design.

座椅婴儿床
Seat Baby Bed

设计 / 黄孕宁、庄锦龙
Design / Huang Yunning, Zhuang Jinlong

座椅婴儿床是针对 1—24 个月左右的婴儿设计的一款多功能家具。专用婴儿床虽然能够满足现实需求，但是在婴儿成长后常常成为家庭存放的负担。该婴儿床设计成可拆分的，在不使用的情况下可以将底部的旋钮旋开，婴儿床就能瞬间变成两把椅子，这样不但节省空间，还对婴儿床进行充分利用，巧妙地实现了婴儿床在其失去服务功能后的全新使用价值，其功能的转化延长了家具的使用周期。

This Seat Baby Bed is multi-functional furniture for the family who has 1-24 month old infants. The specialized infant bed could fulfill the real need; however, it becomes a burden for the family to store it up. This bed is detachable, could be detached to two parts by rotating the knob at the bottom, and the bed becomes two chairs. This design makes the furniture fully used and could extend the existing furniture's life cycle.

虚怀坐墩
Tabour Stool

设计 / 王树茂

Design / Wang Shumao

本产品专注于中国本土文化精神的传承，它审慎地抽取古代家具坐墩的线条，并结合现代生活的起居习惯，借助原竹等多种材料进行组合演绎，将竹材与节气、防腐防蛀、结构与树脂、受力稳定性、造型肌理的纹样美感等诸方面进行综合考虑，重新诠释了当代中国文人的生活美学。独具匠心的中空设计既符合竹子本身的生长特点又给予一种强烈的视觉冲击力，整个侧面的造型流露出自然连贯的感觉。本产品用原竹可实现大批量生产，生产难度低，制作成本低，体现了可持续的设计理念。

The design bamboo stool is inspired by both ancient furniture's line and living habits of modern life. This work is trying to reinterpret the contemporary Chinese literati life aesthetics. Through this stool the designer expresses not only his respect for the wisdom of previous lives but also the appreciation modesty of Chinese nation.

隐约（转椅）
Vaguely

设计 / 安新妹

Design / Ann

隐约（转椅）的设计最终以实物呈现，采用藤条编结，材料合理，使用便捷，满足了人们休闲的多种需求，舒适宜用。藤条的镂空编织通过格式塔视错觉塑造出封闭与通透的空间，藤条编结后的微微透光也为使用者休息带来了安静的氛围和情趣。主体的坐具与照明灯具采用统一的结构，丰富了产品的多样性。坐具尺寸符合人体工程学，多角度旋转可带来多样的变化。

This work is presented as a real object which made with rattan knitting, fulfilling the people's need during the leisure time, bringing a comfortable experience when using. The hollowed out rattan builds a closed but transparent space for people to spend their leisure time. The transmitting of the light creates a quiet atmosphere for the users. The main part is unified with the lighting part, enriches the product's diversity. The sitting part is accordance with ergonomics, the multi-angle rotation brings variety of changes.

CHINA RED STAR DESIGN AWARD

Best Designer Award of Original Design Award

优秀设计师奖

张剑
Zhang Jian

[设计是粒很奇特的种籽，你怎样栽培，她就会开怎样的花。
Design is a magic seed, the blossom depends on how you cultivate it.]

张剑，男，1995 年至 2009 年任教于南京艺术学院设计学院，现任教于广州美术学院工业设计学院生活设计工作室。从事工业设计教育 19 年，一直致力于产品创新设计研究与开发，完成具有研究性作品 250 余件，其中 100 余件（次）在国内外重大设计比赛中获奖入选。多次在北京、上海、广州等地举办个人设计作品展及专题讲座。

Zhang Jian, used to be teaching in School of Design, Nanjing University of the Arts from 1995 to 2009, now teaching at The Life Design Studio of Industrial Design School, Guangzhou Academy of Fine Arts. He has dedicated to design education for 19 year, devoted for in R&D of product innovation. His has done more than 250 pieces of works of research works, 100 of them are prize winners in different design awards. Zhang Jian himself has held many solo exhibitions and seminars.

CHINA RED STAR DESIGN AWARD

Future Star Award of Original Design Award

未来之星奖

林炳塔
Lin Bingta

[设计犹如生活，是一种激情，更是一种享受；是一种感悟，更是一种精神。
Design is like life, is a passion, and a joyful process; it's also an inspiration and spirit.]

林炳塔，男，目前就读于江西财经大学艺术学院工业设计系，担任学院创新型人才培养工作室负责人，带领二十余人的设计团队参加国内外大型工业设计大赛及与企业、公司对接进行实际项目的研发。曾获得过国内外比赛共三十余项奖项，获得国家实用新型专利四项。

Lin Bingta, studies at College of Art, Jiangxi University of Finance and Economics, is in charge of the innovation talent training studio of the College of Art, leading a team of 20 designers to participate design awards, competitions at home and abroad, he also leads his team to take over programs for companies. He has won more than 30 prizes in the awards and competitions, has obtained 4 pieces of China national practical new-type patent.

王树茂
Wang Shumao

[设计源于生活，细节成就品质。
Design derives from life, detail decides quality.]

王树茂，毕业于广东工业大学环境设计专业，大学期间曾获得国家奖学金等奖学金共计十二次。设计作品曾获四十多项专业赛事奖项。多项设计作品曾在国内外重要活动展出，作品《虚怀》入选世博会中国礼品，于 2015 年意大利米兰世博会中国馆展出。设计作品收录于《持续之道国际可持续设计学术研讨会暨设计作品展作品集》《中国大学生美术作品年鉴》等。2015 年创立沣茂研究室（Femo Design），任负责人。

Wang Shumao, majored in Environment Design, graduated from Guangdong University of Technology, has obtained national scholarship for 12 times. His design work has won prizes for 40 pieces competitions and has been showcased in many of events. His work Modesty entered in the national present list of the Shanghai Expo, and displayed in the 2015 Milan Expo. His works have been collected in The Tao of Sustainability, An International Conference and Exhibition on Sustainable Design and its design exhibition, Yearbook of Chinese Art graduates. He's also Femo Design Studio's founder and CEO.

CHINA RED STAR DESIGN AWARD

Excellent Award of Original Design Award

红星原创奖

卧床洗头盆
The In-bed Head-wash Basin

设计 / 加拿大搜罗传媒

Design / Canada Solo Media Inc.

卧床洗头盆是专门为长期卧床的老人（病人）所设计的一款能够在床上使用的洗头盆。设计师积极思考中国正在日益步入老龄化社会的需求，对卧床的人给予关爱与呵护。可在床上使用的洗头盆，只需要一个护理人员即可操作，简单方便。设计了手部柔性喷头代替手持式喷头，双手可同时操控，更加灵巧方便又起到了按摩的作用。头枕也被设计成喷头，可冲洗头后部。不用担心水洒在床上。自供加热。外观新颖，美观，符合人体，使用舒适。安全、节能、环保，结实耐用，成本低，实现性高，并且能够受到老人（病人）喜爱。

This basin is specially designed for the bed-ridden people to wash hair. Designers are thinking about the real need of the Chinese elderly society and the work is showing respect and care to the vulnerable people. By only one nurse it could realize the washing process. This is designed to be hand-like shower nozzle instead of the hand hold shower nozzle for easy operation and massage. The headrest is designed to be a shower which could wash from behind. In addition, the basin is auto-heated.

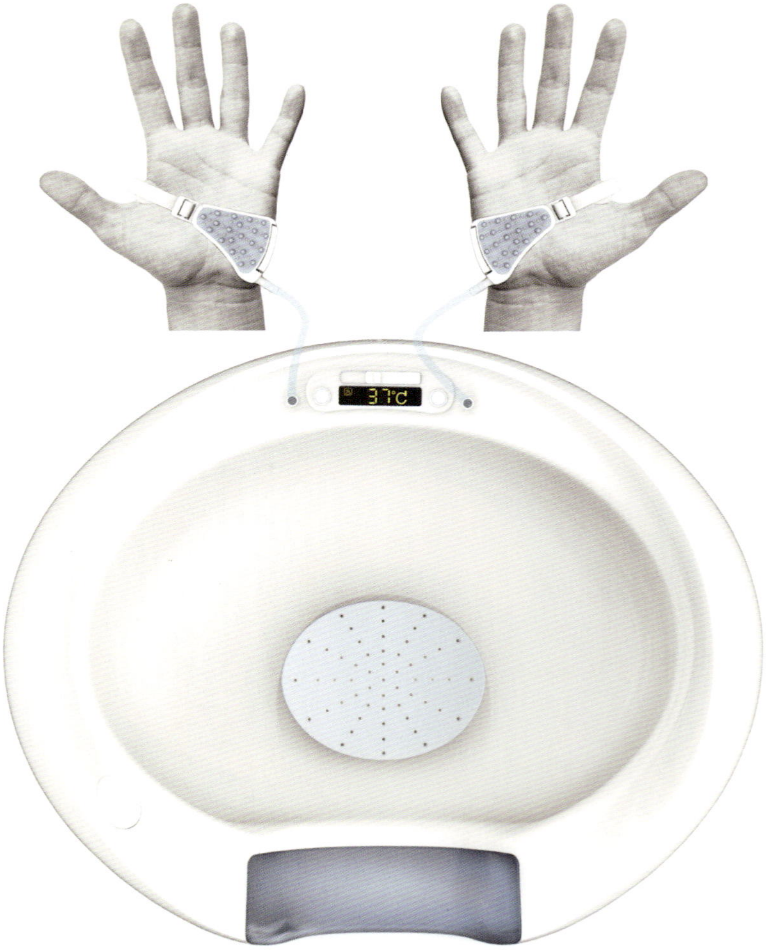

领结—可以平放的酒瓶
Bow tie - the Winebottles that Can be Laid Flatwise

设计 / 张剑

Design / Zhang Jian

这款酒瓶设计可以很简单地解决酒瓶平放的问题，在制作玻璃酒瓶时，在其上半部增加一个横向圆柱体，与酒瓶衔接成为一个“领结”的造型。“领结”造型简单而不失优雅，匹配品酒的环境，与品酒者及酒店服务人员建立起和谐良好的气氛，不但可以起到装饰效果，更重要的是当酒瓶平放在桌面时，起到支点的作用防止酒瓶滚动，使酒瓶可随意平放在桌面上或橱柜里，而不需要额外配置红酒瓶支架。此设计具有很广泛的推广价值，在制作葡萄酒瓶的模具时稍加改动，可批量化投产，成本低廉，解决放置葡萄酒的实际问题。

For wine storage, the bottle needs to be placed horizontally or aslant to keep the contact between cork and wine, so that air is not able to enter through the cork that is fully hydrated. Thus, the wine is prevented from oxidation and can be stored for a long time without going bad. The design of this bottle can easily solve the problem of how to keep the wine bottle being placed horizontally. When making the glass wine bottles, we can add a crosswise cylinder to its upper half to make a bow-tie shape with the bottle itself. This "bow-tie" can be not only the decoration, but also a pivot to prevent the bottle from rolling when the bottle is laid flatwise on the table.

废弃的汽车音响再设计利用
Waste Car Audio Redesign and Recycle

设计 / 惠州学院美术系
Design / Art Department of Huizhou University

本设计主要是解决废弃的底端音响的重新利用问题，以实现节约资源、绿色环保的目的。将废弃的底端音响通过重新设计——加装喇叭、天线、电源转变为家用的组合音响，成为家庭的娱乐、教育、信息中心，创造出简约、极具都市风格的家庭娱乐产品，是“升级再创 upcycling”设计理念的典范。

The design is to solve the problem of re-use abandoned the bottom of the speaker, in order to achieve resource conservation, to achieve the environmental protection purposes. By redesigning the speaker with a loudspeaker, antenna, power supply, the product could become a home music center, an integration product of entertainment, education and information center, creating an upcycling model.

扣子刷
Brush Button

设计 / 李伟斯
Design / Li Weisi

扣子刷整体设计简洁、轻盈、轻薄，极富有设计感。作品的整体造型为夹子形状，附带主刷，方便携带。同时，夹子造型方便用户在使用中固定在酱料杯壁以及清洗后扣挂在绳子上，适合家用以及户外烧烤等多种场景。小小的创意改变，带来生活品质的提升。

The overall design of the Brush button sauce is concise and ultra thin, which is a belt shape, convenient to carry. The clip shape enables users to fix it on the sauce cup and buckle after cleaning. This could be used for barbecue and other outdoor scenario.

环保培养皿
Environmental Dish

设计 / 李伟斯
Design / Li Weisi

环保培养皿是一个由废纸纸浆压模而成的幼苗培养皿，且其表面经过防水处理，这将改变当前市场上大量使用不可降解塑料为原料的现状，体现了设计者的环保设计初心。它减少了工业塑料对土地的污染，减轻了土地的降解压力。相对于塑料培养皿，它更容易降解在土地里面，同时纸浆原材料使幼苗培养皿更具透气性，利于种苗的出芽生长。也降低了产品的生产成本，便于产品市场化生产。

The environment dish is a petri dish for the sprout, made up with wasted paper pulp, processed to be water proof. Comparing with the non-degradable product made by plastics, it reduces the pollution of industrial plastics. In comparison with the plastic one, it is more ventilate for the sprout, good for the growth of the plant, also, it reduces the manufacture cost, easy to be the mass production.

医用折叠担架
Medical Folding Stretcher

设计 / 郭振宇、庄锦龙
Design / Guo Zhenyu, Zhuang Jinlong

医用救护折叠担架具有反应速度快、短时内展开使用的特点，满足了病人突发情况时的需要。设计结构合理，保证折叠担架的灵活多变，也为固定病人提供了更多的支撑和保证。作品在材料方面采用高强度环保塑料面板及航空铝材，使产品更加轻便。外观采用了比较简约的镂空设计，在担架的右侧还设计了一个伸缩支架，方便患者使用吊瓶。作品的色彩合理醒目。多个抓手的设计，为医务人员搬运提供了方便。

The ordinary medical stretcher is used for emergency and first-aid. The reasonable structure enables the flexibility of the stretcher, providing more possibility for carrying patients. It adopts a high-intensity eco-friendly plastic panel, the aviation aluminum is light weight and easy to carry. A stand holder on the right side is designed for transfusion and used by the medicals to move the patients.

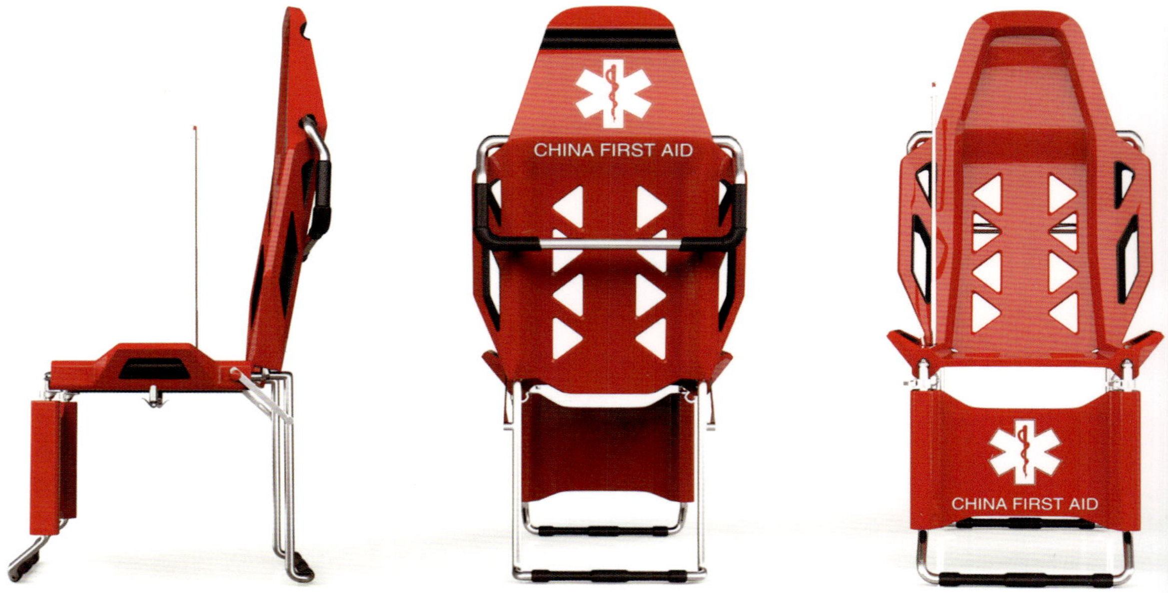

纸巾和袋子设计
Space Saver

设计 / 林炳塔、尤志鹏、罗时武

Design / Lin Bingta, You Zhipeng, Luo Shiwu

本设计是可以随身携带的纸巾袋子。当人们吃完食物后，都会习惯性的从背包里拿出纸巾来擦干净嘴巴。运用该设计作品，便可把擦完嘴巴的纸巾打开，变成一个袋子，把吃剩下的果皮、瓜子壳等垃圾放进袋子里，便于垃圾的整理和丢弃。该设计利用现有纸巾的结构，增加一道简单的工艺，便能将纸巾的双层结构变为一个可收纳食物残渣的袋子，在发挥传统功能后仍能继续重新发挥它的价值。

Tissue with sack is a paper portable bag for rubbish keeping instead of throwing away. Normally people use tissue to clean up after eating; this work could change the tissue into a garbage bag by opening up the tissue, therefore the waste could be collected and abandon afterwards. By one more simple process, Tissue With Sack enables the double-layer tissue become a rubbish bag, maximize the value.

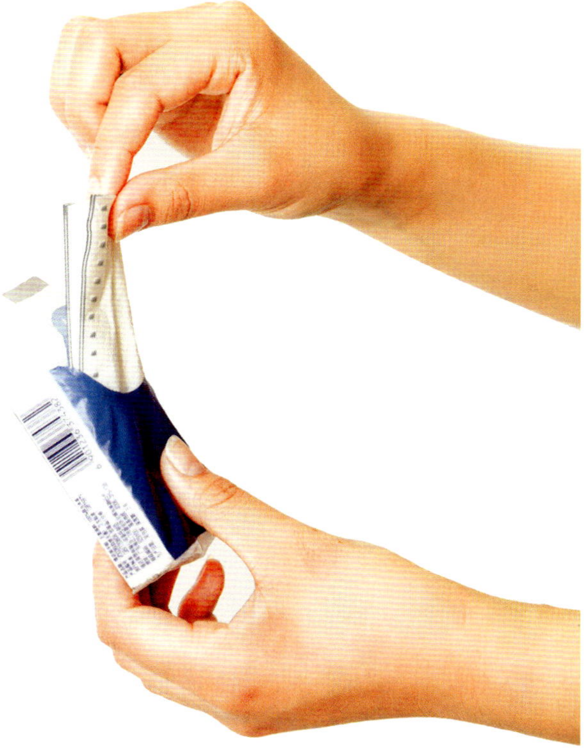

Blooming 雨淋花洒
Blooming Rainshower

设计 / 厦门松霖科技有限公司

Design / Xiamen Solex High-tech Industries Co., Ltd

该雨淋花洒采用柱状造型，运用平抛运动原理，改传统纵向出水为横向出水，实现了小体积花洒大淋浴面积功能。相比以增大花洒尺寸获得大淋浴体验的传统雨淋花洒，更加简洁，节约材料和运输成本。旋转切换旋钮，轻柔发散水如烟花般优雅绽放，如春雨般无声抚过肌肤。同时，环状瀑布水、一柱水为用户提供了更多体验选择。花洒具有多种形态的出水方式，使沐浴成为一种有趣的体验，使用户可享受沐浴的过程和体验淋浴的乐趣。

Adopting the parabola principle, The Blooming Rainshower is shaped in columnar shape, changing the traditional shower direction, maximizing the proportion. Comparing with the traditional shower head, this one is more concise and energy saving. By using the rotation button, the water could turn in to a wcterfall, providing multi options for the users. Different water flow brings fun for life, users could enjoy their bathing with this product.

私人定制自行车设计
Private Custom Bicycle Design

设计 / 河北科技大学艺术学院

Design / College of Art, Hebei University of Science and Technology

私人定制自行车设计是设计师通过软件对具体使用者的身体尺寸进行精密测算，设计出严格符合骑者的人体工程学，满足未来个性化市场的需求的产品。主体车身采用碳纤维材料保证车的结构稳固而又轻便。使用者还可以根据喜好，对外观进行喷涂或者碳纤维纹理的保留，自己动手完成设计的实施，也给设计增加了亮点。

Bicycle design should consider the riding experience of the riders, including the process of riding comfort level and safety. This design is based on the physical data of rider to better the user experience, thus creating a highly conforms to the rider ergonomics bike. Carbon fiber material ensures the bike itself a stable structure and light weight.

拼接凳
Splicing Stool

设计 / 徐乐、杨存园、林炳塔
Design / Xu Le, Yang Cunyuan, Lin Bingta

拼接凳在选材上采用原木（白橡木）、麦秸板和少量塑料，绿色环保。塑料部分可以加固凳面，易更换色彩，缤纷色彩使其具有时尚感，整个设计简约优雅。整个产品巧用传统的榫卯结构，不需要任何一颗螺丝钉，方便牢固，其结构之美很好地展现了前人的智慧。拼接凳由两个部件组成，不需要任何工具或硬件组装和拆卸，它的易拆分也让封装变得很简单，大大地降低运输成本

Splicing Stool is an eco-friendly work which using wood(white oak), OSSB and very little plastic. The Tenon structure is adopted without screw, which is easy to fix, the beauty of structure represents the wisdom of the ancient people. The stool is assembled by two parts, the easy-assemble design makes the cost low.

2015 中国设计红星奖获奖名单

至尊金奖

Yoga3 Pro
设计 / 联想设计与用户体验中心
生产 / 联想
008

金奖

海尔智能机器人
设计 / 青岛海尔智能家电科技有限公司
生产 / 青岛海尔智能家电科技有限公司
012

CRH2G 时速 250 公里高寒动车组
设计 / 南车青岛四方机车车辆股份有限公司
生产 / 南车青岛四方机车车辆股份有限公司
013

OLED 电视
设计 / 冠捷显示科技（厦门）有限公司创新中心 ID 设计团队
生产 / 冠捷显示科技（厦门）有限公司
014

戴森 Pure Cool™ 空气净化风扇
设计 / 戴森
生产 / 戴森
015

海信激光影院
设计 / 海信工业设计中心
生产 / 青岛海信电器股份有限公司
016

探索者
设计 / 深圳零度智能飞行器有限公司
生产 / 深圳雷柏科技股份有限公司
017

蝙蝠无人机
设计 / 北京白鲸创享科技有限公司
生产 / 江苏首控制造技术有限公司
018

QS-M2 无针注射器
设计 / 陈苏宁
生产 / 北京快舒尔医疗技术有限公司
019

银奖

传祺 GS4
设计 / 广州汽车集团股份有限公司汽车工程研究院
生产 / 广州汽车集团股份有限公司
022

Nubia Z9
设计 / 努比亚技术有限公司
生产 / 努比亚技术有限公司
023

XT680 伸缩臂叉装机
设计 / 江苏徐州工程机械研究院工业设计中心
生产 / 徐州工程机械集团有限公司
024

苏州有轨电车 1 号线
设计 / 法国 MBD 工业设计公司
生产 / 南车南京浦镇车辆有限公司
025

赞月池茶盘
设计 / 石大宇
生产 / 北京清庭文创文化发展有限公司
026

“无”衣帽架
设计 / 周安彬、雷南仕
生产 / 广州高尚生活文化传播有限公司
027

介入医疗器械可吸收封堵器
设计 / 深圳市四六区工业产品策划有限公司
生产 / 先健科技（深圳）有限公司
028

定量快开龙头
设计 / 佛山市日丰企业有限公司
生产 / 佛山市日丰企业有限公司
029

FW6108 移动式多功能照明装置
设计 / 海洋王照明科技股份有限公司
生产 / 海洋王照明科技股份有限公司
030

方正榜书行
设计 / 汪文
生产 / 北京北大方正电子有限公司
031

最佳团队奖

联想笔记本设计团队
033

最佳新人奖

李若鑫
035

红星奖

倬茂网络红外摄像机
设计 / 深圳市感叹号产品设计有限公司
生产 / 倬茂企业股份有限公司
038

康佳 BK929 警务智能手机
设计 / 陈万衡
生产 / 深圳康佳通信科技有限公司
039

智能屏风系统
设计 / 深圳市柏斯工业设计有限公司
生产 / 深圳市柏斯工业设计有限公司
039

E 动终端
设计 / 张楠、黄波文
生产 / 福建星网锐捷通讯股份有限公司
039

智能后视镜行车记录仪
设计 / 深圳捷渡科技有限公司
生产 / 深圳捷渡科技有限公司
040

EP404 蜗牛吸盘数据线
设计 / 褚明华、申林
生产 / 深圳市洛斐客文化有限公司
041

云电栈
设计 / 深圳市四六区工业产品策划有限公司
生产 / 深圳市赤道极光信息科技有限公司
042

小型化卫星信号模拟器
设计 / 甄大崴
生产 / 航天恒星科技有限公司
042

掌静脉认证智能终端
设计 / 成都拓成工业产品设计有限公司
生产 / 成都芯软件科技发展有限公司
043

智能行车记录仪
设计 / 深圳捷渡科技有限公司
生产 / 深圳捷渡科技有限公司
043

E 人E 本 T9 商务平板
设计 / 成都浪尖工业设计有限公司
生产 / 北京壹人壹本信息科技有限公司
044

SIM +蓝牙 SIM 卡读卡器
设计 / 深圳市嘉兰图设计股份有限公司
生产 / 深圳市嘉兰图设计股份有限公司
044

能科三防平板
设计 / 郑州市浪尖产品设计有限公司
生产 / 能科节能技术股份有限公司
045

三防手机
设计 / 任敏杰
生产 / 上海数果科技有限公司
045

“启” 移动电源
设计 / 潘润松
生产 / 万莱华国际有限公司（香港）
046

WOW!dea MOCA X7s 多功能便携数据卡
设计 / 北京元隆雅图文化传播股份有限公司
生产 / 北京元隆雅图文化传播股份有限公司
046

多功能光通信工具钳
设计 / 烽火通信科技股份有限公司
生产 / 烽火通信科技股份有限公司
046

OV U-Net
设计 / 深圳市四六区工业产品策划有限公司
生产 / 深圳市锐仁电子有限公司
047

胸卡工作记录仪
设计 / 郑州市浪尖产品设计有限公司
生产 / 郑州华力信息技术有限公司
047

WOW!dea MOCA X8 多功能数据移动电源
设计 / 北京元隆雅图文化传播股份有限公司
生产 / 北京元隆雅图文化传播股份有限公司
047

动捕系统
设计 / 瀚域联华科技（北京）有限公司
生产 / 北京诺亦腾科技有限公司
048

2015 中国设计红星奖获奖名单

悠宝
设计 / 祝正文、陈钟山
生产 / 烽火通信科技股份有限公司
049

旺果儿童手表
设计 / 逸乐工业产品设计（上海）有限公司
生产 / 讯研通信息技术（上海）有限公司
049

中视典全息交互台
设计 / 北京天创易造工业设计有限公司
生产 / 北京中视典数字科技有限公司
050

机器人虚拟图文在线包装系统
设计 / 艾迪普
生产 / 北京东方艾迪普科技发展有限公司
050

智能穿戴式牵伸康复系统
设计 / 成都拓成工业产品设计有限公司
生产 / 四川旭康医疗电器有限公司
051

电子铠甲定位鞋
设计 / 考克（福建）工业设计有限公司
生产 / 福建省莆田市双驰智能信息技术有限公司
051

老年智能手杖
设计 / 北京乐品乐道科技有限公司
生产 / 北京联芯瑞康科技有限公司
052

夹式立体声耳机
设计 / 深圳市四六区工业产品策划有限公司
生产 / 深圳市万诚通电子有限公司
053

iBone 宠物狗关爱智能配件
设计 / 杭州领跑者工业设计有限公司
生产 / 杭州汪星人科技有限公司
053

汉仪旗黑系列
设计 / 北京汉仪科印信息技术有限公司
生产 / 北京汉仪科印信息技术有限公司
054

方正悠黑体
设计 / 仇寅
生产 / 北京北大方正电子有限公司
055

F50LW-B 电热水器
设计 / 美的集团热水器事业部工业设计部
生产 / 芜湖美的厨卫电器制造有限公司
056

净滤宝
设计 / 美的集团热水器事业部工业设计部
生产 / 芜湖美的厨卫电器制造有限公司
056

可以在线买菜的智能冰箱
设计 / 惠而浦（中国）工业设计中心
生产 / 惠而浦（中国）股份有限公司
057

旗舰版空气能热水器
设计 / 广东顺德潜龙工业设计有限公司
生产 / 广东芬尼电器有限公司
058

长虹 CHIQ-Q1V 柜机
设计 / 四川虹微技术有限公司
生产 / 四川长虹电器股份有限公司
059

户外蓝牙音响
设计 / 深圳市感叹号产品设计有限公司
生产 / 深圳市尊特数码有限公司
060

敦拓 磁悬浮蓝牙音箱
设计 / 深圳市感叹号产品设计有限公司
生产 / 深圳市敦拓电子有限公司
060

B18 可变形移动电源
设计 / 深圳市艾狄科技有限公司
生产 / 深圳卡格尔数码科技有限公司
061

Amazing Box Lite 智能家居控制中心
设计 / 张嘉泳
生产 / 大连华信计算机技术股份有限公司
061

极路客 Goluk 智能行车记录仪
设计 / 深圳洛可可工业设计有限公司
生产 / 北京智趣车联科技有限公司
062

圣宝 V5 音响
设计 / 深圳市感叹号产品设计有限公司
生产 / 东莞市圣宝电子制造有限公司
062

旗子 Moretel 智能电话
设计 / 深圳市感叹号产品设计有限公司
生产 / 珠海市齐飞信息技术有限公司
063

iTvTop 移动网络电视宝
设计 / 成都浪尖工业设计有限公司
生产 / 深圳清华大学研究院
063

LEBOND 家用冲牙器
设计 / 广州森迪产品设计有限公司
生产 / 力博得电子科技有限公司
064

ALLER 箱
设计 / 杭州领跑者工业设计有限公司
生产 / 洛克施为空气净化技术（天津）有限公司
064

Smart Care 智能家居套装
设计 / 上海艺凯设计有限公司
生产 / 海尔
065

神妈奶瓶
设计 / 杭州领跑者工业设计有限公司
生产 / 山东麦格信息技术有限公司
065

AR-F40I501 电饭煲
设计 / 龙域设计
生产 / 浙江爱仕达生活电器有限公司
066

海尔 IH 电磁电饭煲 HRC-IFZ502 咖色
设计 / 苏州海歌电器科技有限公司
生产 / 海尔生活家电
066

胚芽米机
设计 / 韩永利
生产 / 北京心觉工业设计有限责任公司
067

AP-F50I104 电压力锅
设计 / 龙域设计
生产 / 浙江爱仕达生活电器有限公司
067

Pulse 无线音乐智能灯
设计 / 浙江生辉照明有限公司
生产 / 浙江生辉照明有限公司
068

咪库 感温调奶棒
设计 / 李伟湛、杨先英
生产 / 重庆伟立仕科技有限公司
068

N 智能运动耳机
设计 / 深圳市恩佳产品策划有限公司
生产 / 深圳市恩佳产品策划有限公司
068

智能湿水牛皮纸包装机
设计 / 宁波市法诺工业产品设计有限公司
生产 / 宁波赛美达环保科技有限公司
069

智能插座
设计 / 深圳市想象力产品策划有限公司
生产 / 深圳市昊达电子有限公司
069

蓝牙触控键盘
设计 / 深圳雷柏科技股份有限公司
生产 / 深圳雷柏科技股份有限公司
070

加湿器
设计 / 联创工业设计中心
生产 / 深圳市联创科技集团有限公司
070

蓝牙户外音箱
设计 / 深圳雷柏科技股份有限公司
生产 / 深圳雷柏科技股份有限公司
071

智能音箱灯
设计 / 深圳市想象力产品策划有限公司
生产 / 深圳市乐百川科技有限公司
071

Core V21 平躺式机壳
设计 / TTdesign
生产 / 曜越科技股份有限公司
072

弓一控制保护开关
设计 / 温州左岸品牌设计推广有限公司
生产 / 德力西电气有限公司
072

Up Box 3D 打印机
设计 / 北京洛可可科技有限公司
生产 / 北京太尔时代科技有限公司
084

iEagle—智能航拍无人机
设计 / 深圳市鼎典工业产品设计有限公司
生产 / 深圳市艾特航空科技股份有限公司
073

长虹“T”空间客厅鲜品区
设计 / 四川虹微技术有限公司
生产 / 四川长虹电器股份有限公司
074

魅厨套系
设计 / 北京圣宝地工业设计有限公司
生产 / 华帝股份有限公司
075

德意吸油烟机 CXW-230-HK2086
设计 / 飞鱼设计（杭州）有限公司
生产 / 浙江德意厨具有限公司
075

美的 436L 法式四门系列冰箱（BCD-436WGPZM/BCD-436WTZM）
设计 / 合肥美的电冰箱有限公司
生产 / 合肥美的电冰箱有限公司
076

长虹五门智能冰箱
设计 / 四川虹微技术有限公司
生产 / 四川长虹电器股份有限公司
077

燃气灶 S902B
设计 / 宁波欧琳厨具有限公司
生产 / 宁波欧琳厨具有限公司
078

家用智能榨油机
设计 / 深圳洛可可工业设计有限公司
生产 / 深圳得力人电器有限公司
078

苏泊尔全景视窗电饭煲
设计 / 宁波浪尖工业产品造型设计有限公司
生产 / 浙江苏泊尔股份有限公司
079

CXW-220-TJ20 吸油烟机
设计 / 帅康集团
生产 / 帅康集团
079

乐凡空气炸锅
设计 / 青鸟工业设计有限公司
生产 / 广东顺德乐凡电器有限公司
080

球釜电饭煲
设计 / 马汉、张胜兰
生产 / 浙江苏泊尔家电制造有限公司
080

启智 A9 集成灶
设计 / 浙江森歌电器有限公司
生产 / 浙江森歌电器有限公司
081

智盒—青芒 智能网络机顶盒
设计 / 深圳智我科技有限公司
生产 / 深圳雷柏科技股份有限公司
082

飞利浦专业级行车记录仪 ADR810
设计 / 上海木马工业产品设计有限公司
生产 / 飞利浦中国投资有限公司上海研发中心
083

智能血糖仪—魔镜
设计 / 上海木马工业产品设计有限公司
生产 / 上海康之元信息技术有限公司
084

软水机“融”
设计 / 贾雪峰、李文锋
生产 / 上海开能环保设备股份有限公司
084

三点式蓝牙音箱
设计 / 杭州凸凹工业设计有限公司
生产 / 杭州凸凹工业设计有限公司
085

“三角鳐”蒸汽地拖
设计 / 杭州凸凹工业设计有限公司
生产 / 杭州凸凹工业设计有限公司
085

除螨吸尘一体机
设计 / 吕知轩、姜鸿胤
生产 / 苏州欧奈电器科技有限公司
086

悦 me 智能机顶盒
设计 / 上海木马工业产品设计有限公司
生产 / 中国电信集团公司智能家居业务运营中心
086

家用智能机器人
设计 / 北京智加问道科技有限公司
生产 / 北京家度科技有限公司
086

怡兰全屋净水机
设计 / 宁波浪尖工业产品造型设计有限公司
生产 / 福建怡兰净水科技有限公司
087

无线吸尘除螨机
设计 / 吕知轩
生产 / 苏州欧奈电器科技有限公司
087

UCON 智能遥控器
设计 /UCON Design Team
生产 / 南京悦控智能科技有限公司
088

震撼者 3D 7.1 全景立体环绕声电竞耳机
设计 /TTdesign
生产 /Thermaltake
088

中兴超简遥控器
设计 / 中兴通讯股份有限公司
生产 / 中兴通讯股份有限公司
089

竹构—月影环形灯
设计 / 杭州凸凹工业设计有限公司
生产 / 杭州凸凹工业设计有限公司
089

军规级抗震防水移动硬盘
设计 / 钟健志、吴家祯
生产 / 广颖电通股份有限公司
090

逸格智能手表
设计 / 深圳意臣工业设计有限公司
生产 / 深圳市宏电技术股份有限公司
090

数码宠物定位器
设计 / 深圳市浪尖设计有限公司
生产 / 郑州派乐数码科技有限公司
091

小米小盒子
设计 / 沈希洁
生产 / 小米科技有限责任公司
091

对开门冰箱 BCD-630WPDGB（鎏金黑）
设计 / 李琦、崔北艳
生产 / 合肥晶弘电器有限公司
092

无霜冷藏冷冻箱
设计 / 杭州领跑者工业设计有限公司
生产 / 杭州华日电冰箱股份有限公司
093

樱花“都市时尚系列”烟炉一体化设计
设计 / 上海木马工业产品设计有限公司
生产 / 樱花工业设计中心
094

老板 5900 油烟机
设计 / 杭州老板电器股份有限公司
生产 / 杭州老板电器股份有限公司
095

海信多门冰箱
设计 / 海信工业设计中心
生产 / 海信容声（广东）冰箱有限公司
096

易清洁燃气灶
设计 / 广东顺德东方麦田工业设计有限公司
生产 / 广东万家乐燃气具有限公司
097

小天鹅比佛利滚筒洗衣机
设计 / 无锡小天鹅股份有限公司工业设计团队
生产 / 无锡小天鹅股份有限公司
097

JBL Control X Wireless
设计 / 哈曼设计团队
生产 / 哈曼国际
098

JBL Grip 100 / JBL Grip 200
设计 / 哈曼设计团队
生产 / 哈曼国际
098

JBL Trip
设计 / 哈曼设计团队
生产 / 哈曼国际
099

Harman Kardon Onyx Studio 2
设计 / 哈曼设计团队
生产 / 哈曼国际
099

2015 中国设计红星奖获奖名单

和而泰电炖锅
设计 / 宁波浪尖工业产品造型设计有限公司
生产 / 深圳和而泰智能控制股份有限公司
100

车载净化器
设计 / 广东顺德东方麦田工业设计有限公司
生产 / 广东顺德博兰尼电器实业有限公司
100

壁挂式空气能热水器
设计 / 广东顺德东方麦田工业设计有限公司
生产 / 广东万家乐燃气具有限公司
101

油烟机 CXW-200-IF6
设计 / 宁波欧琳厨具有限公司
生产 / 宁波欧琳厨具有限公司
101

小天鹅比佛利全自动洗衣
设计 / 无锡小天鹅股份有限公司工业设计团队
生产 / 无锡小天鹅股份有限公司
102

商用跑步机
设计 / 北京艾德沃工业设计有限公司
生产 / 山东大胡子运动器材有限公司
103

弘宜森合空气净化器
设计 /Andre Santos、张雯
生产 / 弘宜森合（北京）科技有限公司
104

威力“极光”系列喷淋自洁桶波轮洗衣机
设计 / 青鸟工业设计有限公司
生产 / 中山东菱威力电器有限公司
104

F6.6-15AQ1 电热水器
设计 / 美的集团热水器事业部工业设计部
生产 / 芜湖美的厨卫电器制造有限公司
105

双面对横式取暖器
设计 / 吉明静、马小康
生产 / 广东美的环境电器制造有限公司
105

miniJ 滚筒洗衣机
设计 / 杭州奥格工业设计有限公司
生产 / 宁波吉德电器有限公司
106

北鼎电水壶 K206
设计 / 张默晗、钟文金
生产 / 深圳市北鼎科技有限公司
107

不用弯腰看火燃气灶
设计 / 赵磊
生产 / 广东顺德东方麦田工业设计有限公司
108

全自动吸油烟机
设计 / 广东顺德东方麦田工业设计有限公司
生产 / 广东万家乐燃气具有限公司
109

小米插线板
设计 / 贺嘉、宋世琦
生产 / 青米（北京）科技有限公司
110

小米体重秤
设计 / 姜婧
生产 / 安徽华米信息科技有限公司
110

小米盒子增强版
设计 / 程兆鹏
生产 / 歌尔声学股份有限公司
111

小米手环
设计 / 王涛
生产 / 安徽华米信息科技有限公司
111

母婴体重秤
设计 / 中山市涅磐产品设计有限公司
生产 / 广东乐心医疗电子股份有限公司
112

拉卡拉支付卡表
设计 / 义乌市浪尖工业设计有限公司
生产 / 拉卡拉集团
113

创维 _G9200 电视
设计 / 深圳创维—RGB 电子有限公司工业设计研究院创新设计中心
生产 / 深圳创维—RGB 电子有限公司
114

NR 系列空气净化器
设计 / 李三新、袁志强
生产 / 广东美的制冷设备有限公司
115

AKG Y23U
设计 / 哈曼设计团队
生产 / 哈曼国际
116

逸曦发烧友入耳式耳机
设计 / 深圳洛可可工业设计有限公司
生产 / 逸曦电子科技有限公司
116

JBL Everest Headphones
设计 / 哈曼设计团队
生产 / 哈曼国际
117

联想双耳无线胶囊耳机
设计 / 联想设计与用户体验中心
生产 / 联想
118

天府通公交手环
设计 / 彭戈、孙智宇
生产 / 成都莫比智能科技有限公司
118

血压计 XY-211
设计 / 杭州奥格工业设计有限公司
生产 / 浙江铭众医疗器械有限公司
119

联想 Yoga 遥控鼠标
设计 / 设计与用户体验
生产 / 联想
119

单手直饮运动水瓶
设计 / 朱熙超、张斌
生产 / 上海思乐得不锈钢制品有限公司
120

儿童益智餐具
设计 / 周龙
生产 / 浙江瑞翔婴童用品有限公司
120

魔盒健身车
设计 / 浙江金棒运动用品有限公司
生产 / 浙江金棒运动用品有限公司
121

D300 锂电智能多功能工具
设计 / 湖洄（上海）设计咨询有限公司
生产 / 浙江恒友机电有限公司
121

RE 系列卷尺
设计 / 湖洄（上海）设计咨询有限公司
生产 / 宁波欧博五金实业有限公司
122

“器”——新型家庭绿植
设计 / 夏旭
生产 / 上海艺凯设计有限公司
122

GYENNO 睿餐勺
设计 / 深圳市佳简几何工业设计有限公司
生产 / 深圳市臻络科技有限公司
123

普朗克过滤水壶
设计 / 李敏
生产 / 厦门建霖工业有限公司
123

Pixel Pro 智能墙面开关
设计 / 北京东成新维设计咨询有限公司
生产 / 北京昊恒天科技有限公司
124

乐活净水机
设计 / 徐智彬
生产 / 厦门建霖工业有限公司
124

茶花易洁系列扫把畚斗套装
设计 / 刘志斌、邱志荣
生产 / 茶花现代家居用品股份有限公司
125

延长水龙头
设计 / 郑金洪
生产 / 厦门建霖工业有限公司
125

婴儿体温计
设计 / 东莞市浪尖产品设计有限公司
生产 / 康之元信息技术有限公司
126

卡易刷
设计 / 深圳市鼎典工业产品设计有限公司
生产 / 深圳市鼎典生活用品有限公司
126

2015 中国设计红星奖获奖名单

竹纤维搅拌碗套件
设计 / 宁波江北矩成创意产品设计有限公司
生产 / 宁波江东诚优进出口有限公司
127

便捷型 COB 工作灯
设计 / 宁波市法诺工业产品设计有限公司
生产 / 宁波市法诺工业产品设计有限公司
127

多功能安全排插
设计 / 骆柏林
生产 / 深圳市绿联科技有限公司
128

"旋霓"茶几
设计 / 梁缘
生产 / 佰墨文化传媒（北京）有限公司
128

至尊水槽
设计 / 殷刘春、卫凯 · 提鲁那嘎鲁
生产 / 珠海普乐美厨卫有限公司
129

一千零一夜
设计 / 北京圣宝地工业设计有限公司
生产 / 河间市万里工艺玻璃制品厂
129

多功能切割机
设计 / 沃伦 · 布朗
生产 / 宝时得机械（中国）有限公司
130

霾星人鼻用空气净化器
设计 / 北京万生人和科技有限公司
生产 / 北京万生人和科技有限公司
130

汽车儿童安全座椅 太空城堡
设计 / 麦克英孚（宁波）婴童用品有限公司
生产 / 麦克英孚（宁波）婴童用品有限公司
131

关怀手持花洒
设计 / 厦门松霖科技有限公司
生产 / 厦门松霖科技有限公司
131

Douho 角阀
设计 / 九牧厨卫股份有限公司
生产 / 九牧厨卫股份有限公司
132

开百合
设计 / 梁振挥、蔡国伟
生产 / PSL Limited
138

开水过滤器
设计 / 马鞍山江东工业设计发展有限公司
生产 / 上海谷奇核孔膜材料科技有限公司
133

卡莱氏滤水壶
设计 / 上海木马工业产品设计有限公司
生产 / 上海卡莱氏净水科技有限公司
133

幻雨魔法师 Select 淋浴管
设计 / 汉斯格雅卫浴产品（上海）有限公司
凤凰设计室
生产 / 汉斯格雅卫浴产品（上海）有限公司
134

正姿护套
设计 / 同济大学 & 晨光文具工业设计部
生产 / 上海晨光文具股份有限公司
134

全能营养料理机
设计 / 青鸟工业设计有限公司
生产 / 广东顺德乐凡电器有限公司
135

榻榻米茶几凳
设计 / 杭州博乐工业产品设计有限公司
生产 / 杭州橙舍文化创意有限公司
135

不锈钢真空保温焖烧罐
设计 / 上海麦扑艺术设计咨询有限公司
生产 / 浙江武义山河工贸有限公司
136

懒时光衣帽架
设计 / 杭州博乐工业产品设计有限公司
生产 / 杭州橙舍文化创意有限公司
137

柜茗器
设计 / 石大宇
生产 / 北京清庭文创文化发展有限公司
137

溪水间茶叶
设计 / 北京光彩无限管理咨询有限公司
生产 / 北京光彩无限管理咨询有限公司
138

便携式烘鞋器
设计 / 杭州博乐工业产品设计有限公司
生产 / 台州市中联电器有限公司
138

实智 P1 智能插排
设计 / 张长东、田春宇
生产 / 实智科技有限公司
139

弹击式汽车安全伞
设计 / 李若权
生产 / 深圳市喜途伞业有限公司
139

果冻重力闹钟
设计 / 深圳市风格派家居用品有限公司
生产 / 深圳市风格派家居用品有限公司
140

小米 LED 随身灯 / 小米随身风扇
设计 / 窦文博
生产 / 江苏紫米电子技术有限公司
140

这里有我的一切（适老厨房）
设计 / 河南省大信整体厨房科贸有限公司
生产 / 河南省大信整体厨房科贸有限公司
141

简 · 爱—4 平微厨
设计 / 饶如泊、林建旋
生产 / 厦门金牌厨柜股份有限公司
141

SILI-CUP 矿化杯
设计 / 黄辉荣
生产 / 广州韩能大健康产品有限公司
142

拔火罐
设计 / 杭州斯帕克造型艺术有限公司
生产 / 杭州斯帕克造型艺术有限公司
142

"小心眼"护眼套装
设计 / 深圳洛可可工业设计有限公司
生产 / 广东三块钱信息科技有限公司
143

流金提梁壶
设计 / 物舍设计团队
生产 / 三度品牌策划有限公司
143

合
设计 / 周安彬、雷南仕
生产 / 广州高尚生活文化传播有限公司
144

叁
设计 / 周安彬、詹秋鸿
生产 / 广州高尚生活文化传播有限公司
144

中老年多功能健康座椅
设计 / 清华大学美术学院健康医疗产业创新设计研究所
生产 / 博奥颐和健康科学技术（北京）有限公司
145

轻扇（屏风）
设计 / 袁媛
生产 / 北京如翌家具有限公司
146

观石（沙发）
设计 / 袁媛
生产 / 北京如翌家具有限公司
146

通气面罩
设计 / 毅达（北京）医疗科技有限公司
生产 / 东莞市毅达电子有限公司
147

婴儿浴盆
设计 / 深圳市问鼎工业设计有限公司
生产 / 深圳市懒妈妈生活用品有限公司
147

五环茶——和之缘
设计 / 焦哲
生产 / 北京老舍茶馆
148

两忘角壶
设计 / 石大宇
生产 / 北京清庭文创文化发展有限公司
148

2015 中国设计红星奖获奖名单

2015 中国设计红星奖获奖名单

PLUS4020 全罩激光切割机
设计 / 武汉玛吉工业设计有限公司
生产 / 武汉卡特激光工程有限责任公司
171

高压清洗机
设计 / 苏州本丞工业设计有限公司
生产 / 苏州洁宝机械有限公司
172

便携式个人新风系统
设计 / 深圳市匠意科技开发有限公司
生产 / 深圳市新乐正环保科技有限公司
172

航母控制台
设计 / 上品设计机构
生产 / 中船重工
173

美容仪
设计 / 深圳市东方艺辰工业设计有限公司
生产 / 深圳市纬安共创生物科技有限公司
173

Kast 3D 打印机
设计 / 深圳市嘉兰图设计股份有限公司
生产 /Photon Fluid Inc.
174

医用胶片打印机
设计 / 深圳市浪尖设计有限公司
生产 / 重庆联佰博超医疗器械有限公司
174

眼科 OCT
设计 / 深圳市浪尖设计有限公司
生产 / 深圳市斯尔顿科技有限公司
175

光纤切割刀
设计 / 深圳市浪尖设计有限公司
生产 / 中国电子科技集团公司第四十一研究所
175

樱花核磁共振成像
设计 / 胡海权、赵妍
生产 / 东软集团股份有限公司
176

FR 云机器人
设计 / 武汉龙兴工业产品设计有限公司
生产 / 武汉奋进电力技术有限公司
176

四维平衡诊断系统
设计 / 温凯翔、刘程
生产 / 上元医疗
177

手持静电纺丝仪
设计 / 青岛桥域产品设计有限公司
生产 / 青岛博纳生物科技有限公司
177

SUN 5 医用升温毯控制器
设计 / 北京谊安工业设计团队
生产 / 北京谊安医疗系统股份有限公司
177

绅宝 CC
设计 / 北汽股份汽车研究院
生产 / 北京汽车股份有限公司
178

绅宝 X65
设计 / 北京汽车股份有限公司
生产 / 北汽（广州）汽车有限公司
178

新型 100 %低地板有轨电车
设计 / 南车青岛四方机车车辆股份有限公司
生产 / 南车青岛四方机车车辆股份有限公司
179

电动独轮车
设计 / 北京梦想者工业设计有限公司
生产 / 北京梦想者工业设计有限公司
180

悦翔 V7
设计 / 重庆长安汽车股份有限公司
生产 / 重庆长安汽车股份有限公司
180

BJ40
设计 / 北京汽车研究总院有限公司
生产 / 北京汽车股份有限公司
181

200km/h 客运机车外形及驾驶室设计
设计 / 西南交通大学人机环境系统设计研究所
生产 / 中国中车股份大同电力机车有限责任公司
182

成都低地板有轨电车
设计 / 西南交通大学人机环境系统设计研究所
生产 / 成都市新筑路桥机械股份有限公司
183

马来西亚 ETS 米轨动车
设计 / 李鹏飞、高楠
生产 / 中国中车株洲电力机车有限公司
184

八轴交流传动快速客运电力机车
设计 / 易琼、高楠
生产 / 中国中车株洲电力机车有限公司
185

Solo Wheel 天蝎
设计 / 北京尚果创想科技有限公司
生产 / 英凡蒂（北京）科贸有限公司
186

乐行 V3 电动独轮车
设计 / 邱宇鹏、蔡优飞
生产 / 深圳乐行天下科技有限公司
186

防雨头盔
设计 / 杭州斯帕克造型艺术有限公司
生产 / 杭州斯帕克造型艺术有限公司
186

传祺 GA6
设计 / 广州汽车集团股份有限公司汽车工程研究院
生产 / 广州汽车集团股份有限公司
187

多生物特征信息智能识别闸机
设计 / 北京智加问道科技有限公司
生产 / 北京海鑫科金高科技股份有限公司
188

公交自动售水机
设计 / 北京乐品乐道科技有限公司
生产 / 北京君汇港沣科技发展有限公司
189

果蔬采购直通车
设计 / 北京智加问道科技有限公司
生产 / 大嘉润商业服务有限公司
189

普罗娜智慧照明路灯系列
设计 / 上海木马工业产品设计有限公司
生产 / 创导（上海）智能技术有限公司
190

“鱼骨”桥梁设计
设计 / 西南交通大学人机环境系统设计研究所
生产 / 西南交通大学建筑勘察设计研究院
191

最受大众欢迎奖

智能后视镜行车记录仪
设计 / 深圳捷渡科技有限公司
生产 / 深圳捷渡科技有限公司
194

Nubia Z9
设计 / 努比亚技术有限公司
生产 / 努比亚技术有限公司
194

CXW-220-TJ20 吸油烟机
设计 / 帅康集团
生产 / 帅康集团
194

乐行 V3 电动独轮车
设计 / 邱宇鹏、蔡优飞
生产 / 深圳乐行天下科技有限公司
194

弹击式汽车安全伞
设计 / 李若权
生产 / 深圳市喜途伞业有限公司
195

智能湿水牛皮纸包装机
设计 / 宁波市法诺工业产品设计有限公司
生产 / 宁波赛美达环保科技有限公司
195

Amazing Box Lite 智能家居控制中心
设计 / 张嘉泳
生产 / 大连华信计算机技术股份有限公司
195

公交自动售水机
设计 / 北京乐品乐道科技有限公司
生产 / 北京君汇港沣科技发展有限公司
195

折角－圆珠笔
设计 / 欧赛笔业
生产 / 杭州欧赛笔业有限公司
195

Winner List of 2015 China Red Star Design Award

Best of the Gold Prize

Yoga3 Pro
Design / Lenovo
Manufacture / Lenovo
008

Gold Prize

Haier Intelligent Robot
Design / Qingdao Haier Intelligent Home Appliance Technology Co.,Ltd
Manufacture / Qingdao Haier Intelligent Home Appliance Technology Co.,Ltd
012

The EMU Resistant to Freezing, Windy and Sandy Conditions
Design / Csr Qqingdao Sifang Co.,Ltd
Manufacture / Csr Qqingdao Sifang Co.,Ltd
013

OLED TV
Design / TPV XMIC ID Design Team
Manufacture / Top Display Technology (Xiamen) Co.,Ltd
014

Dyson Pure Cool
Design / Dyson
Manufacture / Dyson
015

Hisense VIDAA MAX Laser Theater
Design / Hisense ID Center
Manufacture / Qindao Hisense Electroniocs Co.,Ltd
016

Xplorer V
Design / Shenzhen Zero-tech UAV Limited
Manufacture / Shenzhen Rapoo Technology Co.,Ltd
017

BAT
Design / Beluga Design
Manufacture / Jiangsu Capital Holding Manufacturing Technology Limited
018

QS-M2 Needle-free Injector
Design / Chen Suning
Manufacture / Beijing QS Medical Technology Co.,Ltd
019

Silver Prize

Trumpchi GS4
Design / Guangzhou Automobile Group Co., Ltd Automotive Engineering Institute
Manufacture / Guangzhou Automobile Group Motor Co.,Ltd
022

Nubia Z9
Design / Nubia Technology Co, Ltd
Manufacture / Nubia Technology Co, Ltd
023

XT680 Telehandler
Design / ID Center of Jiangsu Xuzhou Construction Machinery Research
Manufacture / Xuzhou Construction Machinery Group Inc.
024

Suzhou Tram Line 1CN
Design / MBD Design France
Manufacture / CSR Nanjing Puzhen Co.,Ltd
025

Praise of Moon Tea Tray Set
Design /Jeff Shi
Manufacture / Dragonfly Design Center
026

Wu
Design / Zhou Anbin, Lei Nanshi
Manufacture / Gaoshang Living (GuangZhou) Co.,Ltd
027

Absorbable ASD Closure System
Design / April 6th Design Co.,Ltd
Manufacture / Lifetech Scientific(Shenzhen) Co.,Ltd
028

Quantitative Quick Tap
Design / Foshan Rifeng Enterprise Co.,Ltd
Manufacture / Foshan Rifeng Enterprise Co.,Ltd
029

FW6108 Portable Multi-functional Lighting Device
Design / Ocean King Lighting Technology Co., Ltd
Manufacture / Ocean King Lighting Technology Co., Ltd
030

FZ Bangshu Xing
Design / Wang Wen
Manufacture / Beijing Founder Electronics Co.,Ltd
022

Best Team Prize

Lenovo Notebook Design Team
033

Best New Designer Prize

Li Ruoxin
035

Excellent Prize

Infrared Camera Network
Design / Shenzhen Exclamation Point Pruduct Design Co.Ltd
Manufacture / Zhuo mao Technology (Shenzhen) Co.,Ltd
038

KONKA BK929
Design / Chen Wanheng
Manufacture / Shenzhen KONKA Telecommunications Techology Co., Ltd
038

Smart Screen Systems
Design / Shenzhen Perth Industrial Design Co.,Ltd
Manufacture / Shenzhen Perth Industrial Design Co.,Ltd
039

E Mobile Terminal
Design / Zhang Nan, Huang Bowen
Manufacture / Fujian Star-net Communication Co., Ltd
039

Smart Rearview Mirror Car Driving Recorder
Design / Jado Technology Co,Ltd
Manufacture / Jado Technology Co,Ltd
040

EP404 Snail Haptor USB Cable
Design / Tim Chu, Shawn Shen
Manufacture / Shenzhen Lofree Culture Co.,Ltd
041

Powerloft
Design / April 6th Design Co.,Ltd
Manufacture / Shenzhen Equator Aurora Information Tech. Ltd
042

Miniaturization of Satellite Signal Simulator
Design / Zhen Dawei
Manufacture / Space Star Technology Co., Ltd.
042

The Palm Meridians Intelligent Terminal Authentication
Design / Chengdu Top-Creative Product Design Co.,Ltd
Manufacture / Chengdu Cinsoft Technology Development Co.,Ltd
044

Smart Driving Data Recorder
Design /Jason
Manufacture / Dawning Information Industry Co., Ltd
043

JolinkTM A600 Remote Teller Machine
Design / Jado Technology Co,Ltd
Manufacture / Jado Technology Co,Ltd
046

Business Tablet
Design / Chengdu Artop Industrial Design Co.,Ltd
Manufacture / Beijing Ereneben Information Technology Co.,Ltd
044

SIM + Bluetooth SIM Card Reader
Design / Shenzhen Newplan Design Co.,Ltd
Manufacture / Shenzhen Newplan Design Co.,Ltd
044

Rugged Tablet PC
Design / Zhengzhou Artop Design Co.,Ltd
Manufacture / Nancal Energy-Saving Technology Co.,Ltd
045

Dustproof, Shockproof and Waterproof Mobile Phone
Design / Ren Minjie
Manufacture / Shanghai Several Fruit Technology Co.,Ltd
045

Winner List of 2015 China Red Star Design Award

"Switch On" Backup Power Bank
Design / Boby Poon
Manufacture / Manova International Limited
046

WOW!dea MOCA X7s Multi-functional Portable Data Card
Design / Beijing Yuanlong Yato Culture Dissemination Co.,Ltd
Manufacture / Beijing Yuanlong Yato Culture Dissemination Co.,Ltd
046

Multi-tool for Optical Communication
Design / Fiberhome Telecommunication Technologies Co.,Ltd
Manufacture / Fiberhome Telecommunication Technologies Co.,Ltd
046

OV U-Net
Design / April 6th Design Co.,Ltd
Manufacture / Shenzhen Ruiren Electronics Co.,Ltd
047

Work Card Recorder
Design / Zhengzhou Artop Design Co.,Ltd
Manufacture / Zhengzhou Huali Infomation Technology Co.,Ltd
047

WOW!dea MOCA X8 Multi-functional Data Portable Charger
Design / Beijing Yuanlong Yato Culture Dissemination Co.,Ltd
Manufacture / Beijing Yuanlong Yato Culture Dissemination Co.,Ltd
047

Perception Neuron
Design / OREA Technology (Beijing) Co.,Ltd
Manufacture / Noitom Ltd
048

Ubox
Design / Zhu Zhengwen, Chen Zhongshan
Manufacture / Fiberhome Telecommunication Technologies Co.,Ltd
049

Mokeen
Design / Yiroo Industrial Products Design Shanghai Co., Ltd
Manufacture / Institute Technology (Shanghai) Co.,Ltd
049

Vistandard HoloStation
Design / Exmade Design Consultants Co.,Ltd
Manufacture / Vistandard (Beijing) Digital Technology Co., Ltd
050

Robot Virtual Graphic Online Packaging System
Design / Ideapool
Manufacture / Ideapool.Ltd
050

Intelligent Wearable Drafting Rehabilitation System
Design / Chengdu Top-Creative Product Design Co.,Ltd
Manufacture / Sichuan Ikcare Medical Electrical Equipment Co.Ltd
051

GPS Shoes in Electronic Armour
Design / Kacke (Fujian) Industrial Design Co.,Ltd
Manufacture / Fujian Province Putian City Shuangchi Intelligent Information Technology Co., Ltd
051

Aged Smart Walking Stick
Design / Beijing LEAD Technology Co.Ltd
Manufacture / Beijing Leadcore Ruikang Technology Co.Ltd
052

Bluetooth Stereo Headset - Clipper
Design / April 5th Design Co.,Ltd
Manufacture / Avantronics Limited
053

iBone Dog Care Smart Accessories
Design / Hangzhou LPZ Industrial Design Co. Ltd
Manufacture / Hangzhou Wangxingren Technology Co.,Ltd
053

HY Qihei
Design / Beijing Hanyi Information Technology Co., Ltd
Manufacture / Beijing Hanyi Information Technology Co.,Ltd
054

Declare of Founder Youhei
Design / Qiu Yin
Manufacture / Beijing Founder Electronics Co.,Ltd
055

F50LW-B water heater
Design / Industrial Design Department of Water Heater Department of Midea Group
Manufacture / Wuhu Midea Kitchen And Bath Appliances Mfg. Co. Ltd
056

Purification and Filtering Chamber
Design / Industrial Design Department of Water Heater Department of Midea Group
Manufacture / Wuhu Midea Kitchen And Bath Appliances Mfg. Co.,Ltd
056

Smart Fridge Which Can OnlineShopping
Design / Whirlpool (China) GCD
Manufacture / Whirlpool (China) Co.,Ltd
057

Heat Pump Flagship Edition
Design / Chinno Industrial Design Co., Ltd
Manufacture / PHNIX Co., LTD
058

CHIQ-Q1V
Design / Homwee Technology (Sichuan) Co., Ltd
Manufacture / Sichuan Changhong Electric Co.,Ltd
059

Outdoor Bluetooth Stereo
Design / Shenzhen Exclamation Point Pruduct Design Co.,Ltd
Manufacture /Shenzhen Jonter digital Co.,Ltd
060

Dotop Extension Maglev Bluetooth Speaker
Design / Shenzhen Exclamation Point Pruduct Design Co.,Ltd
Manufacture /Shenzhen Cager Digital Technology Co.,Ltd
060

B18 Transformable Power Bank
Design / Shenzhen AIDI Technology Co.,Ltd
Manufacture / Shenzhen Cager Digital Technology Co.,Ltd
061

Amazing BOX Life
Design / Mark Cheung
Manufacture / Dalian Hi-Think Computer Technology, Corp
061

Goluk Intelligent Vehicle Traveling Data Recorder
Design / LKK Design Shenzhen Co., Ltd
Manufacture / Beijing Mobnote Technology Co.,Ltd
062

SINGBOX V5 speaker
Design / Shenzhen Exclamation Point Pruduct Design Co.Ltd
Manufacture / Dongguan City Singbox Electronics Manufacturing Co., Ltd
062

Qizi Moretel Smart Phone
Design / Shenzhen Exclamation Point Pruduct Design Co.,Ltd
Manufacture / Zhuhai Qifei Information Technology Co.,Ltd
063

iTvTop Portable TV Box
Design / Chengdu Artop Industrial Design Co.,Ltd
Manufacture / Research Institute of Tsinghua University in Shenzhen
063

LEBOND Teeth Cleaning
Design / Sounded Product Design Co.,Ltd
Manufacture / LEBOND Electronics Technology Co.,Ltd
064

Winner List of 2015 China Red Star Design Award

miniJ Washing Machine
Design / AUG design Co.,Ltd(Hangzhou)
Manufacture /Ningbo Jide Electrical Appliance Co.,Ltd
106

BUYDEEM K206
Design / George Mohan Zhang, Zhong Wenjin
Manufacture / Buydeem Technology (Shenzhen) Co.,Ltd
107

Gas Stove, no Need to Lean Over for Observing the fire
Design / Zhao Lei
Manufacture / East-innovation Shunde GD Co.,Ltd
108

Automatic Range Hood
Design / East-innovation Shunde GD Co.,Ltd
Manufacture / Guangdong Macro Gas Appliance Co.,Ltd
109

MI Power Strip
Design / He Jia, Song Shiqi
Manufacture / QingMi (Beijing) Technology Co.,Ltd
110

MI Body Scale
Design / Jiang Jing
Manufacture / Huami Inc.
110

MI Box Pro
Design / Cheng Zhaopeng
Manufacture / GoerTek Electronics
111

MI Band
Design / Wang Tao
Manufacture / Huami Inc.
111

Weight Scale for Mother and Baby
Design / Zhongshan Nirvana Design Co.,Ltd
Manufacture / Guangdong Transtek Medical Electronics Co.,Ltd
112

Payment Watch
Design / Yiwu Artop Design Co.,Ltd
Manufacture / Lakala Payment Co.,Ltd
113

Skyworth_G9200 TV
Design / Skyworth -RGB Electronics Co., Industrial Design Innovation Design Center and Research Institute
Manufacture / Skyworth-RGB Electronics CO.,Ltd
114

NR Series Air Purifier
Design / Li Sanxin,Yuan Zhiqiang
Manufacture / GD Midea Air-Conditionging Equipment Co.,Ltd
115

AKG Y23U
Design / Harman Design Center
Manufacture / Harman International Industries
116

ECCI Hi-Fi In-ear Headset
Design / LKK Design Shenzhen Co.,Ltd
Manufacture / ECCI Electronic technology Co.,LTD
116

JBL Everest Headphones
Design / Harman Design Center
Manufacture / Harman International Industries
117

Lenovo Earphone 900
Design / Lenovo
Manufacture / Lenovo
118

Tianfu Tong Bus Bracelet
Design / Peng Ge, Sunny
Manufacture / Chengdu Mobi Intelligence ltd
118

Mobile Health Blood Pressure Terminal
Design / AUG design Co.,Ltd (Hangzhou)
Manufacture / Zhejiang Medzone Medical Devices Co.,Ltd(Hangzhou)
119

Lenovo Yoga Remote Mouse
Design / Lenovo
Manufacture / Lenovo
119

Sports Flask
Design / Zhu Xichao, Zhang Bin
Manufacture / Shanghai Solid Stainless Steel Products Co.,Ltd
120

baby training tableware
Design / Aaron
Manufacture / Zhejiang Reshine Babycare Co.,Ltd
120

M-BOX
Design / Zhejiang Jinbang Sports Equipment Co.,Ltd
Manufacture / Joybold Sports
121

Tinkool D300
Design / Sohui (Shanghai) Design and consult Co.,Ltd
Manufacture / Zhejiang Hengyou Machine & electron Co.,Ltd
121

RE Series Tapes
Design / Sohui (Shanghai) Design and Consult Co.,Ltd
Manufacture / Ningbo Oubo Hardware Industrial Ltd
122

Green Life
Design / Xia Xu
Manufacture / GK Design Shanghai Inc
122

GYENNO Spoon
Design / Shenzhen XIVO Design Co.,Ltd
Manufacture / Shenzhen GYENNO Technologies CO., Ltd
123

Planck
Design / Mya li
Manufacture / Runner-corp
123

Pixel Pro Smart Wall Switch
Design / FromD Innovation
Manufacture / HaoHengTian Technology Inc.
124

Lohas
Design / Xu Zhibin
Manufacture / Runner-corp
124

EASY CLEAN OUSTPAN WITH BROOM
Design / Liu Zhibin, Qiu Zhirong
Manufacture / Chahua Modern Housewares Co.,Ltd
125

Lengthen Faucet
Design / Zheng Jinhong
Manufacture / Xiamen Runner Industrial Corporation
125

Baby Thermometer
Design / Dongguan Artop Product Design Co.,Ltd
Manufacture / Sybercare Technology Co., Ltd
126

Swipeasy
Design / Shenzhen Designdo Industrial Design Co., Ltd
Manufacture / Shenzhen Designdo Lifestyle Co., Ltd
126

Bamboo Fiber Mixing Bowl Kit
Design / Ningbo Galachy Creative Product Design Co.,Tld
Manufacture / Brightman Iinternational Tranding Co.,Ltd
127

Portable COB Working Light
Design / Ningbo FANUO Industrial Product Design Co.,Ltd
Manufacture / Ningbo FANUO Industrial Product Design Co.,Ltd
127

Multifunction Charging Station
Design / Luo Bolin
Manufacture / Ugreen Group Limited
128

Water Ripples Tea Table
Design / Liang Yuan
Manufacture / BaiMo Culture Media (Beijing) Co., Ltd
128

Proficency Sink
Design / Yin Liuchun, Venkat Tirunagaru
Manufacture / Primy Corporation Limited
129

Winner List of 2015 China Red Star Design Award

One Thousand and One Nights
Design / CBD Group Corp.
Manufacture / HeJian WanLi Craft Glass Product Factory
129

Blade Runner 2X
Design / Warren Brown
Manufacture / positec machinery (china) co.,Ltd
130

MaiXingRen Nasal Air Purifier
Design / Beijing Winsunny Harmony Science
Manufacture / Beijing Winsunny Harmony Science
130

R102A
Design / MAX-INF(Ningbo) Baby Product Co., Ltd
Manufacture / MAX-INF(Ningbo) Baby Product Co., Ltd
131

Care
Design / Xiamen Solex High-Tech Industries Co.,Ltd
Manufacture / Xiamen Solex High-Tech Industries Co.,Ltd
131

Douho
Design / JOMOO Kitchen & Bath Co.,Ltd
Manufacture / JOMOO Kitchen & Bath Co.,Ltd
132

I-OPENER
Design / Fai Leung, Michael Choi
Manufacture / PSL Limited
132

Hot Water Filters
Design / Ma'an Shan Jiangdong Industrial Design Co.,Ltd
Manufacture / Shanghai GUCH Nuclear Poro Membrane Material Technology Co.,Ltd
133

HydroPure Filter kettle
Design / Shanghai Moma Industrial Product Design Co.,Ltd
Manufacture / Shanghai HydroPure Water Purification Technology Co. Ltd
133

Hansgrohe Rainmaker Select Showerpipe
Design / Hansgrohe Sanitary Products(Shanghai) Co.,Ltd Phoenix Design
Manufacture / Hansgrohe Sanitary Products (Shanghai) Co.,Ltd
134

Corrective Sheath
Design / Tongji University & M&G ID department
Manufacture / Shanghai M&G Stationery INC.
134

Almighty Nutrition Food Machine
Design / Bird Industrial Design
Manufacture / Guangdong Shunde LeFan Electrical Appliances Co.,Ltd
135

Tatami Teapoy Stool
Design / Hangzhou Bole Industrial Design Co.,Ltd
Manufacture / Hangzhou Zen's Cultural and Creative Co.,Ltd
135

Stainless Steel Thermal Insulation Pot
Design / MAP ART&DESIGN
Manufacture / Zhejiang Wuyi Shanhe Industry
136

Lazy Time Coat Stand
Design / Hangzhou Bole Industrial Design Co.,Ltd
Manufacture / Hangzhou Zen's Cultural and Creative Co., Ltd
137

Gui Ming-Qi
Design / Jeff Shi
Manufacture / Dragonfly Design Center
137

Tea of XiShuiJian
Design / Shine Design Consulation Center
Manufacture / Shine Design Consulation Center
138

Portable Shoe Dryer
Design / Hangzhou Bole Industrial Design Co.,Ltd
Manufacture / Taizhou Zhonglian Electrical Co.,Ltd
138

P1 Smart Platooninsert
Design / Zhang Changdong, Tink Tian
Manufacture / iSmart Science and Technology CO.,Ltd
139

Shooting Safety Hambrella
Design / Li Ruoquan
Manufacture / Shenzhen Xitu Umbrella Co.,Ltd
139

Jelly Gravity Control Clock
Design / Shenzhen Stylepie Lifestyle Co., Ltd
Manufacture / Shenzhen Stylepie Lifestyle Co., Ltd
140

MI Portable Light/MI Portable Fan
Design / Dou Wenbo
Manufacture / Zimi Corporation
140

One for All
Design / Henan Province Daxin Whole Cookroom Science
Manufacture / Henan Province Daxin whole cookroom Science
141

Simple Love-Mini Kitchen
Design / Rao Rubo, Lin Jianxuan
Manufacture / Xiamen Goldenhome Co., Ltd
141

Sili-cup
Design / Huang Ruirong
Manufacture / Guangzhou Han Energy & Health Products Co.,Ltd
142

Chinese Cupping
Design / Hangzhou Spark Industrial Design.,Ltd
Manufacture / Hangzhou Spark Industrial Design.,Ltd
142

Care Your Eyes Eye Protection Package
Design / LKK Design Shenzhen Co., Ltd
Manufacture / GuangZhou Three Yuan Information Technology Co., LTD
143

Golden Handle Teapot
Design / MESH design team
Manufacture / Guangzhou Sandu Brand Strategy Planning Co.,Ltd
143

In One
Design / Zhou AnBin, Lei NanShi
Manufacture / Guangzhou Han Energy & Health Products Co.,Ltd
144

SAN
Design / Zhou Anbin, Zhan Giuhong
Manufacture / GaoShang Living (GuangZhou) Co.,Ltd
144

Multi-functional Health Chair for Elderly
Design / Healthcare Design Research Lab, Tsinghua University
Manufacture / CapitalBio eHealth Science & Technology(Beijing)Co.,Ltd
145

Light Fan (Scree)
Design / Yuan Yuan
Manufacture / Beijing Rooy Furnishing Co.,Ltd
146

Stone Vision (Sofa)
Design / Yuan Yuan
Manufacture / Beijing Rooy Furnishing Co.,Ltd
146

Nasal Mask
Design / EDA (Beijing) Medical technology Co.,ltd
Manufacture / Dongguan EDA Electronics Co.,ltd
147

Bathtub
Design /Shenzhen Wing-id Co.,Ltd
Manufacture / Shenzhen Lazymum Daily Supplies Co.,Ltd
147

Five Rings Tea
Design / Kurt Jiao
Manufacture / Beijing Laoshe Tea House
148

Liangwang Teapots Set
Design / Jeff Shi
Manufacture / Dragonfly Design Center
148

OASO Ink Self-sucking Fountain Pen
Design / Shanghai OASO Stationery Co.,Ltd
Manufacture / Shanghai OASO Stationery Co.,Ltd
149

Flod-Ballpen
Design / Ownseas
Manufacture / Hangzhou Ownseas Pen Co.,Ltd
149

FIYTA 3D Time Watch GA8606.BBB
Design / Sun Lei, Gao Rengdong
Manufacture / FIYTA Holdings Ltd
149

Looking Hometown
Design / Yancheng Institute of Technology
Manufacture / Carousel Technology Co.,Ltd
150

City on Backpackers
Design / Yancheng Institute of Technology
Manufacture / Carousel Technology Co.,Ltd
151

SKYJET UV Double Side Printer SDM3300i
Design / Shenyang Sky Air-Ship Digital Printing Equipment Co.,Ltd
Manufacture / Shenyang Sky Air-Ship Digital Printing Equipment Co.,Ltd
152

Universal Motor for Concrete Vibrator
Design / Zhang Jionghui
Manufacture / Shanghai MOTOR Electromechanical Technology Co.,Ltd
152

Remote Intelligent Medicine Cabinet
Design / Shenzhen Perth Industrial Design Co.,Ltd
Manufacture / Shaanxi Shiqiang Industry Co.,Ltd
153

DMC2950
Design / Liu Yongjin, Ben Qin
Manufacture / Sungrow Power Supply Co.,Ltd
153

The Design of Internal and External Protection
Design / Dalian Post-Spring Industrial Design Co.,Ltd
Manufacture / Dalian Jirun Enterprise Group
154

QLYC3015 Laser Cutting Machine
Design / Wuhan Huaxia Star Industrial Products Design Co., Ltd
Manufacture / Wuhan Huaxia Star Industrial Products Design Co., Ltd
154

XG-3015E Cover All Laser Cutting Machine
Design / Wuhan Huaxia Star Industrial Products Design Co., Ltd
Manufacture / Wuhan Huaxia Star Industrial Products Design Co., Ltd
155

Intelligent Deep Groove Turner
Design / Beijing GreenTech Environmental Engineering Ltd
Manufacture / Beijing GreenTech Environmental Engineering Ltd
155

Single Photon Emission Computed Tomography, SPECT
Design / ZCO Design Co., Ltd
Manufacture / Beijing TianDi Zhihui Technology Co.,Ltd
156

XM1003S Milling Machine
Design / ID Center of Jiangsu XuZhou Construction Machinery Research
Manufacture / XuZhou Construction Machinery Group Inc.
156

3C Industry Large Special Laser Engraving Machine
Design / Wuhan Huaxia Star Industrial Products Design Co.,Ltd
Manufacture / Wuhan Huaxia Star Industrial Products Design Co.,Ltd
157

C400K Inclined Rail Type CNC Milling Machine
Design / Wuhan Huaxia Star Industrial Products Design Co.,Ltd
Manufacture / Wuhan Huaxia Star Industrial Products Design Co.,Ltd
157

Automatic Loading and Unloading Car
Design / Wuhan Huaxia Star Industrial Products Design Co., Ltd
Manufacture / Wuhan Huaxia Star Industrial Products Design Co., Ltd
158

DGNXQ300 Sapphire Cutter Machine
Design / Shenyang Fantian Industrial Design Co.,Ltd
Manufacture / Chongqing Machine Tool (Group) Co., Ltd
158

SGTH160 Compound Machine Tool
Design / Shenyang Fantian Industrial Design Co.,Ltd
Manufacture / Chongqing Machine Tool (Group) Co., Ltd
159

The Five-star V Brake Handle
Design / Hangzhou HUMTA Industrial Design co., Ltd
Manufacture / The Five-star Vehicle Industry Co., Ltd
159

Infant Oxygen
Design / Wuhan Huaxia Star Industrial Products Design Co., Ltd
Manufacture / Wuhan Huaxia Star Industrial Products Design Co., Ltd
160

CNC plasma rotary cutting torch
Design / Wuhan Huaxia Star Industrial Products Design Co.,Ltd
Manufacture / Wuhan Huaxia Star Industrial Products Design Co.,Ltd
160

Star3015 Cover All Laser Cutting Machine
Design / Wuhan Huaxia Star Industrial Products Design Co., Ltd
Manufacture / Wuhan Huaxia Star Industrial Products Design Co., Ltd
161

XS395 Single Drum Vibratory Roller
Design / ID Center of Jiangsu XuZhou Construction Machinery Research
Manufacture / Xuzhou Construction Machinery Group Inc.
161

GR215K Motor Grader
Design / ID Center of Jiangsu XuZhou Construction Machinery Research
Manufacture / Xuzhou Construction Machinery Group Inc.
162

Electric Forklift
Design / Hangzhou LPZ Industrial Design Co. Ltd
Manufacture / Hangzhou Yutou Industrial Co.,Ltd
162

Electric Pallet Truck
Design / Hangzhou LPZ Industrial Design Co. Ltd
Manufacture / Hangzhou Yu Tou Industrial Co., Ltd
163

X-Ray Digital Radiographic System
Design / Hangzhou LPZ Industrial Design Co. Ltd
Manufacture / Zhe Jiang Kangyuan Medical Devices Co., Ltd
163

Motlun
Design / Hangzhou LPZ Industrial Design Co. Ltd
Manufacture / Beijing LeiGuo Technology Co., Ltd
164

Intravenous Auxiliary Device
Design / Hangzhou HUMTA industrial design co., LTD
Manufacture / Hangzhou PLJ Biomedical Instrument Co., Ltd
164

SY485H Hydraulic Excavator
Design / Sany Heavy Machinery Ltd
Manufacture / Sany Heavy Machinery Ltd
165

Winner List of 2015 China Red Star Design Award

Solowheel Scorpio
Design / Beijing Sungo Industria Design Co.,Ltd
Manufacture / Invanti Co. Ltd
186

Inmotion SCV V3
Design / Qiu Yupeng, Cai Youfei
Manufacture / Inmotion Technologies Co., Ltd
186

Rain Helmet
Design / Hangzhou Spark Industrial Design.,Ltd
Manufacture / Hangzhou Spark Industrial Design.,Ltd
186

Trumpchi GA6
Design / Guangzhou Automobile Group Co., Ltd Automotive Engineering Institute
Manufacture / Guangzhou Automobile Group Motor Co.,Ltd
187

The Intelligent Identification Turnstile for Biometric Information
Design / ZCO Design Co.,Ltd
Manufacture / Beijing Hisign Technology Co.,Ltd
188

The Fruit and Vegetable Procurement Business Car
Design / ZCO Design Co.,Ltd
Manufacture / Da Jiarun Business Services Ltd
189

Bus automatic water dispenser
Design / Beijing LEAD Technology Co.,Ltd
Manufacture / Beijing Junhui Hong Kong being technology development co.,ltd
189

PRONA Intelligent Lighting Streetlight Series
Design / Shanghai Moma Industrial Product Design Co.,Ltd
Manufacture / ChuangDao Alliance (Shanghai) Co.,Ltd
190

"Fishbone" Bridge Design
Design / Institute of Human Environment and System Design, Southwest Jiaotong University
Manufacture / Survey and Design Institute of Architectural Southwest Jiaotong University
191

Most Popular Product Prize

Smart Rearview Mirror Car Driving Recorder
Design / Jado Technology Co.,Ltd
Manufacture / Jado Technology Co.,Ltd
194

Nubia Z9
Design / Nubia Technology Co.,Ltd
Manufacture / Nubia Technology Co.,Ltd
194

CXW-220-TJ20
Design / Sacon
Manufacture / Sacon
194

INMOTION SCV V3
Design / Qiu Yupeng, Cai Youfei
Manufacture / Inmotion Technologies Co.,Ltd
194

Shooting Safety Hambrella
Design / Li Ruoquan
Manufacture / Shenzhen Xitu Umbrella Co.,Ltd
195

Water Soluble Kraft Paper Packer
Design / Ningbo FANUO industrial product design Co.,Ltd
Manufacture / Ningbo Media Environmental Technology Co.,Ltd
195

Amazing Box life
Design / Mark Cheung
Manufacture / Dalian Hi-Think Computer Technology, Corp
195

Bus Automatic Water Dispenser
Design / Beijing LEAD Technology Co.Ltd
Manufacture / Beijing Junhui Hong Kong Being Technology Development co. ltd
195

Fold-Ballpen
Design / Ownseas
Manufacture / Hangzhou Ownseas Pen Co.,Ltd
195

N+ Series
Design / CBD Group Corp.
Manufacture / Vatti Corporation Limited
195

IQS-M2 Needle-free Injector
Design / Chen Suning
Manufacture / Beijing QS Medical Technology Co.,Ltd
196

DMC2950
Design / Liu yongjin, Ben Qin
Manufacture / Sungrow Power Supply Co.,LTD
196

One for All
Design / Henan Province Daxin Whole Cookroom Science
Manufacture / Henan Province Daxin Whole Cookroom Science
197

Intelligent Deep Groove Turner
Design / Beijing GreenTech Environmental Engineering Ltd
Manufacture /Beijing GreenTech Environmental Engineering Ltd
197

Most Popular Team Prize

JADO Re-DESIGN
199

Winner List of 2015 China Red Star Original Design Award

Silver Award of Original Design Award

Praying Bud - Incense Burning Flame Retardant Device
Design / Zhang Jian
202

Washing Plastic Bag
Design / Kuang Jiaying
203

Seat Baby Bed
Design / Huang Yunning, Zhuang Jinlong
204

Tabour Stool
Design / Shumao wang
205

Vaguely
Design / Ann
206

Best Designer Award of Original Design Award

Zhang Jian
209

Future Star Award of Original Design Award

Lin Bingta
212

Wang Shumao
213

Excellent Award of Original Design Award

The In-bed Head-wash Basin
Design / Canada Solo Media Inc.
216

Bow Tie - the Winebottles That Can be Laid Flatwise
Design / Zhang Jian
216

Waste Car Audio Redesign and Recycle
Design / Art Department of Huizhou University
217

Brush Button
Design / Li Weisi
217

Medical Folding Stretcher
Design / Guo Zhenyu, Zhuang Jinlong
218

Environmental Dish
Design / Li Weisi
218

Space Saver
Design / Lin Bingta, You Zhipeng, Luo Shiwu
219

Blooming Rainshower
Design / Xiamen Solex High-tech Industries Co.,Ltd
220

Private Custom Bicycle Design
Design / College of Art, Hebei University of Science and Technology
220

Splicing Stool
Design / Xu Le,Yang Cunyuan, Lin Bingta
221

国际工业设计协会联合会
认证奖项
Icsid
Endorsement
红星奖
Red Star Design
中国设计红星奖

UNESCO
United Nations
Educational, Scientific and
Cultural Organization
联合国教科文组织
BEIJING
Member of the UNESCO
Creative Cities Network
Since 2012
北京·设计之都

Second
Screening
2015
红星奖
Red Star Design
Award

CHINA RED STAR DESIGN AWARD

Organizer & Jury Committee

主办及专家委员会

中国设计红星奖委员会主席
Chairman of China Red Star Design Award Committee

朱焘 Zhu Tao

闫傲霜 Yan Aoshuang

中国设计红星奖专家委员会
Jury Committee of China Red Star Design Award

柳冠中 Liu Guanzhong
中国 China

清华大学美术学院责任教授、博士生导师、享受政府津贴学者
清华大学美术学院工业设计系系统设计工作室总设计师
中国工业设计协会副会长
香港理工大学名誉教授

Professor & doctoral supervisor of Academy of Arts & Design of Tsinghua University, with governmental subsidies
Chief Designer of System Design Studio of Industrial Design Department of Art College of Tsinghua University
Deputy Chairperson of China Industrial Design Association
Honorary professor of Hong Kong Polytechnic University

何人可 He Renke
中国 China

湖南大学设计艺术学院院长、教授
中国工业设计协会副会长
教育部高等学校工业设计专业教学指导分委员会主任委员
湖南省工业设计创新平台专业委员会委员

Dean & Professor of School of Design, Hunan University
Deputy Chairperson of China Industrial Design Association
Chairman of China National Instructive Committee of Industrial Design Education
President of Design Artists Association of Hunan Province of China

Peter Zec
德国 Germany

2005—2007 国际工业设计协会联合会主席
红点设计奖主席
北威设计中心主席

President of ICSID（2005 - 2007）
President of Red Dot Design Award
Chairman of Design Zentrum Nordrhein Westfalen

Ralph Wiegmann
德国 Germany

德国 IF 设计奖常务理事
欧洲设计管理奖评委会主席

Managing Director of International Forum Design
European Design Management Award Jury Chairman

Brandon Gien
澳大利亚 Australia

2013—2015 国际工业设计协会联合会主席
澳大利亚优秀设计协会总经理
澳大利亚国际设计奖主席

President of ICSID (2013 - 2015)
Managing Director of Good Design Australia
Chair of the Australian International Design Awards

喜多俊之 Toshiyuki Kita
日本 Japan

日本 G-mark 奖评委会前主席

Former Chairperson of the Jury of G-mark Award

鲁晓波 Lu Xiaobo
中国 China

清华大学美术学院院长、教授
清华大学信息艺术设计系主任
中国工业设计协会常务理事
红点设计奖评委

Dean & Professor of Academy of Arts & Design, Tsinghua University
Director of Information Art & Design of Academy of Arts & Design, Tsinghua University
Committeeman of China Industrial Design Association
Jury of Red Dot Design Award

Arturo Dell'Acqua Bellavitis
意大利 Italy

意大利米兰三年展主席

President of the Triennale Design Museum

Chang Donghoon
韩国 Korea

三星电子集团高级副总裁
三星电子集团手机通讯业务手机设计团队负责人
企业设计中心设计战略团队负责人
亚洲电子艺术和设计协会执委

Senior Vice President of Samsung
Head of Samsung's Mobile Design Group of Mobile Communications Business, Samsung Electronics Co., LTD
Head of Design Strategy Team of Corporate Design Center
Board member of Asian Digital Art and Design Association (ADADA)

童慧明 Tong Huiming
中国 China

前广州美术学院设计学院院长
广东省工业设计协会副会长

Former Dean of College of Design of Guangzhou
Academy of Fine Arts Deputy Chairman of Guangdong Industrial Design Association

Michael Young
英国 UK

迈克尔 · 杨工作室创始人

Founder & Director of Michael Young Studio

陈冬亮 Chen Dongliang
中国 China

北京工业设计促进中心主任
北京工业设计促进会理事长
中国设计红星奖委员会执行主席
中国工业设计协会副会长
意大利设计中国巡展华人评委
韩国好设计奖评委
清华大学美术学院工业设计发展顾问

Director of Beijing Industrial Design Center
Director of Beijing Industrial Design Promotion Organization
Executive Chairman of China Red Star Design Award Committee
Deputy Chairperson of China Industrial Design Association
Jury of Italian Design on Tour
Jury of Korean Good Design Award
Industrial Design Development Consultant of Academy of Arts & Design, Tsinghua University

Tapani Hyvönen
芬兰 Finland

Destem 有限公司、ED 设计有限公司 CEO
2009—2011 国际工业设计协会联合会执委会委员
前芬兰设计师协会（Ornamo）主席

CEO of Destem Ltd and ED-Design Ltd.
Member of 2009 - 2011 Executive Board of ICSID
Former President of Ornamo, Finnish Designers Association

Andy Ogden
美国 USA

美国艺术中心设计学院工业设计系研究生院主任
前迪士尼幻想工程研发副总裁、设计师
美国本田研究院汽车设计师

Chair of Graduate Industrial Design at Art Center College of Design
Formerly Vice President, Executive Designer for Walt Disney Imagineering R&D
Automobile designer for Honda Research of America

陈文龙 Wen-long Chen
中国台湾 China Taiwan

台湾创意设计中心执行长
2007—2009 国际工业设计协会联合会执委会委员

President of Taiwan Design Center
Member of 2007 - 2009 Executive Board of ICSID

刘小康 Freeman Lau
中国香港 China Hong Kong

香港设计中心副主席
香港设计总会秘书长
靳刘高设计创办人

Vice Chairman of Hong Kong Design Center
Secretary General of Hong Kong Federation of Design Associations (FHKDA)
Founder of KL & K Design

辛向阳 Xin Xiangyang
中国 China

江南大学设计学院院长
ICID（国际交互设计会议）学术委员会主任
中国工程学会工业设计分会理事

Professor and Dean, School of Design at Jiangnan University
Director of International Conference on Interaction Design Academic Board
National board member of the Industrial Design Group, Chinese Association of Engineers

石大宇 Jeff Shi
美国 USA

清庭设计中心创办人暨创意总监

Dragonfly Design Center Founder and Creative Director

娄永琪 Lou Yongqi
中国 China

同济大学设计创意学院院长
芬兰阿尔托大学设计学院客座教授
国际艺术设计与媒体院校联盟执行委员会委员

Dean of College of Design & Innovation, Tongji University,
Guest professor of Finland Aalto University
Executive Board Member, CUMULUS

许平 Xu Ping
中国 China

南京艺术学院设计学院院长（1999—2002）
中央美术学院设计学院副院长（2002—2010）
中央美术学院研究生处处长

Dean of Design School of Nanjing Arts Institute (1999 - 2002)
Deputy Dean of Design School of China Central Academy of Fine Arts (2002 - 2010)
Head of Graduate Section of China Central Academy of Fine Arts

Andrej Kupetz
德国 Germany

德国设计委员会主席

General Manager of German Design Council

David Kester
英国 UK

英国设计委员会前主席
英国 D&AD 主席（1994—2003）
英国皇家艺术学院执委

Former Chief Executive of Design Council
Chief Executive of D&AD (1994 - 2003)
Council member of the Royal College of Art

官政能 Cheng Neng Kuan
中国台湾 China Taiwan

台湾实践大学副校长、产品与建筑设计研究所所长
台湾实践大学设计学院首任院长

Deputy Principal of Shih Chien University
Chairman of Institute of Industrial & Architecture Design of Shih Chien University
The First Dean of School of Design of Shih Chien University

Christian Schwamkrug
德国 Germany

保时捷设计工作室设计总监

Design Director of Porsche Design Studio

陈汗青 Chen Hanqing
中国 China

上海视觉艺术学院副院长
国家工业设计教学团队负责人
中国工业设计协会常务理事

Vice president, Shanghai Institute of Visual Art
Principal of National industrial design education
Executive Board, China Industrial Design Association

Francois Lenfant
法国 France

通用电气医疗全球设计经理

Global Design Manager for Europe & Middle-East (EMEA)，GE Healthcare

曾辉 Zeng Hui
中国 China

北京国际设计周组委会办公室副主任
歌华创意设计中心主任

Deputy Director of Beijing Design WeekOrganizing Committee
Chairman of Beijing Gehua-Rizzoli Design Communication

Tim Flattery
美国 USA

美国艺术中心设计学院娱乐设计系主任
概念艺术家及电影特效专家
作品包括《加勒比海盗》《饥饿游戏》《蜘蛛侠 II》等

Chair of Entertainment Design at Art Center College of Design
Concept artist and designer with expertise in concept development, design, fabrication and story for the entertainment industry
His works including Pirates of The Caribbean, The Hunger Games, Spiderman 2 etc.

邱丰顺 Kumo Chiu
中国台湾 China Taiwan

北京艺有道工业设计有限公司创办人及总经理
摩托罗拉亚洲区设计总监（2001–2006）

Founder and President of Idea Dao Design Ltd.
Asia Design Director of Mobile Device , Motorola (2001 - 2006)

Jorge Teixeira
葡萄牙 Portugal

葡萄牙设计师协会会员
葡萄牙建筑师协会会员
Ada 工作室合伙人兼 CEO

Member of Portuguese Association of Designers
Member of Association of Portuguese Architects
CEO and Partner of Ada Studio

应放天 Ying Fangtian
中国 China

中国工业设计协会副会长兼秘书长
浙江大学教授，博导

Vice President of China Industrial Design Association
Professor & doctoral supervisor of Zhejiang University

蔡军 Cai Jun
中国 China

清华大学美术学院工业设计系教授
清华大学艺术与科学研究中心设计管理研究所所长
清华大学美术学院工业设计系主任（2006–2009）

Industrial Design Professor of Art College of Tsinghua University
Head of Design Management Research Department of Art & Science Research Center, Tsinghua University
Chief of Industrial Design Department of Art College of Tsinghua University (2006 - 2009)

Park Youngsoon

韩国 Korea

韩国设计协会联盟主席
韩国设计振兴院理事
韩国好设计奖评委会主席（2005）

Chairman of Korea Federation of Design Associations (KFDA)
Director of Korea Institute of Design Promotion (KIDP)
Chairman of Jury committee in Korea Good Design Award (2005)

Lee Soon In

韩国 Korea

2011—2013 国际工业设计协会联合会主席
首尔设计中心主席
国际设计高级研究院院长

President of ICSID (2011 - 2013)
President of the Seoul Design Center
Dean of International Design School for Advanced Studies

殷正声 Yin Zhengsheng

中国 China

同济大学设计创意学院教授
中国工业设计协会常务理事
上海工业设计协会副理事长

Professor of Design Innovation College of Tongji University
Executive member of China Industrial Design Association
Vice President of Shanghai Industrial Design Association

Alpay Er

土耳其 Turkey

伊斯坦布尔技术大学工业产品设计系主任、教授
国际工业设计协会联合会执委（2015–2017）

Chair and Professor, Dept. of Industrial Product Design, Istanbul Technical University (ITU)
Member of 2015 - 2017 Executive Board of ICSID

Harald Leschke

德国 Germany

梅赛德斯奔驰汽车集团设计总监（1978—2007）
Leschke 设计公司自由设计师、顾问（2008）
Litex 汽车公司总经理（2008 年至今）

Head of Mercedes-Benz Advanced Design (1978—2007)
Freelance designer and consultant in "leschke.design" (2008)
General Manager in Litex Motors (since 2008)

Leimei Julia Chiu

日本 Japan

2011—2013 国际平面设计协会联合会主席
日本工业设计振兴会执行主任
武藏野美术大学教授

2011 - 2013 President of Icograda
Executive Director of Japan Institute of Design Promotion (JDP)
Professor of Musashino Art University (MAU)

林衍堂 Lam Yanta

中国香港 China Hong Kong

香港理工大学设计学院副主任
香港设计局董事

Professor of Design & Associate Head school of Design, the Hong Kong Polytechnic University
Director, Hong Kong Design Centre

严扬 Yan Yang

中国 China

清华大学美术学院工业设计系教授

Professor of Industrial Design Department of Academy of Arts & Design, Tsinghua University

Edna dos Santos-Duisenberg
巴西 Brazil

联合国贸易和发展会议创意经济项目主任
联合国贸易和发展会议全球数据银行创始人、主任
联合国贸易和发展会议秘书长首席顾问

Chief of Creative Economy Programme of UNCTAD Founder and Director of the UNCTAD's global data bank
Chief of Cabinet of the Secretary General of UNCTAD

Jeroen Raijmakers
荷兰 Netherlands

飞利浦医疗全球设计总监

Global Design Director of Healthcare at Philips

George M. Beylerian
美国 USA

Material ConneXion 新材料图书馆创始人兼首席执行官（1997 年至今）
Culture & Commerce 设计咨询公司创始人（1994）

Founder and CEO of Material ConneXion（Since 1997）
Founder of Culture & Commerce（1994）

孙大力 Sun Dali
德国 Germany

北京工业大学艺术设计学院院长

Dean of Beijing College of Art & Design, Beijing University of Technology

Tim Fletcher
美国 USA

美国工业设计师协会美国政府联络官 (2011 至今)
美国宾斯法尼亚州匹兹堡 Daedalus 公司业务发展经理（2009 至今）

US Government Liaison Officer of IDSA (Since 2011)
Business Development Manager of Daedalus, Pittsburgh, PA US (Since 2009)

王昀 Wang Yun
中国 China

中国美术学院设计艺术学院副院长
中国美术学院工业设计研究院院长
浙江省工业设计协会副会长

Vice president, Design Art College of China Academy of Art (CAA)
Dean of Industrial Design and Research Institute of CAA
Vice President, Zhejiang Industrial Design Association

袁岳 Victor Yuan
中国 China

零点研究咨询集团董事长
中国信息协会市场研究业分会副会长
北京科技咨询业协会理事长

Chairman of the board, Founder and President of Horizon Research Consultancy Group
Vice President of China Marketing Research Association
President of Beijing Consulting Association (BCA)

周佚 Zhou Yi
中国 China

上海指南工业设计有限公司创始人、总经理
中国工业设计协会理事
广州美术学院客座教授

Founder & General Manager, S Point Design
Board Member, China Industrial Design Association
Guest Professor, Guangzhou Academy of Fine Arts

朱小杰 Zhu Xiaojie
中国 China

澳珀家具艺术总监

Art Director of Opal Furniture

Mark Breitenberg
美国 USA

艺术中心设计学院院长特别助理
国际工业设计协会联合会主席（2009—2011）
帕萨迪纳创新执委会委员

Special Assistant to the President, Art Center College of Design
President of ICSID (2009 - 2011)
Executive Committee, Innovate Pasadena

朱长岭 Zhu Changling
中国 China

中国家具协会理事长

President of China National Furniture Association

周红石 Zhou Hongshi
中国 China

广东工业设计协会秘书长

Secretary General of Guangdong Industrial Design Association

田中一雄 Kazuo Tanaka
日本 Japan

GK 设计株式会社总裁
2007—2009 国际工业设计协会联合会执委会委员

President of GK Design Group Inc.
Member of 2007-2009 Executive Board of ICSID

杨明洁 Jamy Yang
中国 China

杨设计创始人

Founder of Yang Design

温浩 Wen Hao
中国 China

广州美术学院家具研究院院长

The Institute of Furniture Design, Guangzhou Academy of Fine Arts

戴蓓 Dai Bei
中国 China

新浪家居执行总编

Executive Chief Editor of Sina Jiaju

感悟
Inspiration

如果说，20 世纪是中国设计力形成的准备阶段，21 世纪就是设计真正进步的开始。“优秀设计”的概念诞生重新定义了“设计”的范畴，为人类提供了一个新鲜的视角。随着社会的不断创新发展，“优秀设计”已经成为促进社会形成和发展的重要力量，成为创新型国家建设的重要动力。

2006 年，《国民经济和社会发展第十一个五年规划纲要》首次正式提出要鼓励发展专业化的工业设计。

在红点奖、美国 IDEA 设计奖等世界知名设计奖项大放异彩的时候，我们国家还没有自己的优秀设计奖项。国内很多优秀的设计作品由于缺乏平台，迟迟得不到国际的认同。中国的工业设计界要想改变这一局面，取得更多的话语权，就必须要具有一个国际化和中国特色兼备、有自主知识产权的工业设计奖项！

2006 年设立的国家级设计大奖——中国设计红星奖，设立之初就吸引了来自 15 个省市和地区的 200 家企业 400 件产品参评。2006 年红星奖至尊金奖的得主联想与海尔，拿出了惊艳世界的设计产品，联想的全球第一款家庭数字娱乐中心开启了数字家庭产品的新时代，海尔全球 U-HOME 成套家电的上市，代表了智慧家电的发展方向。

国际化的评委构成、评选标准和评选流程，让红星奖从设立之初就代表着中国工业设计界的最高水准出现在全球设计界。借助这一窗口，中国工业设计在较短的时间内获得了国际认可。意大利米兰三年展主席阿尔图 · 拜拉维提斯在参与红星奖评选时感慨到："以前世界对中国产品的印象很糟糕，都是移民在廉价商店里出售的质量很低的商品。但是我在这里看到的大不相同，我看到了无人机、大型机械、高铁等等。我从来没有想过一列火车可以像飞机那么快。真的，我认为你们应该把这些展示给世界看。”红星奖的标准得到了国际企业界的认可，如三星、戴森、哈曼、飞利浦、蔡司等知名企业，都出现在了红星奖的参评企业名录中。

红星奖既是中国好设计走向世界的窗口，也是中国制造走向世界的舞台。2011 年至尊金奖、2012 年金奖、2013 年至尊金奖、2014 年金奖，这是中国高铁的红星奖成绩单，更是以高铁为代表的中国制造跻身世界尖端制造之林的见证。

历经十年磨练的红星奖，让中国制造一次又一次地为全世界带去惊喜。红星奖国际评委、荷兰埃因霍温科技大学副校长阿诺德·布隆巴赫表示，一些中国设计已经达到了世界级的水准，能够看到如此专业的设计让我感到非常骄傲，甚至在这里我要报以谦逊的态度进行评审。

2007 年始，红星奖每年受邀代表中国设计赴韩国，与红点、F、G-mark、IDEA 等共同参加世界优秀设计联展，2009 年受邀亮相米兰国际设计周，2014 年成为全球第一个走进联合国教科文组织总部的全球设计奖项。红星奖前后共举办了 13 站国外巡展，很多参观者惊叹于中国文化的博大精深，以及中国设计所蕴含的创造力。

红星奖所凝聚的创新活力，也得到了国内越来越多的关注，截止 2015 年，红星奖坚持传播好设计，在国内 29 个地市共举办近 130 场巡展，参观人数达到 300 万人、参展企业累计超过 4000 家次。

红星奖一直都保持着对设计师的关注，一些默默无闻的设计师，正是在红星奖这个平台上，逐步成长为拥有独立品牌和设计企业的创业者。来自中国农学院的张岩，凭借“绿色信封”这一充满了生态设计和可持续发展理念的作品获得了 2014 红星奖，并成为了中国邮政的合作伙伴。不少年轻设计师看到张岩的成功，也希望借助红星奖这一平台得到社会认可，实现创业梦想。

双创不仅是小微企业的专利，更是大企业的优势。2006 年至尊金奖得主海尔集团于 2015 年再次获奖。如今的海尔已经由传统家电制造企业转型为一家拥有 183 个小微生态圈、数十个产品品牌和互联工厂的创业平台，在“中国制造 2025”和工业 4.0 的浪潮下，海尔迈开了互联网 + 的步伐。

展望未来，迈向明天。随着“一带一路”国家战略的提出，大到高铁、小到手机，中国设计和中国创造已经越来越得到“一带一路”上各国的欢迎与接纳。从基础设施互联互通，到不同文化交流交融，再到“一带一路”沿线国家人员相知相亲，我们看到“一带一路”战略正在编织几十亿百姓的共同命运。

世界正处在新世纪发展的关键时刻，可持续发展是人类所面临的共同议题。设计产业的发展促进了经济与科技和文化的融合，在促进社会和谐、经济增长、贸易和就业方面发挥日趋重要的作用。

秉承以人为本、绿色、协调、可持续发展的生态设计理念，未来红星奖将更加致力于以设计改善生存环境，加强中国与世界的交互融通，不断迈上新的历史台阶。

中国设计红星奖委员会执行主席
陈冬亮

感悟
Inspiration

If the 20th century was the preparatory stage for the global influence of Chinese design, the 21st century is the real start of progress for Chinese design. The birth of the concept of "excellent design" redefined the field of "design", providing mankind with a fresh perspective. With continuous innovation and development of society, "excellent design" has become an important force for promoting the formation and development of society and an important driving force in building an innovative country.

In 2006, the Eleventh Five-Year Guideline for National Economic and Social Development first formally proposed to encourage the development of specialized industrial design. While the Red Dot Award, the United States IDEA Design Award and other world-renowned design awards had successfully established themselves, China did not have its own national design award. Many excellent domestic design products could not receive international recognition due to a lack of platform. If China's industrial design community wished to change this situation and have their voices heard better, it was necessary to have an industrial design award combining international and Chinese characteristics with independent intellectual property rights.

The national design award, China Red Star Design Award, was established in 2006 and attracted 400 product entries from 200 companies in 15 provinces and regions at the time it was established. The 2006 Red Star Best of Gold Prize winners, Lenovo and Haier, came up with stunning design products that were among the best in the world; Lenovo's world's-first home digital entertainment center opened a new era in digital home products and Haier global U-HOME set of appliances represented the direction of development for smart home appliances.

The Red Star Award made its first appearance in the global design community, representing the highest level of Chinese industrial design through its international jury composition, selection criteria and selection process. With the aid of this award, Chinese industrial design has gained international recognition in a short period of time. Arturo Dell'Acqua Bellavitis, the director of the Milan Triennale, Italy, expressed his impression when serving as a judge for the Red Star Award, stating that:" The previous impression of Chinese products in the world was bad with low quality goods selling in cheap stores. What I have seen here, however, is very different. I have seen unmanned aerial vehicles, large machinery, high-speed rail and so on. I have never thought that a train could reach Shanghai as quickly as an airplane. Really, I think you should show this to the world." The standards of the Red Star Award have been recognized by the international business community: Samsung, Dyson, Harman, Philips, Zeiss and other well-known companies have appeared in the participating enterprises directory of the Red Star Award.

The China Red Star Design Award is abridge to lead Chinese design excellence to the world and to bring Chinese products to the world stage. Chinese high-speed rail, a representative of products made-in-China, has won the 2011 Best of the Gold Prize, 2012 Gold Prize, 2013 Best of the Gold Prize and 2014 Gold Prize of China Red Star Design Award, which is also a testimony to Chinese manufacturing being among the world's leading-edge manufacturing industries.

After a decade of effort and carrying the expectations of Chinese manufacturing being able to challenge the status quo of global leading-edge manufacturing industries, the Red Star Award has repeatedly brought the world the features and surprises of products made-in-China. Aarnout Brombach, of the Red Star Award international jury and the vice-chancellor of Eindhoven University of Technology in Netherlands, said that "some Chinese designs have reached world-class standards and I feel very proud to see such professional designs; I would conduct my assessmentshere in a humble manner."

In each year, starting in 2007, the Red Star Award is invited to South Korea to represent Chinese design and to participate in the World Excellent Design Exhibition with Red Dot, IF, G-mark, IDEA,etc; in 2009 it was invited to debut in the Milan Design Week; in 2014 it became the world's first design award to enter the UNESCO Headquarter. The Red Star

Award has organized a total of 13 foreign tours, in which multitudes of visitors marveled at the profound Chinese culture and the inherent creativity of Chinese design.

The cohesive creative vitality of the Red Star Award has also received more domestic attention. As of 2015, the Red Star Award has persisted in spreading excellent designs and held a total of nearly 130 tours in 29 cities in the country, in which the number of visitors reached 300 million and the total number of exhibitors exceeded 4000.

The Red Star Award has always maintained its focus on designers. Some unknown designers have gradually grown into entrepreneurs of independent brands and design businesses. Zhang Yan from China Agricultural University won the 2014 Red Star Award for the "Green Envelope", a work that is all about eco-design and the concept of sustainable development and Yan has become a partner of China Post. Many young designers who saw the success of Zhang Yan also hope to be recognized by society and realize their entrepreneurial dreams through the Red Star Award platform.

Being doubly awarded is not only the specialty of small enterprises but also the advantage of large enterprises. Haier Group was awarded again in 2015 after its winning of the Best of the Gold Prize in 2006. Today, Haier has been transformed from a traditional home appliance manufacturing enterprise to a business platform with 183 micro eco systems, dozens of product brands and interconnecting factories; Haier has moved forward with Internet+ under the tide of "Made in China 2025" and industrial 4.0.

Look back to the past and look into the future; being at a strategically advantageous position and move towards tomorrow. For the last ten years, the Red Star Award has dedicated itself and done a lot of work to globalize national industrial products, design concepts and the core culture. With the proposal of China's "One Belt, One Road" national strategy, Chinese design and products ranging from high-speed rail to cell phones have been increasingly welcomed and accepted by countries along the "One belt and One road". From the interconnections of infrastructure to the diffusion of various cultures and friendships between people from various countries along the "One belt, One road", we find that the "One belt, One road" strategy is weaving the fate of billions of people together. In the coming decade, the Red Star Award will continue its past tasks of spreading excellent designs, highlighting soft power, communication and interaction as well as promoting industrial development to once again take a new historic step.

The world is at a crucial moment in the new century and sustainable development is a common issue faced by mankind. The development of design industry promotes integration between the economy, technology and culture and plays an increasingly important role in promoting social harmony, economic growth, trade and employment. Adhering to the ecological design concepts of people-oriented, green, coordinated and sustainably developed designs, the Red Star Award proposes innovation, focusing on industry, serving enterprises, nurturing talent and going international; it also proposes to improve the living environment, enhance human care, promote the harmonious development of society and promote the general health and welfare of people through design.

Executive Chairman of China Red Star Design Award Committee
Chen Dongliang

中国好设计

CHINA GOOD DESIGN